FINANCIAL ECONOMICS

for Dagmar

for Roslyn, Geoffrey and Stuart

FINANCIAL ECONOMICS

Jürgen Eichberger
Ian R. Harper

OXFORD UNIVERSITY PRESS

Oxford University Press, Great Clarendon Street, Oxford OX2 6DP

Oxford New York

Athens Auckland Bangkok Bogota Buenos Aires Calcutta
Cape Town Chennai Dar es Salaam Delhi Florence Hong Kong Istanbul
Karachi Kuala Lumpur Madrid Melbourne Mexico City Mumbai
Nairobi Paris São Paolo Singapore Taipei Tokyo Toronto Warsaw
and associated companies in
Berlin Ibadan

Oxford is a registered trade mark of Oxford University Press

Published in the United States by
Oxford University Press Inc., New York

British Library Cataloguing in Publication Data
Data available

Library of Congress Cataloging in Publication Data
Eichberger. Jürgen. 1952-
Financial economics / Jürgen Eichberger and Ian R. Harper.
Includes bibliographical references and index.
1. Finance   2. Economics.   Ian R. Harper,   II. Title.
HG 173.E45   1997   332—dc20   96-32575
ISBN 0 19 877405 2 (Hbk)
ISBN 0 19 877540 7 (Pbk)

10 9 8 7 6 5 4 3

Printed in Great Britain
on acid-free paper by
Bookcraft (Bath) Ltd., Midsomer Norton, Somerset

PREFACE

The idea of this book was conceived at the Australian National University nearly ten years ago when the two authors realized that the courses they taught, 'Uncertainty and Information' in Jürgen Eichberger's case and 'Financial Economics' in Ian Harper's case, had more than a few topics in common. The 'Financial Economics' course focussed on the finance aspects of general equilibrium theory with asset markets. This theory constitutes the intellectual foundation of asset pricing models commonly applied in the analysis of financial markets. The 'Uncertainty and Information' course, on the other hand, focused on the then new theory of contracts in the presence of asymmetric information. Such models can be used to explain the form of contracts widely used in insurance markets and in financial intermediation. Asymmetric information provides a rationale for the standard debt contract and for deposit contracts, and may explain allocative problems including credit rationing and bank runs.

A good deal of our excitement with the subject arose from our different approaches to the material. While one of the authors emphasized the formal logic of models and propositions, the other adopted a more applied approach, searching the theory to find insight into problems faced by the applied financial economist. The challenge to express results in a form amenable to interpretation and appreciation by applied economists has informed the exposition in all sections of the book. As a consequence, we have achieved a book that is rigorous, but not mathematically concise, narrowly focused rather than comprehensive in the selection of topics covered, and innovative in joining the general equilibrium approach of finance theory with the contract approach of the theory of asymmetric information. An overarching interest of both authors is the contrast between financial markets and financial intermediaries as alternative institutional solutions to the problem of intertemporal allocation. This interest serves as our *leitmotiv* and informs both our choice of topics and method of approach. To this extent, at least, our book differs from other texts in the field.

From our experience, there is considerable demand for courses in financial economics which focus on the economic foundations of concepts that are widely used in applied finance and banking. We hope this book offers students a unifying theoretical perspective on the diverse issues addressed by finance and contract theory, as well as preparing them with the background and skills necessary to approach more specialized literature.

Lecture notes prepared by the authors for their courses at the Australian National University formed the early versions of several sections of the book. The book did not take shape, however, until both authors had moved to the University of Melbourne where they again found themselves teaching companion courses in their respective fields. The notion of presenting one course team-taught by the two authors spurred them to action. We are grateful for comments and suggestions from a number of colleagues at different stages of the project. Frank Milno followed the work with encouragement and helpful criticism. Simon Grant and David Kelsey provided us with valuable feedback, particularly on Chapter 1. Anonymous referees offered valuable suggestions on how to link certain sections of the book with the most recent literature. None of these bears any responsibility for shortcomings which may remain.

Many people have played a part in the production of the book, including students of our courses who encouraged us to improve our exposition, even of standard topics. In transforming our handwritten notes into typescript, we were ably supported by Andrew Mills, Susan Waterfall and Nerida Slizys. We wish to acknowledge the Programme in Monetary and Financial Economics at the University of Melbourne and the Ian Potter Centre for International Finance at the Melbourne Business School for providing financial support to cover the costs of technical drawing and word-processing. We also acknowledge the Department of Economics at Monash University who hosted Ian Harper during a period of study leave spent writing parts of the book. The final camera-ready versions of the diagrams were prepared by Sven Boland and Undine Ewald of the University of Saarland. Their care and precision with this task contributed significantly to the final version of the book and deserves special mention.

Our last but by no means least acknowledgment is to our families for their forbearance and support during the many hours spent writing this book.

J.E. and I.R.H.
May 1996

CONTENTS

Contents

7. Deposit Contracts and Banking

8. Regulation of Banks

9. Towards Application: Financial Markets and Financial Intermediaries

Contents

INTRODUCTION

Thirty years ago, students were taught economics and finance as if they were two separate disciplines. Finance majors steered clear of economics because it was 'too theoretical' and, in any case, they were keen to proceed to practical matters of capital budgeting, portfolio selection, and the like, without being unnecessarily encumbered by theoretical niceties. Serious students of economics, on the other hand, were rarely introduced to financial issues, except perhaps in the distant and abstract form of capital theory, since the application of economic principles to problems in finance was underdeveloped, if not non-existent.

During the intervening period up to the present, the research agendas of finance and economic theorists have converged in a remarkable way. Even at a practical level, the disciplines are much more obviously and closely related than at any prior time. Nowadays, certainly at the graduate level but also in undergraduate teaching, a good grounding in microeconomic theory is considered essential to a proper grasp of the principles of finance. In fact, the convergence of the two disciplines is acknowledged in the increasing currency of the term *financial economics* to describe the application of general microeconomic theory to the special problems encountered in finance.

This book aims to introduce students to the main theoretical models used by financial economists. The literature is now so vast that some selection is necessary. Attention is therefore confined to exposition of the essential models from which the various branches of the literature develop. Both economics and finance majors will benefit from this approach. The former will appreciate how finance theory articulates with economic theory; specifically, how the main results of finance theory emerge from suitably specialized versions of general economic models. The latter group will recognize the specific assumptions upon which many results in finance theory depend and will appreciate their importance in deciding how best to apply theory to practice.

Most of modern finance theory is based on the competitive market model where traders have symmetric information about their environment, face market-determined prices, and decide how much to buy and sell of particular goods or assets. In this framework, it is possible to gain important insights which heavily influence application. From a competitive model of asset exchange, for example, we learn that a willingness to insure risk may result from the possibility of diversification or from differences in risk preferences. The law of one price, that perfect substitutes must trade at the same price, has been exploited successfully to determine asset prices by noting that equilibrium prices must be free from arbitrage. Modern asset-pricing methods, such as the Black–Scholes formula, have their roots in the theory of competitive markets under symmetric information.

Parallel with the development of modern finance, new models were developed which allow us to deal with problems of asymmetric information and information-processing. With these instruments, the extremely restrictive assumption underlying the theory of competitive markets that all traders share the same information about market prices and future contingencies can be abandoned. With asymmetric information, competitive markets may no longer be feasible and, if they are, they may no longer produce Pareto-optimal outcomes. Institutions like banks and contracts like loans that are observed in all developed economies emerge as rational responses to a world where information is asymmetrically distributed. Analysis of these models by comparing them with competitive assumptions throws light on the conditions governing the development of new financial markets and instruments.

Structure of the Book

The distinction between models based on symmetric information and competitive markets and those built on asymmetric information and contractual relationships forms the organizing principle of this book. After a brief review of the necessary prerequisites from the theory of decision-making under uncertainty, Part I deals with the theory of competitive asset markets under symmetric information. In this part, we introduce the equilibrium-pricing method which supports the Capital Asset Pricing Model (CAPM) and the arbitrage-pricing method which lies behind the Black–Scholes pricing formula.

Also in Part I we treat the Modigliani–Miller proposition concerning the irrelevance of corporate finance and show the importance of a complete set of financial markets for the successful separation of ownership and control of firms. Though central to the analysis of firms in financial markets, the latter problem is rarely treated in corporate finance texts. We also stress the importance of market completeness for the efficiency of the financial market system and the determinacy of equilibrium prices and allocations.

The assumption of asymmetric information between trading partners is the *leitmotif* of Part II. With symmetric information, a trade contract need only specify the amounts and contingencies for the delivery of goods or assets and the price at which the transaction is to be conducted. If the information about possible contingencies or about characteristics of market participants is not the same for all trading partners, it may be impossible to specify and enforce the contracts required for competitive markets.

Given constraints imposed by these asymmetries, a central question in the literature on institutional arrangements under asymmetric information concerns the optimal form of contracts. Over the past twenty years, a large number of models have been developed which investigate the optimal form of contract under various assumptions about the asymmetry of information. In Part II of this book, we introduce the reader to the most relevant contracts in the context of financial intermediation.

The insurance market serves as our first example for the failure of competitive markets under asymmetric information. We then devise three optimal contracts. Because of their practical relevance and importance, we concentrate on insurance contracts, standard debt contracts, and the deposit contract. The informational conditions which make these contracts optimal is the focus of attention. In the case of the standard debt contract and the deposit contract, we investigate the implications of the contract form. Credit rationing is one of the implications of the debt contract and bank runs are a possible consequence of the deposit contract.

Understanding how informational asymmetries give rise to different forms of contract is a prerequisite to the analysis of whether and to what extent new financial instruments, i.e. contracts, overcome the informational asymmetries and incompleteness of financial market systems.

Target Readership

This book is best suited to instruction at the advanced undergraduate or beginning graduate level. Ideally, intermediate-level courses in both economics and finance will have been taken before a course based on this book. While the level of technical skill required is moderate, a student should be prepared to work through the notation in order to grasp the material. Familiarity with the standard mathematical methods encountered in modern courses in economics and finance will be especially helpful. On the other hand, students who seek to acquire the knowledge and skill necessary to understand more advanced material in finance, including that published in professional journals and in more advanced books like Huang and Litzenberger (1988), Ingersoll (1987), and Jarrow (1988), will find this a useful intermediate book.

Special Features

We consider the careful selection of material covered in this book to be an essential feature.

The first chapter, dealing with decision-making under uncertainty, focuses on those issues which find application in financial economics. The main part of the chapter treats choice among state-contingent outcomes as the primitive notion on which decision-making over probability distributions builds. The relationship between concepts of stochastic dominance and risk preference is given careful exposition. The mean-variance approach is presented as a special case of expected utility theory. All axiomatic considerations germane to a thorough understanding of the concept are included in an appendix. A simple and, to our knowledge, novel proof of the expected utility theorem based on the independence axiom is provided there.

Part I presents material usually covered in finance courses. The close attention given to the implications of incomplete financial markets is, however, a special feature of this book. The implied non-optimality and the dependence of the equilibrium allocation on the choice of numeraire commodity incorporate results drawn from the most recent research in this field. The treatment of incomplete markets allows us to question the concept of profit or value maximization as an appropriate objective function for a firm.

Part II introduces contract models and incentive concepts which are not commonly treated at all in finance texts. Incorporating economic analysis developed over the past twenty years under the heading of the 'economics of uncertainty and information' is another special feature of this book. In this regard, our book links those parts of the economics and finance literature of most relevance to financial economists. It facilitates access to related work in books by Hirshleifer and Riley (1992) and Laffont (1989).

How to Use This Book

The book begins with a brief introduction to the theory of choice under uncertainty. The main concepts and techniques used elsewhere in the book are introduced at this stage. For readers who are familiar with these concepts, it is recommended to read Section 1.5 on the mean-variance approach only. In Appendix A, we review some concepts from probability theory and, in Appendix B, introduce the axiomatic foundations of expected utility theory. Though quite important as background reading, these appendices can be omitted from a first reading without loss of continuity.

Chapters 2 to 5 constitute Part I. Chapter 2 discusses Portfolio Choice Theory and some of its derivatives. One difference in approach compared with most other texts is the emphasis placed on the general equilibrium economic foundations of the models developed. The familiar results from basic finance theory, including Mean-Variance Analysis and the Capital Asset-Pricing Model, are covered but with an explicit link to their general equilibrium economic foundations.

Chapter 3 explores systems of financial markets. The ideal conception of Arrow–Debreu securities is introduced and contrasted with ordinary securities markets. Conditions under which stock markets might approach the ideal of complete contingent claims markets are derived and the implications of the incompleteness of markets are explored.

Chapter 4 deals with the important principle of arbitrage in asset pricing, and applies it to derive an option-pricing formula. It is shown how repeated trading of a security can enlarge the state space, allowing assets with many possible pay-offs to be priced.

Chapter 5 explores the role of the firm in the context of financial markets. Since a firm's production decision determines not only the amount of goods in the various states of nature, but also the number of independent assets available to hedge against risks, in general shareholders will only agree on the production decision of a firm if markets are complete. A second issue treated in this chapter is the Modigliani–Miller 'irrelevance' result. The analysis grounds the result in the framework of general equilibrium economics. It is then straightforward to show why the value of the firm is no longer invariant to financial structure or dividend policy when the firm does not operate in a world of perfect markets. Though essential for an understanding of the role of firms in an economy and of the limitations of general equilibrium models when extended to economies with production, one can treat the two sections of this chapter as independent of each other.

Part II begins with Chapter 6 where we consider models with insurance contracts and debt contracts and the related phenomena of adverse selection and credit rationing. The nature of the debt contract as an incentive-compatible arrangement between two agents unable to verify certain aspects of each other's behaviour is stressed.

Chapter 7 discusses the deposit contract and banking as particular institutional responses to asymmetric information in financial markets. Discussion of the nature of the deposit contract and its optimality in certain circumstances leads naturally to an analysis of the phenomenon of bank runs. The issue of false signals, like rumours about the soundness of a bank, as possible triggers for bank runs, is given particular attention.

Chapter 8 follows with a discussion of bank regulation, placing it in the context of the model of bank runs presented in Chapter 7. The main forms of bank regulation including reserve requirements, suspension rules, capital-adequacy requirements and deposit insurance, are analysed in simple diagrammatic terms. The capacity of bank regulations to forestall bank runs is investigated in each case.

Chapters 7 and 8 form a unit that should be covered jointly. Readers not interested in regulatory issues can drop Chapter 8. It is, however, impossible to fully understand Chapter 8 without first reading Chapter 7. Chapters 6, 7, and 8 form the core of Part II. Chapter 9 concludes the book with a general discussion of the evolution of financial markets and financial intermediaries.

Some Remarks on Notation

Most of the notation will be familiar to readers with some background in statistics. However, we consistently use a few conventions of which the reader should be aware.

1. To avoid additional notation, we use the same capital letter to denote a set and the last element of the set if it is finite. For example, we may write

$$S = \{1,\ldots,S\}$$

to indicate a set consisting of the finite elements 1,2,3,.....S with S as the last element of the list. A typical element of a set will often be indicated by the same small letter, e.g. $s \in S$.

2. Functions will be indicated either by

$$f: A \rightarrow B,$$

a notation that stresses that each element of the set A has an associated element of the set B which is identified by the function f, or by

$$f(a) = b$$

which stresses the dependence of the variable b on the variable a.

3. The equality sign (=) can sometimes cause confusion. It may indicate that there is an argument, say x, for which two functions, say f and g, have the same value

$$f(x) = g(x).$$

In other cases, the equality sign may indicate that an expression, say an integral $\int u(x)\, \mathrm{d}F$, can be viewed as a function, say of F, $H(F)$. In this case, we write

$$H(F) := \int u(x)\, \mathrm{d}F.$$

The colon indicates the side of the equality where one finds the function sign $H(F)$. On the side without the colon, one finds the defining expression. This notation is often convenient because one can also write unambiguously

$$\int u(x)\, \mathrm{d}F =: H(F).$$

DECISION-MAKING UNDER UNCERTAINTY

This first chapter covers the basic theoretical framework for choice under conditions of uncertainty. We begin with a formal characterization of uncertainty and develop two ways of looking at choice under uncertainty: (i) as a choice amongst state-dependent outcomes; and (ii) as a choice amongst different probability distributions over outcomes. We then explain how the expected utility representation of preferences can be interpreted as a utility function over state-dependent outcomes (the 'state-preference approach') or as a utility function over probability distributions. Following a discussion of attitudes to risk and stochastic dominance, we introduce a special application of expected utility theory commonly encountered in financial economics, viz. mean-variance analysis. Two appendices provide a brief collection of results on probability distributions and a short exposition of the axiomatic derivation of the expected utility representation.

Financial decisions are intertemporal decisions: they involve choices whose consequences extend into the future. Since the future is unknown, financial decisions are inevitably taken under conditions of uncertainty. To begin our study of financial economics, we must first establish a conceptual distinction between 'certainty' and 'uncertainty'. On this foundation, we can then construct the formal superstructure of decision-making under uncertainty. An understanding of the principles of decision-making under uncertainty is essential to a full appreciation of the various themes of financial economic analysis.

1.1 Certainty and Uncertainty: What's the Difference?

When economic agents choose amongst actions which are feasible for them, they choose on the basis of consequences which the chosen actions produce.

Very often, however, actions alone are not sufficient to determine particular consequences. Other factors may interact with an action chosen to produce a particular consequence. These other factors, which are beyond the control of economic agents, are summarized as the *state of the world*. Numerous states of the world are possible and, at any point in time, economic agents will be uncertain as to the future states which will apply as the history of the world unfolds. They will therefore be uncertain of the future consequences of any actions they take in the present.

More formally, if A is the set of feasible actions, S the set of possible states of the world, and C the set of consequences, a combination of an action $a \in A$ and a state $s \in S$ will produce a particular consequence $c \in C$. Thus there is a function f which maps actions and states into consequences:

$$(s, a) \rightarrow c = f(s, a).$$

At the time of deciding upon a course of action, an agent is uncertain about the state of the world which will co-determine the consequence of the chosen action. Uncertainty about the state of the world will often be modelled by a probability measure on S. Some important properties of probability measures are therefore reviewed in Appendix A.

Choosing an action a determines a consequence for each state of the world, $f(s, a)$. The decision over actions in A can therefore be viewed as a decision over *state-dependent* (or *state-contingent*) consequences. Thus a choice of some action a_1 corresponds to the choice of the state-contingent outcomes $\{f(s, a_1) \mid s \in S\}$. If the set of states is finite, $S = \{1, \ldots, S\}$, one can write the state-contingent consequences associated with action a_1 as a vector $(c_{11}, \ldots, c_{s1}, \ldots, c_{S1})$, where the first index lists the state and the second the action, i.e. $c_{s1} =: f(s, a_1)$. From this point of view, choosing a_1 over a_2 is the same as choosing $(c_{11}, \ldots, c_{s1}, \ldots, c_{S1})$ over $(c_{12}, \ldots, c_{s2}, \ldots, c_{S2})$.

A decision made under certainty is easily distinguished from a decision made under uncertainty by looking at the function f. If f is constant with respect to the state of the world, i.e. the state of the world does not influence the consequence which arises, the decision is said to be taken *under certainty*. If, on the other hand, different states lead to different consequences, the decision is said to be *under uncertainty*. Thus to assume that decisions are taken under certainty need not imply that there is no uncertainty in the world; rather the uncertainty which is present does not bear on the problem at hand.

When variables do not affect the values of functions, they are usually not included as arguments. Accordingly, states of the world are mostly left unmentioned in problems of decision-making under certainty, as in the following familiar economic example.

Example 1.1. Consider a price-taking firm which maximizes profit by choosing a single input, say, labour ℓ. Given a production function $\Phi(\ell)$, and prices w for the input and p for the output, the firm's profit function becomes:

$$\pi(\ell) := p \cdot \Phi(\ell) - w \cdot \ell.$$

In this example, an *action* is the choice of an input level ℓ from the feasible set of all non-negative real numbers. The *consequence* is the resulting profit level $\pi(\ell)$. Figure 1.1 depicts this decision problem for a standard production function Φ.

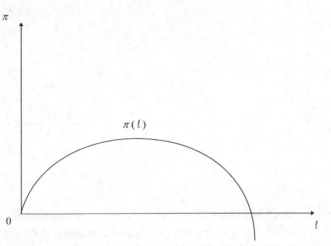

Fig. 1.1

Note that in this example the choice of an action (a particular level of labour input) leads to a consequence (a particular level of profit) independently of the state of the world. This is a problem of decision-making under certainty.

Assume now that the level of output is not determined solely by the level of labour input ℓ but depends in addition on some other factor, for example, the weather. Relevant states of the world are weather conditions: say, rain s_1, and sunshine s_2. The set of states of the world is $S = \{s_1, s_2\}$. The fact that output now depends on the state of the world is reflected in the production function which is written as $\Phi(s, \ell)$ where $s \in S$.

Assume further that the firm is more productive in fine weather than foul, i.e.:

$$\Phi(s_2, \ell) > \Phi(s_1, \ell) \text{ for all } \ell.$$

Then the firm's profit will be higher at each level of labour input when there is sunshine than when there is rain:

$$\pi(s_2, \ell) := p \cdot \Phi(s_2, \ell) - w \cdot \ell > p \cdot \Phi(s_1, \ell) - w \cdot \ell =: \pi(s_1, \ell).$$

If there is uncertainty about future weather conditions, the question of what level of input (i.e. what action) to choose becomes a problem of decision-making under uncertainty. The consequence of an action depends on the state of the weather, i.e. $f(s,\ell) = \pi(s,\ell)$, $s \in S$. Figure 1.2 illustrates the case.

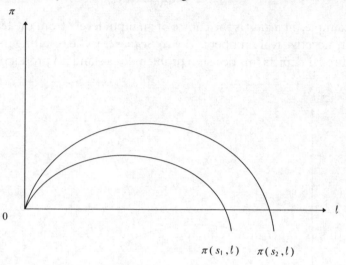

Fig. 1.2 ∎

It should be clear from this example that decision-making under certainty is just a special case of decision-making under uncertainty. If $\Phi(s_2,\ell) = \Phi(s_1,\ell)$, then $\pi(s_2,\ell) = \pi(s_1,\ell)$ and the firm's level of profit is independent of the prevailing weather conditions. In this case, the two profit functions of Figure 1.2 coincide, and the choice problem is identical to that depicted in Figure 1.1.

1.2 Decision-Making under Uncertainty: An Alternative Representation

There is another way to think about decision-making under uncertainty. It is in essence identical to that described above but is sometimes easier to work with. Since the relationship among actions, states of the world, and consequences is described by the function $f\colon S \times A \to C$ and since a probability measure[1] is defined on S, there is an induced probability distribution on the set of consequences for each action. In other words, for each action $a \in A$, there is a probability distribution on C defined as follows:

[1] i.e., there is a well-defined probability distribution on S. A review of basic concepts of probability theory is provided in Appendix A.

For any (measurable) subset of consequences $K \subset C$
$$\text{prob } \{K\} := \text{prob } \{s \in S \mid f(s,a) \in K\}.$$

This simply says that the probability of a particular consequence is equal to the probability of the states of the world which lead to this consequence given a particular action. Note that the probability of a consequence depends upon the action a which is chosen. So one could equally well say that the choice of an action amounts to the choice of a probability distribution on consequences. An equivalent way to view decision-making under uncertainty is to think about it as a choice amongst alternative probability distributions (or *lotteries*, *prospects*, *gambles*, etc.).

Example 1.1. (*continued*). Given the probabilities of state 1 and state 2, for each non-negative input level ℓ, the firm faces a probability distribution over the resulting profit levels:

$$\text{prob } \{\pi(s_1,\ell)\} = \text{prob } \{s_1\}$$
$$\text{prob } \{\pi(s_2,\ell)\} = \text{prob } \{s_2\}.$$

To make the example more concrete, assume the particular production function:

$$\phi(s,\ell) = \begin{cases} \sqrt{\ell} & \text{for} \quad s = s_1 \\ 2 \cdot \sqrt{\ell} & \text{for} \quad s = s_2 \end{cases}$$

and the particular probability distribution:

$$\text{prob } \{s_1\} = \frac{3}{4}; \text{prob } \{s_2\} = \frac{1}{4}.$$

For prices $p = 2$ and $w = 1$, choosing $\ell = 1$ implies the following probability distribution over profits:

$$\text{prob } \{\pi = 1\} = \frac{3}{4}; \text{prob } \{\pi = 3\} = \frac{1}{4}.$$

Similarly, for $\ell = 4$, the firm faces the probability distribution:

$$\text{prob } \{\pi = 0\} = \frac{3}{4}; \text{prob } \{\pi = 4\} = \frac{1}{4}. \qquad \blacksquare$$

The choice of an action in an uncertain world may be viewed either as the choice of a state-dependent outcome or as the choice of a probability distribution over outcomes. The distinction is represented diagrammatically in the following example.

Example 1.1. (*continued*). Suppose that the set of actions A consists of two actions only. Recall that actions were levels of labour input ℓ. Hence consider $A = \{\ell_1, \ell_2\}$ to be the set of feasible actions.

In the state-space approach, a choice of action ℓ_i is viewed as a choice of the state-contingent profit levels ($\pi(s_1,\ell_i)$, $\pi(s_2,\ell_i)$). Indicating the state by a subscript to simplify notation, the two possible levels of labour input lead to two pairs of state-dependent profit levels:

$$\{(\pi_1(\ell_1), \pi_2(\ell_1)\,), (\pi_1(\ell_2), \pi_2(\ell_2)\,)\}.$$

These two state-contingent profit pairs may be illustrated as two points in a diagram with π_1 and π_2 on the axes (Figure 1.3).

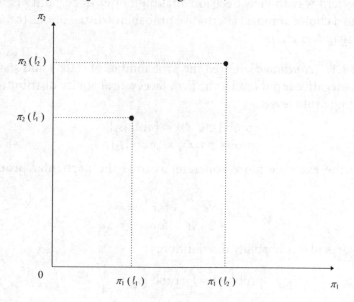

Fig. 1.3

Alternatively, given a probability distribution on the set of states $S = \{s_1, s_2\}$, the choice of an action ℓ_i can be viewed as the choice of a probability distribution on the four profit levels:

$$\{\pi_1(\ell_1), \pi_2(\ell_1), \pi_1(\ell_2), \pi_2(\ell_2)\}.$$

As explained in greater detail in Appendix A, such a probability distribution can be represented by a vector $p = (p_1, p_2, p_3, p_4)$ where:

$$p_1 = \text{prob}\,\{\pi_1(\ell_1)\}; p_2 = \text{prob}\,\{\pi_2(\ell_1)\};$$
$$p_3 = \text{prob}\,\{\pi_1(\ell_2)\}; p_4 = \text{prob}\,\{\pi_2(\ell_2)\}.$$

Hence the choice between two actions can be viewed as the choice amongst probability vectors p. For example, suppose that the probability of s_1 is 0.4 and the probability of s_2 is 0.6. Then the choice between the two levels of labour input corresponds to the choice between the following probability distributions:

	$\pi_1(\ell_1)$	$\pi_2(\ell_1)$	$\pi_1(\ell_2)$	$\pi_2(\ell_2)$
ℓ_1	0.4	0.6	0	0
ℓ_2	0	0	0.4	0.6

    ■

If there are only three basic outcomes, probability distributions are vectors with three components $p = (p_1,p_2,p_3)$ and it is possible to depict them in a two-dimensional diagram. The following example illustrates this possibility.

Example 1.2. Consider the choices of a firm about eight different input levels and suppose that there are three states $\{s_1,s_2,s_3\}$ which occur with equal probability. Assume that only three profit levels are possible (π_A,π_B,π_C) which are ranked $\pi_A < \pi_B < \pi_C$. The mapping from states and actions (input levels) to outcomes (profit levels) is as follows:

Action

		ℓ_1	ℓ_2	ℓ_3	ℓ_4	ℓ_5	ℓ_6	ℓ_7	ℓ_8
	s_1	π_A	π_A	π_A	π_A	π_A	π_A	π_B	π_C
States	s_2	π_B	π_A	π_C	π_B	π_A	π_A	π_B	π_C
	s_3	π_C	π_C	π_C	π_B	π_B	π_A	π_B	π_C

    ■

Any probability distribution associated with the three profit levels (π_A,π_B,π_C) is represented by a point with three non-negative co-ordinates (p_A,p_B,p_C) that sum to one, where p_A denotes the probability of profit level π_A, p_B that of level π_B and p_C that of π_C.

Since $p_B = 1 - p_A - p_C \geq 0$ is unambiguously determined for any two probabilities (p_A,p_C), one can depict any probability distribution on (π_A,π_B,π_C) by a point in Figure 1.4. The probability distributions induced by the actions in the table are indicated in Figure 1.4 by the symbol '•'.

Choosing between actions randomly induces further probability distributions over these outcomes. For example, if the choice between input levels ℓ_1 and ℓ_2 is made by tossing a coin, choosing ℓ_1 if 'heads' comes up and ℓ_2 if 'tails' results, one obtains the following probability distribution over the profit levels (π_A,π_B,π_C):

- π_A occurs if 'heads' results and state 1 occurs and if 'tails' comes up and either state 1 or state 2 occurs; hence with probability $0.5 \cdot 1/3 + 0.5 \cdot (1/3 + 1/3) = 0.5$,
- π_B occurs if 'heads' comes up and state 2 occurs, i.e. with probability $0.5 \cdot 1/3 = 1/6$, and
- π_C occurs if state 3 occurs and either 'heads' or 'tails' results, hence with probability $0.5 \cdot 1/3 + 0.5 \cdot 1/3 = 2/6$.

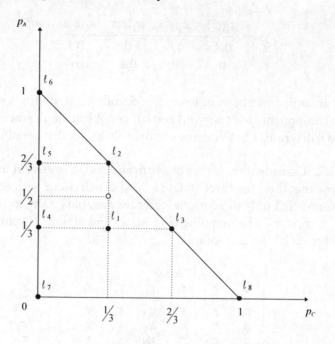

Fig. 1.4

This probability distribution is indicated by the symbol '○' in Figure 1.4. Clearly one can obtain any probability distribution over the three outcomes by using an appropriate randomization over actions. ∎

1.3 Decision-Making and Expected Utility

The two previous sections have argued that a decision-maker who faces uncertainty about the outcomes of her actions can view the objects of her choice either as state-contingent outcomes or as probability distributions. This raises the question of whether the decision-maker's preferences should order

- the set of state-contingent outcomes, or
- the set of probability distributions over outcomes.

Both approaches are possible and have been used in the literature.

The former is usually referred to as the 'state-preference' approach. If the set of states is finite, one can write state-contingent outcomes as vectors $(c_1, \ldots, c_S)$ from the set of all state-contingent outcomes:

$$C^S := \{(c_1, \ldots, c_S) \mid c_s = f(s,a), a \in A\}.$$

If preferences on the set C^S satisfy the usual assumptions of *completeness, transitivity,* and *continuity,* they can be represented[2] by $V(c_1, \ldots, c_S)$, a utility function $V: C^S \to \mathbb{R}$. Notice that, in this case, it is not necessary to specify probabilities over states or outcomes. It suffices to know what outcomes from an action will occur in each state.

Figure 1.5 shows indifference curves for such a utility function for the case of two states, $S = 2$. Three indifference curves $V(c_1, c_2) = k_i$, for $k_1 > k_2 > k_3$, are drawn. It is assumed that the outcome is something desirable in each state. Hence, the decision-maker prefers to get more rather than less of the outcome in each state. This implies that the level of utility increases in the direction of higher values of the state-contingent outcomes.

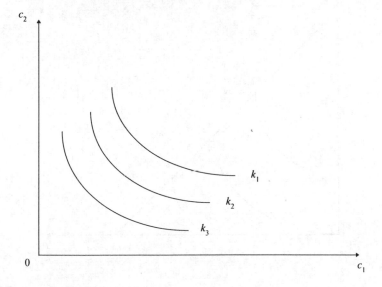

Fig. 1.5

Similarly, given a set of outcomes C and a probability distribution on the set of states,[3] each action induces a probability distribution on the outcomes in C. If the set of consequences is finite, say $C := \{c_1, \ldots, c_n\}$, then each action determines a vector of probabilities from the set

$$\Delta^n := \{(p_1, \ldots, p_n) \in \mathbb{R}^n_+ \mid \sum_{i=1}^{n} p_i = 1\},$$

the $(n-1)$-dimensional simplex, with $p_i = \text{Prob}(\{s \in S \mid f(s,a) = c_i\})$.

---

[2] For an exposition of the general representation theorem, see e.g. Varian (1992, 111–15).
[3] The function $f(s,a)$ must also be measurable. Since this condition is satisfied for all functions one practically works with, it is not mentioned.

A preference ordering over such probability distributions will order the set Δ^n. Once again, if preferences are *complete*, *transitive*, and *continuous*, they can be represented by a utility function $U(p_1,\ldots,p_n)$, $U: \Delta^n \to \mathbb{R}$. Figure 1.6 shows such a preference ordering for the case of three outcomes, $n = 3$. Indifference curves $U(p_1,p_2,p_3) = k_i$, for levels $k_1 > k_2 > k_3$, have been drawn in this diagram. Note that they increase in the direction of p_3. This indicates that the consequence c_3 is the most preferred outcome, since this decision-maker prefers a probability distribution that puts higher probability on this outcome.

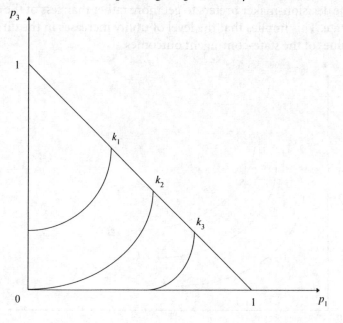

Fig. 1.6

The *expected utility approach* makes additional assumptions on the decision-maker's preferences over probability distributions. If these preferences satisfy a further condition,[4] that of *independence*, indifference curves over probability distributions will be linear and parallel. Moreover, the utility representation of preferences that comply with the independence assumption has the following form:

$$\sum_{i=1}^{n} p_i \cdot u(c_i)$$

for some utility function over outcomes $u: C \to \mathbb{R}$.

---

[4] Appendix B of this chapter provides a brief introduction to the axiomatic approach to expected utility theory.

This representation evaluates a probability distribution simply by computing the expected value of the utilities of the outcomes, $u(c_i)$. A decision-making rule of this type had been suggested by the Swiss mathematician Daniel Bernoulli as early as 1738. John von Neumann and Oscar Morgenstern (1944) were the first, however, to recognize the *independence axiom* (together with *completeness, transitivity*, and *continuity*) as a necessary and sufficient condition for such an *expected utility representation*. The utility function over outcomes $u(c_i)$ is therefore often referred to as the *von Neumann–Morgenstern (expected) utility index*.

In economics and finance, the expected utility approach has become the dominant paradigm of decision-making under uncertainty. This is at least partly due to two attractive features of this special representation. The curvature of the von Neumann–Morgenstern utility index can be interpreted as the decision-maker's attitude towards risk and this interpretation turns out to be consistent with many statistical decision rules (see Section 1.4). Furthermore, one can view the expected utility representation either as a utility function over state-contingent outcomes or as a utility function over probabilities.

For given consequences $\{c_1, \ldots, c_n\}$ and a given von Neumann–Morgenstern utility function, u, one can treat

$$\sum_{i=1}^{n} p_i \cdot u(c_i)$$

as a function of the probability distribution $(p_1, \ldots, p_n)$. Hence, in this perspective, the expected utility representation is a special case of a utility function on probabilities,

$$U(p_1, \ldots, p_n) = \sum_{i=1}^{n} p_i \cdot u(c_i).$$

Figure 1.7 shows indifference curves of this utility function over probabilities in Δ^3.

Substituting for p_2 ($:= 1 - p_1 - p_3$), the following formula describes an indifference curve:

$$p_3 = \frac{k - u(c_2)}{u(c_3) - u(c_2)} - \frac{u(c_1) - u(c_2)}{u(c_3) - u(c_2)} \cdot p_1.$$

Indifference curves are obviously linear and upward-sloping if

$$u(c_3) > u(c_2) > u(c_1).$$

This case has been assumed in the diagram. Furthermore, since changing the utility level k shifts only the intercept of an indifference curve, leaving the slope unchanged, indifference curves must be parallel.

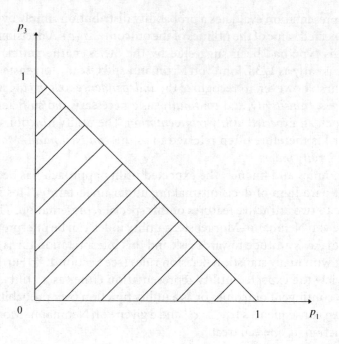

Fig. 1.7

On the other hand, if one interprets the indices $i = 1,\ldots,n$ as states for which the probability distribution is given, $(p_1,\ldots,p_n)$, one can view the expected utility representation as a special case of a utility function ranking state-contingent consumption vectors $(c_1,\ldots,c_n)$,

$$V(c_1,\ldots,c_n) = \sum_{i=1}^{n} p_i \cdot u(c_i).$$

Figure 1.8 gives an example for two states (c_1, c_2).

To obtain the convex shape of the indifference curves, it is assumed that the von Neumann–Morgenstern utility function $u(\cdot)$ is *concave*. If they are differentiable as well, one can derive the slope of an indifference curve by implicitly differentiating the equation of the indifference curve,

$$p_1 \cdot u(c_1) + p_2 \cdot u(c_2) = k,$$

to yield:

$$\frac{dc_2}{dc_1} = -\frac{p_1 \cdot u'(c_1)}{p_2 \cdot u'(c_2)},$$

where $u'(\cdot)$ denotes the derivative of the expected utility index $u(\cdot)$. A special property of the expected utility representation interpreted as a utility function over state-contingent outcomes is the fact that the slope of each indifference

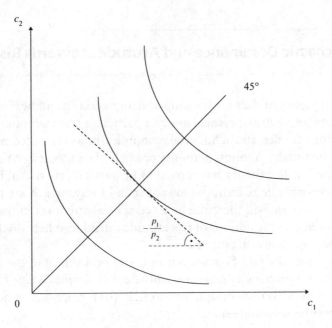

Fig. 1.8

curve on the 45°- line is always equal to $-p_1/p_2$. This is easy to see from the formula for the slope since, on the 45°– line, $c_1 = c_2$ and therefore $u'(c_1) = u'(c_2)$ no matter what specific functional form the utility index u may have.

Up to this point it has been assumed that the set of states and outcomes is finite. This need not be the case. Some probability distributions considered in finance and economics are characterized by continuous distribution functions. Fortunately, the expected utility approach can be extended to cover this case. For probability distributions over continuous sets of states or outcomes, one can no longer assign probabilities to single points.[5] Hence, one cannot form a sum to obtain an expected utility but must integrate the von Neumann–Morgenstern utility index over states or outcomes. In such cases, the following notation is used

$$\int_C u(c)\, g(c)\, \mathrm{d}c$$

for probability distributions given by a *density function* $g(c)$, or

$$\int_C u(c)\, \mathrm{d}G(c)$$

for probability distributions given by a *distribution function* $G(c)$. In both cases, integration takes place over the set C.

---

[5] For more on the distinction between discrete and continuous distributions, see Appendix A.

1.4 Stochastic Dominance and Attitudes towards Risk

The general theory of decision-making under uncertainty allows for all kinds of consequences, such as, personal injury, a particular team winning a contest, consumption bundles, etc. In financial economics, however, outcomes or consequences are usually amounts of money or levels of wealth. It is in this context that expected utility theory has proven to be particularly useful because it allows us to characterize attitudes towards risk in ways which are intuitively appealing. This case will therefore be given special attention in this section. Note, however, that the notions of risk attitude introduced here do not extend easily to more general outcome sets.

In this section, the set of consequences C will be a subset of the real numbers, $C \subset \mathbb{R}$, and probability measures will be either simple (where C is a finite set) or represented by distribution functions. In the former case, expected utility can be written as a finite sum:

$$U(p) = \sum_{x_i \in C} u(x_i) \cdot p_i,$$

where $U(\cdot)$ denotes the expected utility function, u is the expected utility index (or Von Neumann–Morgenstern utility index), $C := \{x_1, \ldots, x_n\}$ is the finite set of consequences, and $p = (p_1, \ldots, p_n)$ is a probability distribution. In the latter case, expected utility is expressed as an integral:

$$U(G) = \int_C u(x) \, dG(x),$$

where $G: \mathbb{R} \to [0,1]$ is a distribution function representing the probability distribution over outcomes.

Characterizing intuitive notions of 'riskiness' is easier for probability distributions defined over monetary outcomes since it seems natural to assume that more money is preferred to less. The following example illustrates this point.

Example 1.3. Consider the following lotteries:

$$\Gamma_A = \begin{cases} 100 \text{ with probability } 0.5 \\ 0 \text{ with probability } 0.5 \end{cases}$$
$$\Gamma_B = \{ 100 \text{ with probability } 1.0$$
$$\Gamma_C = \begin{cases} 250 \text{ with probability } 0.5 \\ 0 \text{ with probability } 0.5 \end{cases}$$
$$\Gamma_D = \begin{cases} 150 \text{ with probability } 0.5 \\ 50 \text{ with probability } 0.5 \end{cases}$$

It seems natural to assume that 'rational' decision-makers will prefer Γ_B over Γ_A and Γ_C over Γ_A since Γ_B and Γ_C yield at least as much or more under all contingencies. Similarly, Γ_D appears to dominate Γ_A because Γ_D has a higher outcome in the best and in the worst case than Γ_A and the best and worst outcomes occur with the same probability. But what about a comparison of Γ_B and Γ_D? Under some contingencies, Γ_D is better than Γ_B and under others Γ_B is better than Γ_D. The expected values of Γ_B and Γ_D are the same, however. One may interpret a decision-maker's choice between Γ_B and Γ_D as an indication of risk-aversion or risk-affinity. Similarly, a preference for Γ_B over Γ_C can be interpreted as a stronger degree of risk-aversion since the expected value of Γ_C is higher than 100. Figure 1.9 shows the distribution functions of these lotteries.

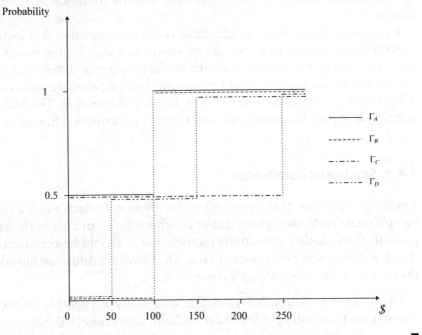

Fig. 1.9 ■

Since the definitions and results of the following subsections hold for discrete as well as continuous probability distributions, it is convenient to use a notation which covers both cases. Continuous probability distributions are usually given by a distribution function which associates with a number x the probability that an outcome less than or equal to x occurs. For continuous probability distributions, one cannot generally assign a probability to each outcome as one usually does in the case of discrete probability distributions. It is, however, possible to characterize discrete probability distributions by a

Decision-Making under Uncertainty

distribution function. For example, the discrete probability distribution $(p_1, \ldots, p_n)$ on the outcomes $\{x_1, \ldots, x_n\}$ can be described by the distribution function

$$G_p(x) := \text{Prob}\{y \in C \mid y \le x\} = \sum_{i \in I(x)} p_i,$$

where $I(x) := \{i \mid x_i \le x\}$ denotes the set of indices i for which the outcome x_i is less than or equal to x.

Figure 1.9 shows the distribution functions for the four simple probability distributions of Example 1.3. Notice that distribution functions of discrete probability distributions are step functions with discontinuous jumps at those outcomes which have a positive probability. In contrast, continuous probability distributions have distribution functions that rise continuously from zero to one.

It is a useful fact that every right-hand continuous function that increases monotonically from zero to one can be viewed as a distribution function of some probability distribution. A second useful property of distribution functions is that the area above a distribution function and below the value $G(x) = 1$ represents the expected value of the probability distribution. The following definitions of risk-dominance are cast in terms of distribution functions.

1.4.1 Stochastic dominance

Example 1.3 suggests that a probability distribution F which yields a higher pay-off under each contingency and/or attaches a higher probability to higher pay-offs than another probability distribution G should be preferred by a decision-maker who prefers more to less. The following definition introduces the notion of *first-order stochastic dominance*.

DEFINITION 1.1. A probability distribution F *dominates* another probability distribution G according to *first-order stochastic dominance* (FSD) if

$$F(x) \le G(x) \text{ for all } x \in C.$$

Two examples will help to clarify this definition.

Example 1.4. Consider the distribution functions:

$$F(x) = \begin{cases} 0 & \text{if } x < 2.5 \\ 0.4 & \text{if } 2.5 \le x < 3.5, \\ 1 & \text{if } 3.5 \le x \end{cases} \quad G(x) = \begin{cases} 0 & \text{if } x < 2 \\ 0.5 & \text{if } 2 \le x < 3 \\ 1 & \text{if } 3 \le x \end{cases}$$

Since $F(x) \le G(x)$ for all x, F dominates G by FSD.

16

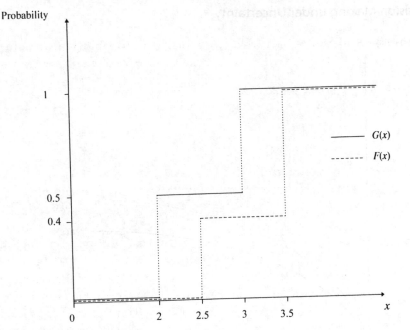

Fig. 1.10 ■

Example 1.5. Consider the following two probability distributions represented in Figure 1.11:

$$F(x) = \begin{cases} 1 - e^{-x} & \text{if } x \geq 0 \\ 0 & \text{if } x < 0, \end{cases} \quad G(x) = \begin{cases} 1 - e^{-2x} & \text{if } x \geq 0 \\ 0 & \text{if } x < 0. \end{cases}$$

Obviously, $F(x) \leq G(x)$ for all x and F dominates G by FSD. ■

An expected-utility-maximizing agent who prefers more to less unambiguously prefers first-order stochastically dominant probability distributions. This property of first-order stochastic dominance is stated formally as:

LEMMA 1.1. *F* dominates *G* by FSD if and only if

$$\int_C u(x)\, dF(x) \geq \int_C u(x)\, dG(x)$$

for all *strictly increasing* expected utility indexes $u(x)$.

The lemma implies that it is sufficient to rank any two probability distributions by FSD that expected-utility-maximizing agents with strictly increasing utility indexes are unanimous in preferring one of the two distributions. Unfortunately, this is rarely the case. As Example 1.3 shows, individuals who prefer more to less may nevertheless differ in their attitudes to risk. As a result, FSD is unable to provide a complete ordering of probability distributions.

A more refined ordering can be achieved by ranking distributions with the same or higher expected values according to a measure of their dispersion or spread. The following definition introduces the notion of *second-order stochastic dominance*.

17

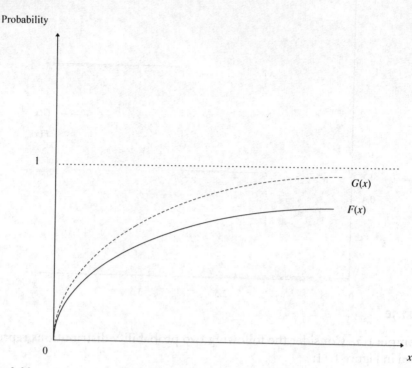

Fig. 1.11

DEFINITION 1.2. A probability distribution F dominates another probability distribution G according to *second-order stochastic dominance* (SSD) if, for all $x \in C$:

$$\int_{-\infty}^{x} F(y)\, dy \leq \int_{-\infty}^{x} G(y)\, dy.$$

This definition requires the dominant distribution to have a smaller area beneath the distribution function for any $x \in C$. Once again, two examples will help to clarify the definition.

Example 1.6. Consider the following distribution functions:

$$F(x) = \begin{cases} 0 & \text{if} \quad x < 10 \\ 1 & \text{if} \quad 10 \leq x, \end{cases} \qquad G(x) = \begin{cases} 0 & \text{if} \quad x < 5 \\ 0.5 & \text{if} \quad 5 \leq x < 15. \\ 1 & \text{if} \quad 15 \leq x \end{cases}$$

Note that $F(x) < G(x)$ for $x \in [5,10)$ and $F(x) > G(x)$ for $x \in [10,15)$. Figure 1.12 depicts the two distribution functions.

From the figure it is clear that the area below F is smaller than the area under G for all $x < 15$ and for $x \geq 15$ the areas are equal. ∎

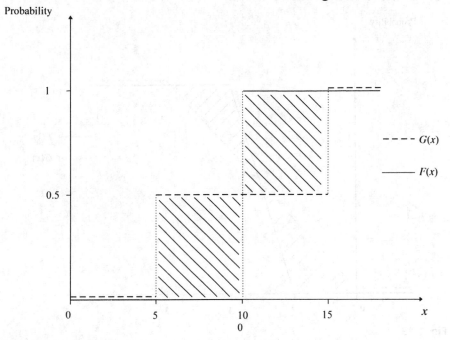

Fig. 1.12

Example 1.7. Let the two distribution functions be as follows:

$$F(x) = \begin{cases} 0 & \text{if } x < 1 \\ (x-1) & \text{if } 1 \le x < 2, \\ 1 & \text{if } 2 \le x \end{cases} \quad G(x) = \begin{cases} 0 & \text{if } x < 0 \\ \frac{x}{3} & \text{if } 0 \le x < 3. \\ 1 & \text{if } 3 \le x \end{cases}$$

Figure 1.13 illustrates these distribution functions. Comparing the areas beneath the respective distribution functions up to any point x, it is clear that the condition for F to dominate G by SSD is satisfied. ∎

As in the case of first-order stochastic dominance, there is a relationship between the expected utilities of two distributions which is both necessary and sufficient for one to dominate the other by SSD.

LEMMA 1.2. F dominates G by second-order stochastic dominance if and only if

$$\int_C u(x) \, dF(x) \ge \int_C u(x) \, dG(x)$$

for all *increasing* and *concave* expected utility indexes $u(x)$.

LEMMA 1.2 implies that it is sufficient to rank any two probability distributions by SSD that expected-utility-maximizing agents with *increasing* and *concave* expected utility indexes are unanimous in preferring one of the two

19

Probability

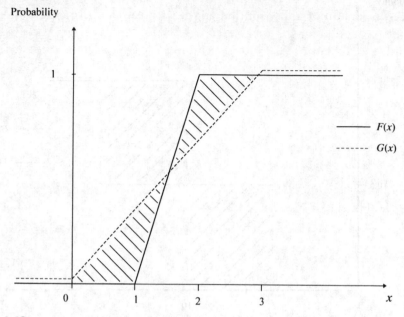

Fig. 1.13

distributions. There will be a greater degree of unanimity amongst agents in this class than amongst the broader class whose expected utility indexes are strictly increasing only.

In general, the more narrowly one defines the characteristics of the expected utility index, the greater the degree of unanimity amongst the agents in that class and the more complete the ordering of probability distributions. Third, fourth, and higher orders of stochastic dominance have been suggested as ways of progressively refining and completing the ordering of distributions. The difficulty is that the set of agents whose expected utility indexes satisfy the increasingly more proscriptive conditions becomes an ever smaller subset of the universe of economic agents. The ordering of distributions can only be made more complete by narrowing the range of opinion considered.

1.4.2 Curvature of the expected utility index and attitudes to risk

Two probability distributions with the same expected value which can be ranked by second-order stochastic dominance will be distinguished by the 'weight' of the probability mass in the tails of their density functions. The SSD-dominant distribution will have less mass in its tails, i.e. will be more concentrated about the mean or less dispersed than the distribution it dominates.

Since dispersion of a distribution about its mean is one measure of risk, second-order dominance can be used to rank distributions with equal means according to their riskiness. Moreover, the link between SSD and the strict concavity of the expected utility index implies that the curvature of the expected utility index is related to an individual's attitude to risk.

Two questions can be asked of a decision-maker to reveal his attitude to risk:

- would he prefer to receive the expected value of a lottery with certainty than to receive the lottery itself?
- what sum would he be willing to pay to avoid the risk involved in a lottery?

The following definition introduces two concepts which correspond to the answers to these questions.

DEFINITION 1.3. The *certainty equivalent* of a probability distribution F is the real number $c(F)$ which satisfies:

$$u(c(F)) = \int_C u(x)\, dF(x) =: U(F).$$

The *risk premium* is the real number $q(F)$ which satisfies:

$$q(F) = \mu(F) - c(F),$$

where $\mu(F) := \int_C x\, dF(x)$ denotes the expected value of the distribution F.

The *certainty equivalent* measures a decision-maker's willingness to pay for a lottery. The *risk premium* is simply the difference between the expected value of a lottery and its certainty equivalent. If a decision-maker is prepared to pay more for a probability distribution than the expected value of it, then the risk involved in the probability distribution appears to be valuable for her. Hence, one feels entitled to call her *risk-loving*. On the other hand, a decision-maker who would pay less for a probability distribution than its expected value seems to require compensation for the risk involved and may therefore be characterized as *risk-averse*. These considerations suggest calling a decision-maker:

$$\left\{ \begin{array}{l} \textit{rise-averse} \\ \textit{risk-neutral} \\ \textit{risk-loving} \end{array} \right\} \quad \text{if} \quad \left\{ \begin{array}{l} q(F) > 0 \\ q(F) = 0 \\ q(F) < 0 \end{array} \right\} \quad \text{for all probability distributions } F.$$

This characterizes an agent's attitude to risk according to her willingness to pay to secure a certain (i.e. riskless) outcome.

A second approach is to characterize an agent's attitude to risk according to whether or not she prefers a probability distribution to its expected value. In this approach, an agent is said to be:

- *risk-averse* if, for any probability distribution, she prefers the expected value of the distribution to the distribution itself;
- *risk-neutral* if, for any probability distribution, she is indifferent between the expected value of the distribution and the distribution itself; and
- *risk-loving* if, for any probability distribution, she prefers the distribution to its expected value.

It is easy to see that the two characterizations of risk-attitudes are identical. From Definition 1.3:

$$u(\mu(F) - q(F)) = u(c(F)) = \int u(x)\, dF(x) =: U(F).$$

Since $u(x)$ is strictly increasing, it follows that:

$$q(F) \left\{ \overset{\geq}{\underset{<}{=}} \right\} 0 \Leftrightarrow u(\mu(F)) \left\{ \overset{\geq}{\underset{<}{=}} \right\} U(F),$$

where $\mu(F)$ denotes the expected value of the distribution F and $U(F)$ is the expected utility of the distribution F.

The second of these two equivalent characterizations links an agent's attitude to risk directly to the curvature of his expected utility index $u(x)$. In particular, an agent is:

$$\left\{ \begin{array}{l} \text{risk-averse} \\ \text{risk-neutral} \\ \text{risk-loving} \end{array} \right\} \Leftrightarrow u(\mu(F)) \left\{ \overset{\geq}{\underset{<}{=}} \right\} U(F)$$

for all probability distributions F. The necessary and sufficient condition is equivalent to a statement about the curvature of $u(x)$.

Example 1.8. Consider an arbitrary probability distribution F that is concentrated on two outcomes $x_1, x_2 \in C$. Then:

$$u(\mu(F)) := u(p_1 \cdot x_1 + p_2 \cdot x_2) \left\{ \overset{\geq}{\underset{<}{=}} \right\} p_1 \cdot u(x_1) + p_2 \cdot u(x_2) =: U(F)$$

depending upon whether the agent is $\left\{ \begin{array}{l} \text{risk-averse} \\ \text{risk-neutral} \\ \text{risk-loving} \end{array} \right\}.$

Now recall that a function $u: \mathbb{R} \to \mathbb{R}$ is $\left\{ \begin{array}{l} \text{concave} \\ \text{linear} \\ \text{convex} \end{array} \right\}$ if:

$$u(\lambda \cdot x_1 + (1 - \lambda) \cdot x_2) \left\{ \overset{\geq}{\underset{<}{=}} \right\} \lambda \cdot u(x_1) + (1 - \lambda) \cdot u(x_2)$$

holds for arbitrary $\lambda, 0 \leq \lambda \leq 1$.

Substituting $\lambda = p_1$ establishes the result that an expected-utility-maximizing agent is:

$$\left\{\begin{array}{l}\text{risk-averse}\\\text{risk-neutral}\\\text{risk-loving}\end{array}\right\} \text{ if } u(x) \text{ is } \left\{\begin{array}{l}\text{concave}\\\text{linear}\\\text{convex}\end{array}\right\}.$$

Figure 1.14 illustrates this result.   ∎

Finally, note that curvature properties are usually local characteristics. Thus, as shown in Figure 1.15, an agent may be risk-averse with respect to some gambles and risk-loving with respect to others.

Note that a decision-maker with risk preferences as depicted in Figure 1.15 is *risk-loving* for gamble F which is concentrated on the outcomes x_1 and x_2 but *risk-averse* for the lottery $\bar{F}$ which is concentrated on the outcomes $\bar{x}_1$ and $\bar{x}_2$.

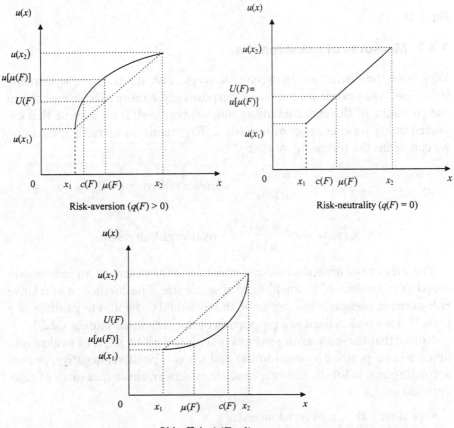

Fig. 1.14

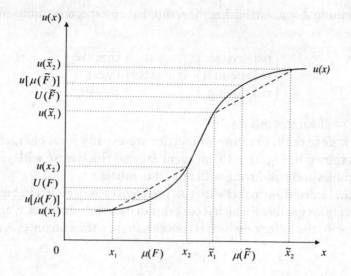

Fig. 1.15

1.4.3 Measures of risk-aversion

Very often the distinction between risk-averse, risk-neutral, and risk-loving behaviour is too crude for analytical purposes and a more precise measure of the curvature of the expected utility index is required. If we assume that expected utility indexes are continuously differentiable and strictly increasing, we can define the following measures,

$$R_a(x) := -\frac{u''(x)}{u'(x)} \qquad \textit{absolute risk-aversion;}$$

$$R_r(x) := -x \cdot \frac{u''(x)}{u'(x)} \qquad \textit{relative risk-aversion.}$$

The measure of absolute risk-aversion gauges the degree of an individual's aversion to gambles of a (small) fixed absolute size. The coefficient of relative risk-aversion measures the degree of an individual's aversion to gambles of a (small) size which is fixed as a proportion of the individual's initial wealth.

Notice that these measures may vary with the point $x \in C$ of evaluation. Since $u'(x)$ is positive by assumption and $u''(x)$ is positive, negative, or zero according as u is locally convex, concave, or linear, these measures of risk-aversion are:

- positive if the agent is risk-averse;
- negative if the agent is risk-loving; and
- zero if the agent is risk-neutral.

It is easy to check that linear transformations of the expected utility index do not affect these measures of risk-aversion.

Many comparative-static results depend upon the degree of risk-aversion a decision-maker possesses. In portfolio choice problems, for example, a decision-maker's degree of absolute risk-aversion determines whether or not he responds to an increase in wealth by increasing his demand for a risky asset. This problem is examined in Example 1.9.

The following lemma identifies classes of expected utility indexes which demonstrate constant, absolute, or relative risk-aversion.

LEMMA 1.3. (i) The expected utility index u has *constant absolute risk-aversion* of α if it has the following functional form:

$$u(x) = \begin{cases} c^{\alpha x} & \alpha > 0 \\ & \text{for} \\ 1 - c^{\alpha x} & \alpha < 0 \end{cases},$$

where c is an arbitrary number.

(ii) The expected utility index u has *constant relative risk-aversion* of ε if it has the following functional form:

$$u(x) = \begin{cases} (1 - \varepsilon)x^{1-\varepsilon} & \varepsilon \neq 1 \\ & \text{for} \\ \ln x & \varepsilon = 1 \end{cases}.$$

This section concludes with an example of an investor choosing a portfolio. The comparative statics of this approach depend crucially on the measure of absolute risk-aversion.

Example 1.9. (*Portfolio choice*). Consider an investor who can buy a risky asset a or a riskless asset b. Denoting the return from the risky asset in state s by r_s and the return from the riskless asset as R, one obtains the following return from the portfolio (a,b) in state s:

$$W_s(a,b) := r_s \cdot a + R \cdot b.$$

Let the price of the risky asset be q and the price of the riskless asset be the numeraire. Hence the investor's budget constraint is given by

$$q \cdot a + b = W_o,$$

where W_o denotes the initial wealth of the investor. Assuming perfect markets, such that short selling of assets is feasible so long as state-dependent wealth $W_s(a,b)$ of the portfolio remains positive, the problem can be simplified by substituting for the riskless asset, $b = W_o - q \cdot a$. Assuming a finite set of states

$S = \{1, \ldots, S\}$ with probability distribution $p = (p_1, \ldots, p_s, \ldots, p_S)$, one can write the optimization problem of an expected utility-maximizing investor in the following form:

Choose the portfolio (a,b) to maximize

$$\sum_{s \in S} p_s \cdot u(W_s(a,b))$$

subject to

$$q \cdot a + b = W_o.$$

Substituting the budget constraint $b = W_o - q \cdot a$, this can be re-expressed as the unconstrained problem:

Choose a to maximize

$$\sum_{s \in S} p_s \cdot u(R \cdot W_o + (r_s - R \cdot q) \cdot a).$$

The first-order condition for this problem is

$$\sum_{s \in S} p_s \cdot u'(R \cdot W_o + (r_s - R \cdot q) \cdot a) \cdot [r_s - R \cdot q] = 0,$$

where $u'(\cdot)$ denotes the first derivative of $u(\cdot)$. If the investor is risk-averse, i.e. $u''(\cdot)$, the second derivative of $u(\cdot)$, is strictly negative, then the second-order condition is

$$\sum_{s \in S} p_s \cdot u''(R \cdot W_o + (r_s - R \cdot q) \cdot a) \cdot [r_s - R \cdot q]^2 < 0.$$

A solution to the first-order condition must therefore be a maximum if the investor is risk-averse. This will be assumed for the remainder of the example.

The optimal choice of the risky asset characterized by the first-order condition depends on the rates of return, r_s and R, the asset price q, and initial wealth W_o. Of particular interest is the question of whether the demand for the risky asset is increasing or decreasing in initial wealth, i.e. whether investors with a higher initial wealth level demand more or less of the risky asset. The following lemma provides the answer to this question. Suppressing all arguments except initial wealth, W_o, one can write the demand function for the risky asset as $a^* = a(W_o)$. Letting $a'(\cdot)$ and $R_a'(\cdot)$ denote the first derivatives of the demand function $a(\cdot)$ and the absolute risk-aversion function $R_a(\cdot)$, respectively, we have:

LEMMA 1.4.

$$a'(W_o) > 0 \text{ if } R_a'(x) < 0,$$
$$a'(W_o) = 0 \text{ if } R_a'(x) = 0,$$
$$a'(W_o) < 0 \text{ if } R_a'(x) > 0.$$

PROOF. Since the demand function $a(W_o)$ is the optimal solution to the portfolio choice problem, it must satisfy the first-order condition:

$$\sum_{s\in S} p_s \cdot u'(R \cdot W_o + (r_s - R \cdot q) \cdot a(W_o)) \cdot [r_s - R \cdot q] = 0.$$

Differentiating this identity with respect to W_o, one obtains

$$\sum_{s\in S} p_s \cdot u''(R \cdot W_o + (r_s - R \cdot q) \cdot a(W_o)) \cdot [r_s - R \cdot q] \cdot R$$
$$+ \sum_{s\in S} p_s \cdot u''(R \cdot W_o + (r_s - R \cdot q) \cdot a(W_o)) \cdot [r_s - R \cdot q]^2 \cdot a'(W_o) = 0.$$

Solving for $a'(W_o)$, one has

$$a'(W_o) = -\left[\sum_{s\in S} p_s \cdot u''(R \cdot W_o + (r_s - R \cdot q) \cdot a(W_o)) \cdot [r_s - R \cdot q]^2\right]^{-1} \cdot$$
$$R \cdot \left[\sum_{s\in S} p_s \cdot u''(R \cdot W_o + (r_s - R \cdot q) \cdot a(W_o)) \cdot [r_s - R \cdot q]\right].$$

If the investor is risk-averse, $u''(\cdot) < 0$ and

$$\left[\sum_{s\in S} p_s \cdot u''(R \cdot W_o + (r_s - R \cdot q) \cdot a(W_o)) \cdot [r_s - R \cdot q]^2\right]$$

is negative. The sign of $a'(W_o)$ must therefore be the same as the sign of

$$\left[\sum_{s\in S} p_s \cdot u''(R \cdot W_o + (r_s - R \cdot q) \cdot a(W_o)) \cdot [r_s - R \cdot q]\right] \qquad (1.1)$$

Since $[r_s - R \cdot q]$ is positive for some states and negative for others, the sign of the expression (1.1) cannot be determined without further assumptions.

Recall the definition of the degree of absolute risk-aversion,

$$R_a(x) := -\frac{u''(x)}{u'(x)}.$$

Substituting for $u''(x) = -R_a(x) \cdot u'(x)$ and rearranging terms, one can transform (1.1) to yield

$$-\sum_{s\in S} p_s \cdot u'(R \cdot W_o + (r_s - R \cdot q) \cdot a(W_o)) \cdot [r_s - R \cdot q] \cdot R_a(R \cdot W_o$$
$$+ (r_s - R \cdot q) \cdot a(W_o)). \qquad (1.2)$$

Now note that, for all $s \in S$,

$$[r_s - R \cdot q] \cdot R_a(R \cdot W_o) \gtreqless [r_s - R \cdot q] \cdot R_a(R \cdot W_o + (r_s - R \cdot q) \cdot a(W_o)) \qquad (1.3)$$

if and only if $R_a'(x) \lesseqgtr 0$ holds.

Figure 1.16 illustrates inequality (1.3) for the case of decreasing absolute risk-aversion, $R_a'(x) < 0$. In this case,

$$[r_s - R \cdot q] \cdot R_a(R \cdot W_o) > [r_s - R \cdot q] \cdot R_a(R \cdot W_o + (r_s - R \cdot q) \cdot a(W_o)) \qquad (a)$$

Decision-Making under Uncertainty

must hold because,

$$\text{for } [r_s - R \cdot q] > 0, R \cdot W_o + (r_s - R \cdot q) \cdot a(W_o) > R \cdot W_o,$$

and by decreasing absolute risk-aversion

$$R_a(R \cdot W_o) > R_a(R \cdot W_o + (r_s - R \cdot q) \cdot a(W_o)), \qquad (b)$$

and

$$\text{for } [r_s - R \cdot q] < 0, R \cdot W_o + (r_s - R \cdot q) \cdot a(W_o) < R \cdot W_o,$$

and by decreasing absolute risk-aversion

$$R_a(R \cdot W_o) < R_a(R \cdot W_o + (r_s - R \cdot q) \cdot a(W_o)). \qquad (c)$$

Figure 1.16 illustrates this argument. The inequality (a) follows from multiplying the inequalities (b) and (c) by $[r_s - R \cdot q]$ which is positive for (b) and negative for (c).

Using 1.3, equation (1.2) therefore satisfies the following inequality,

$$-\sum_{s \in S} p_s \cdot u'(R \cdot W_o + (r_s - R \cdot q) \cdot a(W_o)) \cdot [r_s - R \cdot q] \cdot R_a(R \cdot W_o + (r_s - R \cdot q) \cdot a(W_o))$$

$$\gtreqless, -R_a(R \cdot W_o) \cdot [\sum_{s \in S} p_s \cdot u'(R \cdot W_o + (r_s - R \cdot q) \cdot a(W_o)) \cdot [r_s - R \cdot q]] = 0,$$

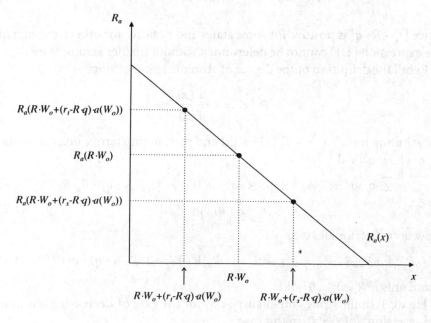

Fig. 1.16

where the expression in square brackets equals zero by the first-order condition. This completes the proof of the lemma. ∎

1.5 Mean-Variance Analysis: A Special Case of the Expected Utility Approach

In this section, we deal with economic agents whose preferences over probability distributions can be represented by a function of the mean and the variance of these probability distributions alone. This is known as *mean-variance analysis*.

In Section 1.3, we demonstrated that, under the usual assumptions on preferences (completeness, transitivity, and continuity), it is possible to represent these preferences by a utility function over the set of probability distributions. In this section, as in the previous one, only probability distributions over wealth will be considered.

It is a general result from probability theory that any probability distribution can be completely characterized by all of its statistical moments. Thus the utility of an agent can be construed as depending on the moments of the probability distributions. A restrictive version of this approach is to consider representations that depend only on the first two statistical moments (i.e. mean and variance) of distributions. Even more restrictive is to impose the independence assumption in addition, so that one considers only preferences that can be represented by an expected utility function and that depend only on mean and variance. This section investigates conditions which, in the context of the expected utility approach, lead to a utility function that depends exclusively on the mean and variance of probability distributions.

Throughout this section, we consider (discrete or continuous) probability distributions over wealth that are characterized by their distribution functions. For any distribution function P, denote by

$\mu(P) := \int W \, dP(W)$, the *expected value* or *mean* of P,

$\sigma^2(P) := \int [W - \mu(P)]^2 \, dP(W)$, the *variance* of P, and

$\sigma(P) := \sqrt{(\sigma^2(P))}$, the *standard deviation* of P.

How can a utility function $V(\mu, \sigma)$, which depends only on the first two moments of a probability distribution, be justified in terms of expected utility theory? There are two possible explanations: one involves placing restrictions on the probability distribution P; the other involves placing restrictions on the expected utility function $u(\cdot)$ (the function defined on consequences).

investigate this question, consider an expected utility function defined on wealth levels $u(W)$ and a wealth distribution function P. One can show that any distribution function is characterized by its statistical moments. We write $P(\cdot \mid M)$ to indicate that the distribution function P is determined by M, where M is the set of moments of the distribution. For the expected utility of a probability distribution, we have therefore in general:

$$V(M) := U(P(\cdot \mid M)) = \int u(W) \, dP(W \mid M),$$

i.e. expected utility is a function of all moments of the distribution P.

If a distribution is completely described by its first two moments (μ, σ), the expected utility function based upon this distribution will also be a function of these two moments, and these two moments only. Thus one way to use expected utility theory to obtain a preference function on mean and variance is to restrict the set of possible probability distributions to those which depend upon their first two moments only.

Unfortunately, the normal distribution is the only (stable) distribution which is fully characterized by its first two moments. The support of the normal distribution is the entire real line, however, and this makes it unsuitable for many economic applications. Moreover, since expected utility must be bounded, an additional constraint must be imposed on the expected utility index u, namely $u(W) \le \alpha \, e^{\beta W^2}$, for some $\alpha, \beta > 0$.

A second possibility, which places no constraints on the distribution function P, is to require $u(W)$ to be quadratic. Suppose $u(W)$ has the following form:

$$u(W) = \alpha W^2 + W, \qquad \alpha \in \mathbb{R}.$$

Then, for arbitrary P, we have:

$$\int u(W) \, dP(W) = \alpha \cdot \int W^2 \, dP(W) + \int W \, dP(W) = \alpha \cdot [\sigma^2(P) + \mu(P)^2] + \mu(P).$$

To obtain the expression in the square brackets, notice that:

$$\sigma^2 = \int (W - \mu)^2 \, dP(W) = \int [W^2 - 2\mu W + \mu^2] \, dP(W)$$
$$= \int W^2 \, dP(W) - 2 \cdot \mu \cdot \int W \, dP(W) + \mu^2$$
$$= \int W^2 \, dP(W) - \mu^2,$$

where σ^2 rather than $\sigma^2(P)$ and μ rather than $\mu(P)$ have been used for notational ease.

Thus, for a quadratic expected utility index $u(W)$, the expected utility function depends exclusively upon the mean and variance of arbitrary distributions. No higher moments appear as arguments. Figure 1.17 graphs the quadratic utility function for different values of α. From the diagram it is clear that $\alpha > 0$ implies risk-loving behaviour, $\alpha = 0$ risk-neutrality, and $\alpha < 0$

risk-aversion. Note that when $\alpha < 0$, $u(W)$ is decreasing in W for $W > -1/2\alpha$. This property of the quadratic utility function is inconvenient since it violates the axiom of non-satiation. The function can be applied, however, where the distribution is concentrated on some bounded interval $[0,A]$ where $A \leq -1/2\alpha$ and α is sufficiently small in absolute value.

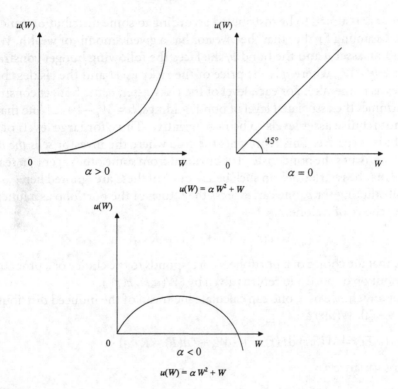

Fig. 1.17

A further property of a quadratic utility function is that for $\alpha < 0$ it demonstrates increasing absolute risk-aversion. To see this, note that

$$R_a(W) = -\frac{2\alpha}{(2\alpha W + 1)} \text{ and therefore } R'_a(W) = \frac{4\alpha^2}{(2\alpha W + 1)^2} > 0.$$

As we saw in Example 1.9 in Section 1.4, this implies that the risky asset is an inferior good, a result which appears implausible.

The following example illustrates the most common application of the mean-variance approach. The portfolio choice problem with two assets is a special case of the more general approach studied in Chapter 2.

Example 1.10. Consider an investor who must choose a portfolio (a,b) consisting of quantities of a riskless bond, b, which has a constant return of R, and a risky asset, a, which yields a random return of r. Different returns of the risky asset coincide here with states of the world. The return on the portfolio (a,b) is:

$$R \cdot b + r \cdot a,$$

where r is assumed to be distributed according to some distribution function $F(r)$. Assuming further that the investor has a given amount of wealth, W_o, to spend on asset a and the bond b, she faces the following budget constraint: $q \cdot a + b = W_o$, where q is the price of the risky asset and the riskless bond serves as numeraire. For each level of the risky asset, a, the budget constraint determines the associated level of bond holdings, $b = W_o - q \cdot a$. Note that we do not require asset levels to be non-negative. Thus, for large levels of a, b might be negative. This represents the case where the investor *sells the bond short*, i.e. issues the bond instead of buying it from some other agent. In reality, there may be restrictions on such behaviour but these are ignored here.

Substituting for b, one can express the return of the portfolio as a function of the choice of a alone:

$$W(a;r) = R \cdot W_o + (r - R \cdot q) \cdot a.$$

Note that the choice of a portfolio a corresponds to the choice of a probability distribution of portfolio returns given by $(W(a;r), F(r))$.

For any choice of a, one can calculate the mean of the induced distribution over wealth $W(a;r)$ as:

$$\mu_W(a,F) := \int W(a;r)\, dF(r) = R \cdot W_o + (\mu(F) - R \cdot q) \cdot a$$

and its variance as:

$$
\begin{aligned}
\sigma_W^2(a, F) &:= \int (W(a;r) - \mu_W(a,F))^2\, dF(r) \\
&= \int (R \cdot W_o + (r - R \cdot q) \cdot a - R \cdot W_o - (\mu(F) - R \cdot q) \cdot a)^2\, dF(r) \\
&= (r - \mu(F))^2 \cdot a^2\, dF(r) = a^2 \cdot \sigma^2(F),
\end{aligned}
$$

where $\mu(F)$ and $\sigma^2(F)$ denote the mean and variance of the return to the risky asset, respectively. This yields two equations relating the mean $\mu_W(a,F)$ and standard deviation $\sigma_W(a,F)$ to the portfolio choice a:

$$\mu_W(a,F) = R \cdot W_o + (\mu(F) - R \cdot q) \cdot a \quad \text{and} \quad \sigma_W(a,F) = \pm a \cdot \sigma(F).$$

Omitting the arguments of these functions and writing μ_W for the portfolio mean and σ_W for the portfolio standard deviation, and μ and σ for the mean and standard deviation of $F(r)$ respectively, one can express the budget constraint as a relationship between the portfolio mean and portfolio standard deviation. Eliminating a, we have a relationship between μ_W and σ_W which depends upon (μ, σ), i.e. the mean and variance of the distribution $F(r)$, only:

$$\mu_W = R \cdot W_o \pm \frac{\mu - R \cdot q}{\sigma} \cdot \sigma_W.$$

Note that, for every combination (μ_W, σ_W), there is exactly one a, i.e. one and only one portfolio. Choosing a portfolio a is therefore equivalent to choosing a combination (μ_W, σ_W) of desired mean and variance of portfolio return. Figure 1.18 shows the set of feasible combinations of (μ_W, σ_W) for the case where the average return on the risky asset exceeds the return on the secure asset.

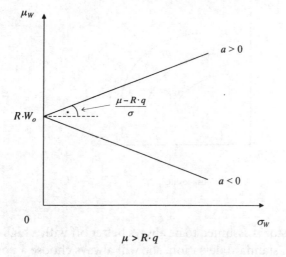

Fig. 1.18

Given the feasible combinations of (μ_W, σ_W), as represented in these diagrams, one needs only a utility function that depends on (μ_W, σ_W) in order to describe portfolio choice. For such a utility function simple considerations suggest the following shapes (Figure 1.19):

- a *risk-averse* investor requires higher and higher expected return to compensate for increased risk as measured by the standard deviation of portfolio returns, i.e. indifference curves must be upward-sloping;
- a *risk-neutral* investor is indifferent to σ_W and ranks according to μ_W only; his indifference curves will be parallel to the σ_W-axis;
- a *risk-loving* investor is willing to sacrifice more and more expected return to obtain an increase in risk; thus her indifference curves will be downward-sloping.

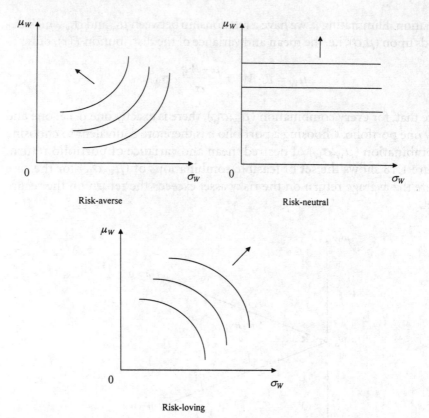

Fig. 1.19

Since the investor is assumed to be always better off with a higher portfolio mean for a given standard deviation, she will always choose a portfolio corresponding to a (μ_W, σ_W) combination on the upper branch of the budget constraint. The portfolio choice problem of an investor with mean-variance preferences will be further investigated in Chapter 2. ∎

In summary, application of the (μ, σ) approach requires restrictions to be placed either on the probability distributions considered or on the expected utility index. Nevertheless, because of its intuitive appeal, mean-variance analysis is still widely used as an approach to decision-making under uncertainty, especially in finance and investment theory.

Probability Distributions

Probability distributions (on states and consequences) play a major role in decision-making under uncertainty. This appendix provides a review of concepts from probability theory which are useful in this context.

The basic concept in probability theory is not a single state of the world but an *event*. This is because, in many applications, states are described by real numbers and not integers. For example, a state of the world relevant to some problem might be the temperature in a city. If one wanted to associate with each real number a probability, i.e. a positive real number smaller than one, these numbers would sum to infinity, even if one were to count temperatures between 5 and 6 degrees only. Fortunately, it is not necessary to distinguish that finely. One can assign a probability of zero to an individual state, say 5.7 degrees, but a positive probability to an event, like the temperature being between 5 and 6 degrees.

In general, an event E is a subset of the set of states of the world S, i.e. $E \subset S$. To guarantee that one can assign *consistent* probabilities to all events, i.e. probabilities which sum to one over the set of all possible states and whose sum does not exceed one when assigned to mutually exclusive events, it is necessary to consider only subsets which are well behaved, like intervals and single points and unions and intersections of such sets. These well-behaved sets are called *events* or *measurable sets* and the set of these events S is called a *sigma-algebra*.

Given a set of states of the world S and an associated set of appropriate subsets S, a sigma-algebra, it is possible to define a probability measure σ on S by associating with each event E in S the probability of this event $\sigma(E)$.

DEFINITION A.1. A probability measure is a mapping $\sigma: S \to \mathbb{R}_+$ with the following properties:

(i) $\sigma(E) \geq 0$ for all $E \in S$;
(ii) $\sigma(S) = 1$; and
(iii) if $F_i \in S$ for $i = 1, 2, 3, \ldots$ and $F_i \cap F_j = \emptyset$

for all i, j ($i \neq j$), then $\sigma\left(\bigcup_{i=1}^{\infty} F_i\right) = \sum_{i=1}^{\infty} \sigma(F_i)$.

A triple (S, S, σ) is called a *probability space*. It is usually possible to associate many probability measures $\sigma, \rho, \mu, \ldots$ with the same sigma-algebra.

In most economic applications, only two types of sets of states of the world are commonly encountered: *finite-state spaces* and *real-number spaces*. These are considered briefly in turn.

If the set of states of the world S is finite, i.e. has only a finite number of states, the appropriate set of events $\boldsymbol{S}$ is the set of all subsets of S. In this case, any function which associates with each state $s \in S$ a number between zero and one such that the sum of these numbers equals unity is a probability measure. Probability measures with a finite set S are sometimes called *simple probability measures*. A convenient feature of simple probability measures is that one need only list the probabilities of the single point sets in order to describe them completely. Thus if the set of states S has n elements, i.e. $S = \{s_1, s_2, s_3, \ldots, s_n\}$, any vector $p = (p_1, p_2, p_3, \ldots, p_n) \in \Delta^n$ can be viewed as a probability measure, where $\Delta^n = \{p \in \mathbb{R}^n_+ \mid \sum_i^n p_i = 1\}$ denotes the $(n-1)$ dimensional unit simplex[6] of $\mathbb{R}^n$. Δ^n is the set of all probability measures on n states of the world.

Example A1. Let rain s_1 and sunshine s_2 be the relevant states of the world. Then:

$$S = \{s_1, s_2\} \qquad \text{set of states of the world}$$
$$\boldsymbol{S} = \{\varnothing, \{s_1\}, \{s_2\}, S\} \qquad \text{set of events (sigma-algebra)}$$
$$\sigma(\varnothing) = 0; \ \sigma(\{s_1\}) = \frac{1}{2}; \qquad \text{probability measure}$$
$$\sigma(\{s_2\}) = \frac{1}{2}; \ \sigma(S) = 1$$

Thus $(S, \boldsymbol{S}, \sigma)$ as given above is a probability space. There are of course many more probability measures which can be associated with the same set of events $\boldsymbol{S}$, e.g. for any $\alpha \in [0,1]$:

$$p(\varnothing) = 0; \ p(\{s_1\}) = \alpha; \ p(\{s_2\}) = 1 - \alpha; \ p(S) = 1. \qquad \blacksquare$$

Example A2. Let the outcome of the toss of a coin be the relevant state of the world, i.e. $s_1 = $ 'head'; $s_2 = $ 'tail'. If the coin is fair, the associated probability space can be described formally as follows:

$$S = \{s_1, s_2\} \qquad \text{set of states of the world}$$
$$\boldsymbol{S} = \{\varnothing, \{s_1\}, \{s_2\}, S\} \qquad \text{set of events (sigma-algebra)}$$
$$\sigma(\varnothing) = 0; \ \sigma(\{s_1\}) = \frac{1}{2}; \qquad \text{probability measure}$$
$$\sigma(\{s_2\}) = \frac{1}{2}; \ \sigma(S) = 1. \qquad \blacksquare$$

---

[6] The $(n-1)$ dimensional unit simplex of $\mathbb{R}^n$ is the set of all non-negative vectors of real numbers with n components which sum to unity.

Example A3. Suppose the outcome of an election is the relevant state of the world. One of ten candidates will be elected. According to your assessment, only candidates 3 and 7 have a chance of being elected. Candidate 7 has a somewhat better chance, say, 70 per cent, of being elected than candidate 3. Denote the states as: s_1 = 'candidate 1 is elected'; s_2 = 'candidate 2 is elected'; and so on up to s_{10} = 'candidate 10 is elected'. The associated probability space would look like this:

$$S = \{s_1, s_2 \ldots, s_{10}\} \qquad \text{set of states of the world}$$
$$\boldsymbol{S} = \{\text{all subsets of } S\} \qquad \text{set of events (sigma-algebra)}$$

$$\sigma(E) = \begin{cases} 0 & \text{if } s_3 \notin E \text{ and } s_7 \notin E \\ 0.3 & \text{if } s_3 \in E \text{ and } s_7 \notin E \\ 0.7 & \text{if } s_3 \notin E \text{ and } s_7 \in E \\ 1 & \text{if } s_3 \in E \text{ and } s_7 \in E \end{cases} \qquad \text{Probability measure}$$

■

If the state space S is an interval of the real line, e.g. $(-\infty, \infty)$, $(-\infty, 10]$, $[1,2]$, $[0, \infty)$, then the set of open intervals in S together with their complements form the natural set of events $\boldsymbol{S}$. This is known as the *Borel sigma-algebra*. In such cases, positive numbers must be associated with events such that the integral over the whole space S equals unity.

Example A4. Suppose that the relevant state space is the range of temperatures from 0 to 25 degrees Celsius. In this case, events are subintervals or points between 0 and 25 degrees. Suppose the decision-maker considers each state equally likely. This can be represented formally as follows:

$$S = [0,25] \qquad \text{state space}$$
$$\boldsymbol{S} = \{\text{any interval and its complement in } [0,25]\} \qquad \text{set of events}$$
$$\sigma((a,b)) = \sigma([a, b)) = \sigma((a,b]) = \sigma([a, b]) = \frac{(b-a)}{25},$$

for any a, b with $0 \le a \le b \le 25$.   *probability measure*

Note that the probability of a single point, say 3 degrees, $\{3\} = [3,3]$, is zero since $\sigma(\{3\}) = (3-3)/25 = 0$, and the probability of the whole state space $[0,25]$ is unity since $\sigma([0,25]) = (25-0)/25 = 1$. This probability measure is called the *uniform distribution*.   ■

Instead of writing $\sigma((a,b))$ for the probability that a state between a and b occurs, one can define a probability measure in such cases by specifying only the intervals from zero to some upper level, e.g. $\sigma([0,a))$. The measure $\sigma((a, b))$ can now be written as $\sigma([0,b)) - \sigma([0,a))$. To simplify notation, one can write $G(a)$ for $\sigma([0,a))$ since it suffices to indicate the upper end of the interval

$[0,a)$. The function $G(a)$ is called the *distribution function* and is equivalent to the measure σ.

Example A5 (*Exponential distribution*). Consider the following distribution function (for $\alpha > 0$):

$$G(x) = \begin{cases} 1 - e^{-\alpha \cdot x} & \text{for } x \geq 0 \\ 0 & \text{for } x < 0. \end{cases}$$

The probability space defined by this distribution function can be described formally as follows:

$S = \mathbb{R}$ *state space*
$\boldsymbol{S}$ = {any interval and its complement}   *sigma-algebra*
$\sigma(\,(a, b)\,) = G(b) - G(a)$,
     for any a,b with $a \leq b$.   *probability measure*

Note that $\sigma(\mathbb{R}) = \lim_{x \to \infty} G(x) - \lim_{x \to -\infty} G(x) = 1 - 0 = 1$, i.e. the probability of the state space (all real numbers) is unity as required by the definition of a probability measure. In addition, for any interval (a, b), it is true that $\sigma(\,(a, b)\,) \geq 0$. Finally, consider the two intervals $(0,1)$ and $[1,4)$:

$$\sigma(\,(0,1) \cup [1,4)\,) = G(1) - G(0) + G(4) - G(1)$$
$$= (1 - e^{-\alpha}) - (1 - e^0) + (1 - e^{-4\alpha}) - (1 - e^{-\alpha}) = (1 - e^{-4\alpha}) \geq 0.$$

Clearly, for a single point, such as the degenerate interval $[a, a]$:

$$\sigma(\,(a, a)\,) = G(a) - G(a) = 0.$$

Once again, this is a probability measure where a single point has 'measure zero'. ∎

Example A6 (*Normal distribution*). The following distribution function describes the familiar normal distribution where α represents the standard deviation and β the mean of the distribution:

$$G(x) = \int_{-\infty}^{x} (\alpha \cdot \sqrt{2\pi})^{-1} \cdot e^{-(y-\beta)^2/2\alpha^2} \, dy.$$

The probability space defined by this distribution function can be described formally as follows:

$S = \mathbb{R}$ *state space*
$\boldsymbol{S}$ = {any interval and its complement}   *sigma-algebra*
$\sigma(\,(a, b)\,) = G(b) - G(a)$,
     for any a, b with $a \leq b$.   *probability measure*

It is easy to check that a single point has measure zero and that an interval (a, b) has measure:

$$\sigma(\,(a, b)\,) = \int_{a}^{b} (\alpha \cdot \sqrt{2\pi})^{-1} \cdot e^{-(y-\beta)^2}/_{2\alpha^2} \, dy. \qquad \blacksquare$$

It is occasionally useful to consider a state space S which contains subsets with measure zero. In such cases, the state space itself is not the smallest set of states with probability one. The *support* (or sometimes, *carrier*) of a measure, denoted $supp(\cdot)$, is the smallest (closed) subset of S with measure one. In Example A.4, the support of σ was $[0,25]$, the state space itself; while, in Example A.5, the support of σ was $\mathbb{R}_{+}$, a strict subset of the state space.

The discussion of the two views of decision-making under uncertainty in Section 1.2 illustrates that a probability measure on one set can induce, through a function, a probability measure on another set. Thus the probability measure on the states of the world, together with a function which associates a particular outcome with each state, leads to a probability measure on the outcomes. In general, not every function from states to outcomes is suitable as a device to induce a probability distribution on outcomes. Basically, one must take care that the range of the function is a space with a sigma-algebra and that the function is *measurable*, i.e. maps in an appropriate way. Measurability is, however, a weak requirement. In fact, most functions that one encounters are measurable. In particular, all continuous functions and all step functions are measurable.

Formally, let $f\colon S \to B$ be a measurable function, B be an interval of real numbers, and $(S, \mathbf{S}, \sigma)$ be a measure space. In this case, all the subintervals of B and their complements constitute the set of events $\mathbf{B}$, i.e. the sigma-algebra of B. The following measure γ, induced by f on B, makes $(B, \mathbf{B}, \gamma)$ a measure space:

$$\gamma(K) := \sigma(\{s \in S \mid f(s) \in K\}) \text{ for all } K \in B.$$

This simply says that the probability of an element $b \in B$ being in K according to the probability measure γ equals the probability of a state $s \in S$ occurring for which the functional value $f(s)$ lies in K. For this definition to make sense, the set $\{s \in S \mid f(s) \in K\}$ must be an element of $\mathbf{S}$, i.e. an event, since only events have probability values associated with them. If a function is measurable, all sets of the type $\{s \in S \mid f(s) \in K\}$ will be events for S provided K is an event for B.

Sometimes it is necessary to combine two or more probability measures to form a new probability measure, e.g. if someone decides according to the toss of a coin whether to play one lottery or another.

Example A7. Consider the following two gambles:

gamble 1:   pay \$2 for a 50 per cent chance of winning \$5;
gamble 2:   pay \$10 for a 25 per cent chance of winning \$100.

Formally, one can write:

$$\text{gamble } 1 = \begin{cases} 3 & \text{with probability of } 0.5 \\ -2 & \text{with probability of } 0.5, \end{cases}$$

$$\text{gamble } 2 = \begin{cases} 90 & \text{with probability of } 0.25 \\ -10 & \text{with probability of } 0.75. \end{cases}$$

Should the decision-maker decide to play each of these gambles with probability 0.5 (toss a coin), she would face the following compound gamble:

- win \$90 with probability $0.5 \cdot 0.25 = 0.125$,
- win \$ 3 with probability $0.5 \cdot 0.5 = 0.25$,
- lose \$ 2 with probability $0.5 \cdot 0.5 = 0.25$,
- lose \$10 with probability $0.5 \cdot 0.75 = 0.375$.

Or formally:

$$\text{gamble } 3 = \begin{cases} 90 & \text{with probability } 0.125 \\ 3 & \text{with probability } 0.25, \\ -2 & \text{with probability } 0.25 \\ -10 & \text{with probability } 0.375 \end{cases}$$

Note that the outcome set of the compound gamble 3 is the union of the outcome sets of gambles 1 and 2. One could have written gambles 1 and 2 in terms of the outcome set of gamble 3 as follows:

$$\text{gamble } 1 = \begin{cases} 90 & \text{with probability } 0 \\ 3 & \text{with probability } 0.5, \\ -2 & \text{with probability } 0.5 \\ -10 & \text{with probability } 0 \end{cases}$$

$$\text{gamble } 2 = \begin{cases} 90 & \text{with probability } 0.25 \\ 3 & \text{with probability } 0. \\ -2 & \text{with probability } 0 \\ -10 & \text{with probability } 0.75 \end{cases}$$

In general, the set of outcomes in a probability space can be made larger by assigning probability zero to the 'new' events, i.e. the *support* of a probability measure need not be the same as the set of basic outcomes. Naturally, some outcomes will be assigned zero probability if this is the case.

The following procedure allows one to construct the appropriate state space for a compound probability distribution.

Consider two probability measures with finite support $(S_1, \boldsymbol{S}_1, \sigma_1)$ and $(S_2, \boldsymbol{S}_2, \sigma_2)$. Let $S_{12} := S_1 \cup S_2$ and let $\boldsymbol{S}_{12}$ be the sigma-algebra of S_{12}. One can then write $(S_1, \boldsymbol{S}_1, \sigma_1)$ and $(S_2, \boldsymbol{S}_2, \sigma_2)$ equivalently as $(S_{12}, \boldsymbol{S}_{12}, \tilde{\sigma}_1)$ and $(S_{12}, \boldsymbol{S}_{12}, \tilde{\sigma}_2)$, respectively, where:

$$\tilde{\sigma}_i(s) := \begin{cases} \sigma_i(s) & \text{if } s \in S_i \\ 0 & \text{otherwise} \end{cases} \quad \text{for } i = 1,2.$$

Then any $\delta \in [0,1]$ defines a new probability measure σ_δ on S_{12} as follows:

$$\sigma_\delta(s) := \delta \cdot \tilde{\sigma}_1(s) + (1 - \delta) \cdot \tilde{\sigma}_2(s) \quad \text{for all } s \in S_{12}.$$

Example A.7 is an illustration of this procedure. ∎

Expected Utility Theory

In Section 1.3, it was claimed that four axioms imply the expected utility representation of preferences over probability distributions. This appendix focuses on the most important of these assumptions, viz. the *independence axiom*. It is shown that, together with the usual assumptions of *completeness*, *transitivity*, and *continuity*, independence implies the existence of an expected utility representation. In addition, some properties of the expected utility representation and some criticisms of the independence axiom are discussed.

To simplify the exposition, attention is restricted in this appendix to probability distributions over a finite number of consequences $\{c_1, \ldots, c_n\}$ which are given by vectors in the $(n-1)$-dimensional simplex

$$\Delta^n := \{p \in \mathbb{R}^n_+ \mid \sum_{i=1}^{n} p_i = 1\}.$$

With appropriate modifications, the results derived for this special case apply to preference orderings over more general probability distributions.

B1 Assumptions on Preferences

Assume that a decision-maker's preferences order probability distributions p, $q \in \Delta^n$ such that any two probability distributions are either equally good for the decision-maker or one is better than the other. An important question concerns the possibility of assigning a utility index number to each probability distribution, $U(p)$ and $U(q)$, so that

- the two probability distributions are assigned the same number if and only if they are equivalent in the eyes of the decision-maker, $U(p) = U(q)$, and
- two different numbers are assigned if the decision-maker prefers one distribution, say p, over the other, $U(p) > U(q)$.

It is well known that the following three assumptions guarantee the existence of a representation of preferences by a continuous utility function:[7]

[7] Debreu (1959, 55–9) proves this result. Varian (1992, 111–15) provides a simpler proof under the additional assumption of *monotonicity*.

(i) *Completeness* requires the ordering to order any pair of probability distributions in Δ^n.

(ii) *Transitivity* is a consistency requirement implying that a decision-maker who prefers p over q and q over r will prefer p over r.

(iii) *Continuity* guarantees that preferences for probability distributions do not change abruptly, i.e. a continuous transformation of a probability distribution p into another probability distribution q, that is strictly preferred to p, should in the course of transformation lead to a probability distribution that is indifferent to any probability distribution ranked between p and q.

From these assumptions one can deduce the following result.

PROPOSITION B1. If a preference ordering over the probability distributions in Δ^n satisfies *completeness*, *transitivity*, and *continuity*, there exists a utility function $U: \Delta^n \to \mathbb{R}$ that represents this preference ordering. The utility function $U(\cdot)$ is unique up to a monotone transformation.

It follows from this proposition that, for analytical purposes, one can work equivalently with the utility function $U(\cdot)$ (which is usually easier) or with the preference relation directly. However, there is no natural interpretation that one can associate with this representation.

In fact, as the last sentence of the proposition states, there are many equivalent utility functions. In particular, one can take any strictly increasing function $f: \mathbb{R} \to \mathbb{R}$, e.g. $f(x) = x^3$ or $f(x) = \exp(x)$, to obtain another equivalent utility function $\tilde{U}(p) := f(U(p))$. This is easy to see, since a strictly increasing function has the property that, for any two numbers x and y, $x > y$ implies $f(x) > f(y)$ and $x = y$ implies $f(x) = f(y)$. Therefore, it must be true for any $p, q \in \Delta^n$, that p has a higher value than q according to the utility function $U(\cdot)$ exactly if it has a higher value according to $\tilde{U}(\cdot)$,

$$U(p) \geq U(q) \text{ if and only if } \tilde{U}(p) := f(U(p)) \geq f(U(q)) =: \tilde{U}(q).$$

Representing preferences over probability distributions by a utility function $U(\cdot)$ suffices for the analysis of many situations where one wants to model a decision-maker facing uncertainty. To derive meaningful results in economics and finance, however, such a representation is often not specific enough. In particular, the fact that this representation does not analytically separate the influence of changes in the riskiness (the probabilities) from changes in outcomes is unfortunate. From Bernoulli (1738) on, the applied literature on decision-making under uncertainty assumed a more specific representation of preferences over probabilities which distinguishes probabilities and outcomes:

$$\hat{U}(p) := \sum_{i=1}^{n} p_i \cdot u(c_i).$$

This representation evaluates a probability distribution $p = (p_1, \ldots, p_n)$ over outcomes $\{c_1, \ldots, c_n\}$ by forming a weighted average of the utilities $u(c_i)$ derived from the different outcomes using the probabilities as weights, i.e. by computing the *expected utility*. Von Neumann and Morgenstern (1944) discovered that only one further assumption is necessary to represent preferences over probability distributions in the form of expected utility.

Recall that a convex combination of any two probability distributions is again a probability distribution:

$$\alpha \cdot p + (1 - \alpha) \cdot q = \alpha \cdot \begin{pmatrix} p_1 \\ \vdots \\ p_n \end{pmatrix} + (1 - \alpha) \cdot \begin{pmatrix} q_1 \\ \vdots \\ q_n \end{pmatrix} = \begin{pmatrix} \alpha \cdot p_1 + (1 - \alpha) \cdot q_1 \\ \vdots \\ \alpha \cdot p_n + (1 - \alpha) \cdot q_n \end{pmatrix},$$

with $p, q \in \Delta^n$ and $\alpha \in [0,1]$. The following statement of the *independence axiom* takes as given a preference relation represented by a utility function $U(\cdot)$.

ASSUMPTION B2 (*independence axiom*). The preference relation on Δ^n represented by the utility function $U(\cdot)$ satisfies, for any $p, q, r \in \Delta^n$ and any $\alpha \in [0,1]$,

$$U(\alpha \cdot p + (1 - \alpha) \cdot r) \geq U(\alpha \cdot q + (1 - \alpha) \cdot r) \text{ if and only if } U(p) \geq U(q).$$

The independence axiom asserts that the decision-maker ranks probability distributions solely according to the parts of the distributions that are different from each other. The strength of this assumption derives from the fact that one can decompose any two probability distributions into parts that are identical and parts that are different. Figure 1.B1 illustrates this assumption for the case of two outcomes, $n = 2$.

A convex combination (or *mixture*) of two probability distributions, say p and r, can be viewed as a compound two-stage random experiment: in stage 1 the probability distributions p and r are selected with probabilities α and $(1 - \alpha)$ respectively. In stage 2, a consequence from the set $\{c_1, c_2\}$ will be chosen according to the probability distribution selected in stage 1. The induced probability of outcome c_i is, of course, $\alpha \cdot p_i + (1 - \alpha) \cdot r_i$, $i = 1,2$.

The independence axiom requires that the decision-maker's ranking of two probabilities should be always the same as her ranking of the differing parts of a compound probability distribution. In Figure 1.B1, the ranking of the two-stage more complex probability distributions should be the same as the ranking of the much simpler distributions p and q.

The logic of this axiom may appear quite intuitive. Experimental studies have shown, however, that decision-makers systematically violate the independence axiom. Before discussing objections to the independence axiom, the expected utility representation theorem is stated and proved.

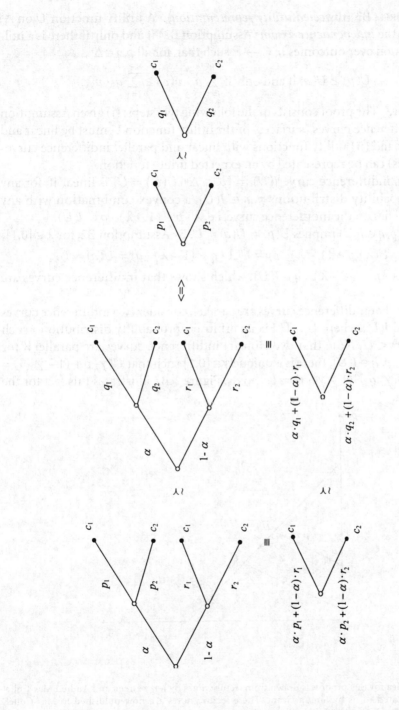

Fig. 1.B1

45

THEOREM B3 (*expected utility representation*). A utility function U on Δ^n satisfies the *independence axiom* (Assumption B2) if and only if there is a utility function over outcomes $u: C \to \mathbb{R}$ such that, for all $p,q \in \Delta^n$,

$$U(p) \geq U(q) \text{ if and only if } \sum_{i=1}^{n} p_i \cdot u(c_i) \geq \sum_{i=1}^{n} q_i \cdot u(c_i).$$

PROOF.[8] The proof consists of the following two steps: (i) given Assumption B2, indifference curves (surfaces) of the utility function U must be linear and parallel; and (ii) utility functions with linear and parallel indifference curves (surfaces) can be represented by an expected utility function.

(i) An indifference curve $I(\bar{U}) := \{p' \in \Delta^n | U(p') = \bar{U}\}$ is linear if, for any two probability distributions $p, q \in I(\bar{U})$, a convex combination with any $\lambda \in [0,1]$ lies on the indifference curve, i.e. $\lambda \cdot p + (1 - \lambda) \cdot q \in I(\bar{U})$.

Now, $p, q \in I(\bar{U})$ implies $U(p) = U(q) = \bar{U}$. By Assumption B2, for $\lambda \in [0,1]$,

$$U(\lambda \cdot p + (1 - \lambda) \cdot q) = U(\lambda \cdot q + (1 - \lambda) \cdot q) = U(q) = \bar{U}.$$

Hence, $\lambda \cdot p + (1 - \lambda) \cdot q \in I(\bar{U})$, which shows that indifference curves are linear.

To see that indifference curves are parallel, consider two indifference curves $I(\bar{U})$ and $I(\tilde{U})$ where $\bar{U} > \tilde{U}$. Fix an arbitrary probability distribution r such that $U(r) < \tilde{U}$. Note that two (linear) indifference curves are parallel if for arbitrary $p, q \in I(\bar{U})$, there is a unique $\gamma \in [0,1]$ such that $U(\gamma \cdot p + (1 - \gamma) \cdot r) = \tilde{U}$ and $U(\gamma \cdot q + (1 - \gamma) \cdot r) = \tilde{U}$ holds. Figure 1.B2 illustrates this fact for the case of Δ.

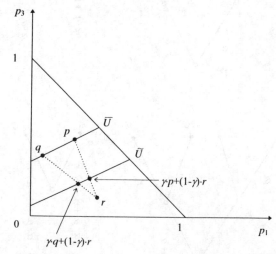

Fig. 1.B2

[8] The idea for this proof was drawn from lecture notes by Jerry Green and Andreu Mas-Collel communicated to us by Simon Grant. These lecture notes are now published in Mas-Collel, Whinston, and Green (1995).

Consider two arbitrary probability distributions $p, q \in I(\bar{U})$ and assume that, for $\lambda \in [0,1]$, $U(\lambda \cdot p + (1 - \lambda) \cdot r) = \bar{U}$ holds. By Assumption B2, for the same λ,

$$U(\lambda \cdot q + (1 - \lambda) \cdot r) = U(\lambda \cdot p + (1 - \lambda) \cdot r) = \bar{U}$$

follows, because $U(p) = U(q) = \bar{U}$. Hence, $\lambda \cdot p + (1 - \lambda) \cdot r \in I(\tilde{U})$ must be true, showing that indifference curves are parallel.

(ii) A linear surface in $\mathbb{R}^n$ is defined as the set:

$$\{p \in \mathbb{R}^n | \sum_{i=1}^{n} p_i \cdot u_i = k\}$$

for some vector of constants $(u_1, \ldots, u_n)$ and some constant k. Parallel linear surfaces are given by the sets:

$$\{p \in \mathbb{R}^n | \sum_{i=1}^{n} p_i \cdot u_i = k'\}$$

for $k' \neq k$.

Let $(u_1, \ldots, u_n)$ be the vector of constants characterizing the linear indifference curves of the utility function U.

For any $p \in \Delta^n$, define:

$$\hat{U}(p) := \sum_{i=1}^{n} p_i \cdot u_i.$$

This utility function generates the same family of indifference curves as $U(\cdot)$ and therefore represents the same preferences as $U(\cdot)$. Setting

$$u(c_i) = u_i \qquad i = 1, \ldots, n$$

completes the proof. ∎

The proof uses the fact that preferences are described by indifference curves. The independence axiom is equivalent to the assumption that indifference curves are linear and parallel. The representation theorem follows directly from the fact that linear functions have linear and parallel indifference curves. Note, however, that there are non-linear utility functions with linear and parallel indifference curves. That is why one cannot conclude that the utility function $U(\cdot)$ which is supposed to describe the preferences in the first place is linear itself. According to Proposition B1, however, the expected utility function $\hat{U}(\cdot)$ must be a monotone transformation of the utility function $U(\cdot)$.

B2 Properties of Expected Utility Indexes

Up to this point no properties of the utility function on consequences, i.e. the von Neumann–Morgenstern utility index $u(\cdot)$, have been derived. This section investigates two important properties of expected utility indexes. The first one is an immediate consequence of the fact that the common gradient of the indifference curves is determined by preferences. The second is of importance only if more than a finite number of consequences are considered.

B2.1 Uniqueness of expected utility indexes

Unlike expected utility functions, expected utility indexes are unique only up to a *linear affine* transformation. Any linear affine transformation of an expected utility index u(x) represents the underlying preference ordering as well as the index itself. A linear affine transformation is a function of the type:

$$v(x) = a + b \cdot u(x)$$

for some $a, b \in \mathbb{R}$ with $b > 0$.

As the following example shows, such a transformation affects neither the slope nor the shape of the indifference curves of the expected utility function $U(\cdot)$.

Example B1. Consider lotteries with three outcomes $\{x_1, x_2, x_3\}$ which are valued as $u(x_1) > u(x_2) > u(x_3)$ by the decision-maker. The set of all such lotteries is Δ^3 where $p = (p_1, p_2, p_3) \in \Delta^3$ are the probabilities of the outcomes x_1 to x_3, respectively. Figure 1.B3 shows all possible vectors p. Note that $p_2 = 1 - p_1 - p_3$.

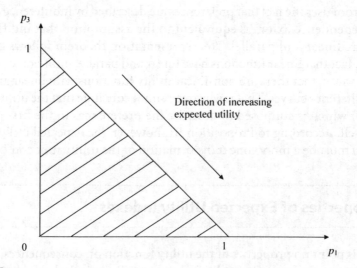

Direction of increasing expected utility

Fig. 1.B3

For different levels of $\bar{U}$, indifference curves of the expected utility function are given by:

$$\bar{U} = p_1 \cdot u(x_1) + p_2 \cdot u(x_2) + p_3 \cdot u(x_3)$$
$$= p_1 \cdot [u(x_1) - u(x_2)] + p_3 \cdot [u(x_3) - u(x_2)] + u(x_2)$$

or

$$p_3 = \frac{\bar{U} - u(x_2)}{u(x_3) - u(x_2)} - \frac{u(x_1) - u(x_2)}{u(x_3) - u(x_2)} \cdot p_1.$$

Since $u(x_1) > u(x_2) > u(x_3)$ these indifference curves are upward-sloping straight lines which represent increasing levels of expected utility $\bar{U}$ as they approach the point $p_1 = 1$.

Now consider the linear affine transformation:

$$v(x) = a + b \cdot u(x).$$

Indifference curves of the expected utility function derived for this transformation of the expected utility index are given by the equation:

$$p_3 = \frac{\bar{V} - v(x_2)}{v(x_3) - v(x_2)} - \frac{v(x_1) - v(x_2)}{v(x_3) - v(x_2)} \cdot p_1$$

$$= \frac{\dfrac{(\bar{V} - a)}{b} - u(x_2)}{u(x_3) - u(x_2)} - \frac{u(x_1) - u(x_2)}{u(x_3) - u(x_2)} \cdot p_1.$$

Obviously, the slope and shape of these indifference curves are unchanged; only the level of expected utility $(\bar{V} - a)/b$ assigned to each curve has changed (i.e. the curves have been relabelled). Hence, the same preferences are represented by the von Neumann–Morgenstern indexes u and v. ∎

B2.2 Boundedness of expected utility indexes

There is an old puzzle in the theory of decision-making under uncertainty called the 'St Petersburg Paradox'. It neatly illustrates the fact that expected utility indexes must be bounded.

Example B2 (*St Petersburg Paradox*). Consider the following lottery: A fair coin is tossed infinitely many times. If 'heads' (H) appears after n tosses for the first time, the prize will be $\$2^n$. Would a rational person pay $\$100$ to take part in this lottery?

The probability that H turns up for the first time after n tosses is just $(1/2)^n$. The expected value of the lottery is therefore infinite:

$$\mu := \sum_{i=1}^{\infty} \left(\frac{1}{2}\right)^i \cdot 2^i = 1 + 1 + 1 + \ldots = \infty.$$

A coªmparison of the expected value of the lottery with its purchase price suggests that the lottery ought to be accepted. Indeed, this would be true for any finite purchase price. When people are faced with such a lottery in experimental trials, they refuse to pay more than a finite price (usually low!) to enter. Recognizing this fact, Bernoulli (1738) proposed a concave function for the pay-offs. More precisely, he suggested the logarithm as an expected utility index: $u(x) := \ln x$. Clearly,

$$\sum_{i=1}^{\infty} \left(\frac{1}{2}\right)^i \cdot u(2^i) := \sum_{i=1}^{\infty} \left(\frac{1}{2}\right)^i \cdot \ln 2^i = (\ln 2) \cdot \sum_{i=1}^{\infty} \left(\frac{i}{2^i}\right) < \infty,$$

i.e. the expected utility of the lottery is finite.

But, as Carl Menger was first to observe, this solution is not robust to a slight change in the terms of the lottery. Suppose the prize for H after n tosses were e^{2^n}. The paradox now reappears even with the concave logarithmic expected utility index $u(x) = \ln x$. In general, if u is unbounded, one can construct a St Petersburg Paradox.

The St Petersburg Paradox shows that not all strictly increasing functions are possible as expected utility indexes because the expected utility function may not be properly defined. Since the expected utility representation theorem extends to all kinds of probability distributions, it must cover the case of lotteries like the one described in the St Petersburg Paradox as well. The representation theorem guarantees that there is a well-defined expected utility function. Hence, neither a linear function (a risk-neutral index) nor a logarithmic function (a particular risk-averse index) can be an appropriate expected utility index in this case. Indeed, if one includes lotteries of the St Petersburg type amongst the set of probability distributions, only a bounded expected utility index will lead to a well-defined, i.e. finite, expected utility function.

In financial economics and finance theory, it is quite common to encounter unbounded utility indexes like the logarithmic function, $\ln x$, and the exponential function, x^α. Why do these functions not give rise to the St Petersburg Paradox? So long as the set of probability distributions to which the expected utility function is applied contains only distributions with bounded supports (which includes finite distributions) or with infinite supports but which are nevertheless 'well behaved' (which includes the normal and alpha distributions, for example), there will be no problem. Applied to such distributions, the expected utility index will be bounded and the St Petersburg Paradox will not arise.

Example B.3. For $a, b > 0$, consider the set of probability distributions defined on the interval $[a, b]$. Let $u(x) = \ln x$. As Figure 1.B4 shows, the expected utility index $\ln x$ is clearly unbounded. The expected utility *function* is bounded, however, since the support of the relevant set of probability distributions is bounded, i.e. $u(a) < u(x) < u(b)$ for all outcomes x.

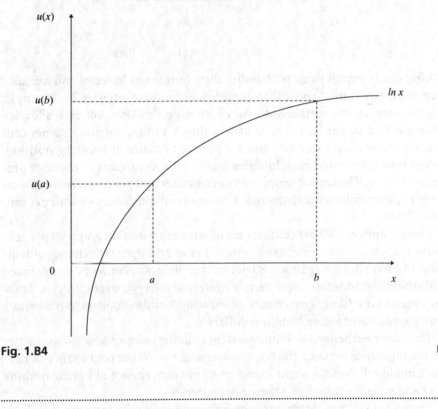

Fig. 1.B4

B3 Critique of the Independence Axiom

Proposition B1 shows that the independence axiom is a necessary and sufficient condition for the expected utility representation. Objections to the independence axiom are therefore necessarily objections to the expected utility approach and vice versa. This fact has been used to design experiments in order to test whether the behaviour of decision-makers actually conforms with the expected utility approach. One of the most famous among these tests is the experiment by the French economist Maurice Allais. Allais (1952) suggested the following experiment. Consider probability distributions over these three outcomes (in dollars):

$$c_1 = 5 \text{ million}, c_2 = 1 \text{ million}, c_3 = 0.$$

The probability distributions are as follows:

	prob$\{c_1\}$	prob$\{c_2\}$	prob$\{c_3\}$
p	0	1	0
q	0.1	0.89	0.01
r	0.1	0	0.9
s	0	0.11	0.89

One can interpret these probability distributions as lotteries and ask subjects in an experiment about their preferences for these lotteries. For example, p corresponds to the certain outcome of winning 1 million dollars, while q is a lottery with a 10 per cent chance of winning 5 million dollars, a 89 per cent chance of winning 1 million, and a 1 per cent chance of winning nothing. Asked how they would rank lotteries p and q, most subjects of the tests preferred p over q. Thus, most people did not consider a 10 per cent chance of winning 5 million dollars worth the risk of losing 1 million dollars with a 1 per cent probability.

Lottery r offers a 10 per cent chance of winning 5 million and a 90 per cent chance of winning nothing, while lottery s gives an 11 per cent chance of winning 1 million dollars against a 89 per cent chance of winning nothing. Faced with these two lotteries, most people preferred lottery r over lottery s. Thus, they preferred a 10 per cent chance of winning 5 million dollars to the extra 1 per cent chance of losing 1 million dollars.

This observed behaviour is inconsistent with the independence axiom. After all, the difference between the two choices is just an 89 per cent chance of having 1 million dollars for p and q, and an 89 per cent chance of having nothing for r and s. Figure 1.B5 shows these four lotteries.

Figure 1.B5 shows clearly that the line connecting the lotteries p and q is parallel to the line connecting the lotteries r and s. Indifference curves of utility functions that satisfy the independence axiom are parallel straight lines. Hence, one of the following must be true for such preferences:

(i) $U(p) > U(q)$ and $U(s) > U(r)$,   or
(ii) $U(q) > U(p)$ and $U(r) > U(s)$,   or
(iii) $U(p) = U(q)$ and $U(r) = U(s)$.

The behaviour of the individuals in the experiments thus violates the independence axiom by ranking p over q and r over s. Consequently, one cannot

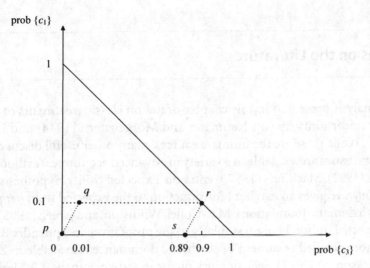

Fig. 1.B5

model their preferences by an expected utility function. This is the so-called *Allais Paradox*.

There are other experiments showing behaviour that is inconsistent with the expected utility hypothesis. The literature on alternative models for decision-making under uncertainty is too large to be reviewed here. The interested reader will find an excellent survey in Machina (1987*a*).

Notes on the Literature

The analysis presented in this chapter draws on classic treatments of choice under uncertainty by von Neumann and Morgenstern (1944) and Debreu (1959). While these are the ultimate sources, many other useful discussions of the same issues are available in a variety of advanced economics textbooks, e.g. Varian (1992). Machina's (1987*b*) entry on 'Expected Utility Hypothesis' in the *New Palgrave* gives an excellent introduction to the expected utility approach and its axiomatic foundations. Mas-Collel, Whinston, and Green (1995) prove the expected utility theorem similarly to the proof given in Appendix B.

A more detailed treatment of stochastic dominance is available in Ziemba and Vickson (1975). The classic work on mean-variance analysis is Markowitz (1952) but most finance textbooks include at least an introductory discussion on this topic, e.g. Copeland and Weston (1988). More detail on the mathematical foundations of probability theory is provided in Feller (1966).

Exercises

1. *Consider three states of the world, $S = \{s_1, s_2, s_3\}$, and three consequences, $C = \{\alpha, \beta, \gamma\}$ with $\alpha, \beta, \gamma \in \mathbb{R}$ and $\alpha > \beta > \gamma$.*
   (a) Show in a table all conceivable functions $f \colon S \to C$.
   (b) Draw a diagram showing all possible state-contingent outcomes.
   (c) Draw a diagram showing the probability distributions on the outcomes $\{\alpha, \beta, \gamma\}$ induced by the functions given in the table derived in (a) for the case where all three states are equally likely.

2. *Consider the following lotteries on the outcomes $\{5, 1, 0\}$:*

$$p = (0.00, 1.00, 0.00), \qquad q = (0.10, 0.89, 0.01),$$
$$r = (0.10, 0.00, 0.90), \qquad s = (0.00, 0.11, 0, 89).$$

   (a) Show that there are lotteries on the outcomes $\{5, 1, 0\}$, say x and y, and a number $\alpha \in [0,1]$ such that

$$p = \alpha \cdot p + (1 - \alpha) \cdot p, \qquad q = \alpha \cdot x + (1 - \alpha) \cdot p,$$
$$r = \alpha \cdot x + (1 - \alpha) \cdot y, \qquad s = \alpha \cdot p + (1 - \alpha) \cdot y.$$

   (b) Show that an agent who satisfies the expected utility hypothesis will rank these lotteries as follows:

$$p \geq q \Leftrightarrow s \geq r.$$

3. *Consider the expected utility function of a risk-averse decision-maker:*

$$\sum_{i=1}^{n} u(x_i) \cdot p_i, \text{ with } x_i \in \mathbb{R} \text{ for all } i = 1, \dots n.$$

   (a) For $n = 2$ and given p, draw the indifference curves of the expected utility function in a state-contingent outcome diagram.
   (b) For $n = 3$ and given outcomes $\{x_1, x_2, x_3\}$, draw the indifference curves of the expected utility function in a diagram representing the probability distributions on $\{x_1, x_2, x_3\}$.

4. *Assume that a decision-maker ranks lotteries according to the following mean-variance functional: $V(\mu, \sigma^2) = \mu \cdot (10 - \sigma)$.*
   (a) Show that this decision-maker prefers a lottery p which pays 10 with probability 1 to a lottery q that pays 10 or 20 with probability 1/2.

(b) Give a definition of first-order stochastic dominance and show that q dominates p in this sense.

(c) Does an expected utility maximizer respect first-order stochastic dominance?

(d) Is the mean-variance approach in general incompatible with the expected utility approach?

5. *Consider the following von Neumann–Morgenstern utility functions:*

$$u(x) = A^{b \cdot x} \qquad\qquad A, b \in \mathbb{R}$$
$$u(x) = (1 - \alpha) \cdot x^{(1 - \alpha)} \qquad \alpha \in \mathbb{R}, \alpha \neq 1$$
$$u(x) = \ln x$$
$$u(x) = a \cdot x^2 + x \qquad\qquad a \in \mathbb{R}$$

(a) Draw diagrams of these functions for different parameter values.

(b) Derive the measures of absolute and relative risk-aversion.

(c) For which parameter values do these functions have decreasing absolute risk aversion?

6. *Consider an investor with the von Neumann–Morgenstern utility function* $u(x) = x - 0.05 \cdot x^2$ *and an initial wealth of* W_o*. Suppose that there are two assets, a stock and a bond, for investment. A bond has a price of* 1 *and returns one unit of money per unit invested. The stock costs* q *per unit and returns* 2 *units of money under good market conditions and nothing otherwise. The investor assesses the probability of good market conditions as* 0.5*.*

(a) Derive the demand/supply function for the stock under the assumption of a stock price $q < 1$.

(b) Draw a diagram of the stock demand/supply function. Is the stock a normal good for this investor? Explain your answer.

(c) Suppose the stock price were equal to or greater than one. Derive the demand/supply schedule for the bond for this case. What changes if short sales of the assets are impossible?

7. *Reconsider the investor in Question 6.*

(a) Show that her expected utility function can be viewed as a mean-variance utility function and draw the indifference curves of the function in a mean-variance diagram.

(b) Draw a diagram showing the mean-variance combinations that arise from portfolios satisfying the budget constraint.

PART I

SYMMETRIC INFORMATION: MARKETS

2
...

PORTFOLIO CHOICE

The subject of this chapter is the problem of portfolio choice. The chapter begins by establishing the equivalence of the problem of choosing assets to hold in portfolio and the problem of choosing state-contingent wealth. The equivalence of these two problems reveals limits on the relationship between the payoffs and the prices of assets in equilibrium. If trade in asset markets is not to produce unbounded wealth, asset pay-offs and prices must be such that riskless arbitrage is not possible. The conditions under which this is true are developed in Section 2.1.1. Section 2.1.2 goes on to investigate general equilibrium in portfolio space.

The later part of the chapter addresses the special case of mean-variance utility. Portfolio choice in the context of mean-variance utility is perhaps the most familiar piece of analysis in modern finance theory. An aim in this discussion is to point to the special assumptions which are needed to derive these results from the more general framework provided by financial economics. While not denying the usefulness of mean-variance analysis, and ultimately the Capital Asset-Pricing Model which emerges from this approach, we are concerned to point out how these popular results are subsumed within the broader framework of a general asset-market equilibrium.

....

2.1 Portfolio Choice
....

Consider an economy with assets $k = 1, \ldots, K$. Assets are characterized by the non-negative pay-offs r_{sk} they generate in different states:

$$r_k = (r_{1k} \ldots, r_{sk} \ldots, r_{Sk}).$$

Consumers can buy or sell assets in unlimited quantities at given positive prices q_k per unit of the asset. Denote by a_k the quantity of asset k which a consumer holds or wants to hold. For $a_k > 0$, the consumer holds an entitlement to receive payments in each state of the world according to the pattern indicated by the state-contingent pay-off vector r_k. For $a_k < 0$, the consumer is obliged to make state-contingent payments according to the same pattern. A portfolio $a = (a_1, \ldots, a_k, \ldots, a_K)$ specifies quantities of the different assets held by a consumer. Each consumer is endowed with an initial portfolio of assets $\bar{a} = (\bar{a}_1, \ldots, \bar{a}_k, \ldots, \bar{a}_K)$.

As usual in an exchange economy, consumers trade assets freely at given asset prices $q = (q_1, \ldots, q_k, \ldots, q_K)$. The value of a consumer's initial endowment $W_0 \equiv \sum_{k=1}^{K} q_k \cdot \bar{a}_k$ is her initial wealth. Furthermore, associated with each portfolio a, there is a state-dependent wealth vector:

$$W(a) = (W_1(a), \ldots, W_s(a), \ldots, W_S(a)),$$

where $W_s(a) \equiv \sum_{k=1}^{K} r_{sk} \cdot a_k$ is the wealth generated by portfolio a in state s.

Assuming that our consumer is an expected utility maximizer, her net demand for the various assets can be derived as the solution to the following optimization problem:

$$\underset{a}{\text{Max}} \sum_{s=1}^{S} p_s \cdot u(W_s(a))$$

$$\text{subject to} \sum_{k=1}^{K} q_k \cdot a_k = W_0.$$

Note that there are no non-negativity constraints on the choice of assets since short sales are allowable.

A solution to this optimization problem is an optimal portfolio a^* which will depend upon:

- the prices of assets q_k
- the pay-off vectors of all assets r_k
- the initial asset endowment $\bar{a}$ (or equivalently, the initial wealth W_0).

Formally, for $k = 1, \ldots, K$,

$$a_k^* = f_k(q_1, \ldots, q_K; r_1, \ldots, r_K; \bar{a}_1, \ldots, \bar{a}_K).$$

Given a set of consumers, $i = 1, \ldots, I$, each endowed with an asset holding $\bar{a}^i = (\bar{a}_1^i, \ldots, \bar{a}_K^i)$; and each with preferences represented by an expected utility index u^i, an equilibrium is an asset price vector

$$q^* = (q_1^*, \ldots, q_k^*, \ldots, q_K^*)$$

and an asset allocation

$$a^{i*} = (a_1^{i*}, \ldots, a_K^{i*})$$

for each agent such that, for all asset markets $k = 1, \ldots, K$:

$$\sum_{i=1}^{I} f_k^i(q_1, \ldots, q_K; r_1, \ldots, r_K; \bar{a}_1^i, \ldots, \bar{a}_K^i) = \sum_{i=1}^{I} \bar{a}_k^i.$$

To illustrate some of the properties of optimal portfolios, we develop the special case of two assets and two states.

2.1.1 Optimal portfolio choice with two assets and two states

For the two-asset, two-state world, the agent's choice problem is written formally as follows:

$$\underset{a_1,a_2}{\text{Max}}\ p \cdot u(r_{11} \cdot a_1 + r_{12} \cdot a_2) + (1-p) \cdot u(r_{21} \cdot a_1 + r_{22} \cdot a_2)$$

subject to $\hspace{10cm}$ (2.1)

$$q_1 \cdot a_1 + q_2 \cdot a_2 = W_o$$

Note that the argument of the utility function $u(\cdot)$ is state-contingent wealth, i.e. $W_s(a) = r_{s1} \cdot a_1 + r_{s2} \cdot a_2$. Note also that there are no restrictions placed on the values of a_1 and a_2 which may be negative, i.e. either asset may be sold short.

This problem is represented in Figure 2.1. The shape of the indifference curves depends on the asset return vector since assets affect wealth through their state-contingent pay-offs.

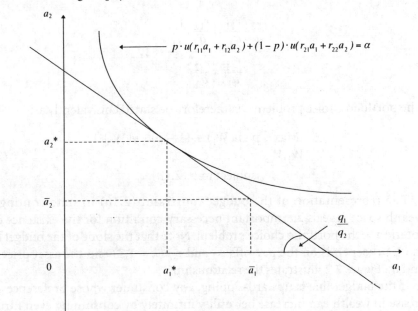

Fig. 2.1

There is an alternative way to represent this problem. Recall that:

$$W_1 = r_{11} \cdot a_1 + r_{12} \cdot a_2 = \frac{r_{11}}{q_1} \cdot q_1 \cdot a_1 + \frac{r_{12}}{q_2} \cdot q_2 \cdot a_2$$

and

$$W_2 = r_{21} \cdot a_1 + r_{22} \cdot a_2 = \frac{r_{21}}{q_1} \cdot q_1 \cdot a_1 + \frac{r_{22}}{q_2} \cdot q_2 \cdot a_2.$$

Solving these two equations for a_1 and a_2 and substituting into the budget constraint (2.1) yields:

$$W_2 = \frac{\dfrac{r_{21}}{q_1} - \dfrac{r_{22}}{q_2}}{\dfrac{r_{11}}{q_1} - \dfrac{r_{12}}{q_2}} \cdot W_1 + \frac{\dfrac{r_{22} \cdot r_{11}}{q_2 \cdot q_1} - \dfrac{r_{12} \cdot r_{21}}{q_2 \cdot q_1}}{\dfrac{r_{11}}{q_1} - \dfrac{r_{12}}{q_2}} \cdot W_o. \qquad (2.1a)$$

Now (2.1a) is a budget line in state-contingent wealth space (W_1, W_2), with a

slope of $\dfrac{\dfrac{r_{21}}{q_1} - \dfrac{r_{22}}{q_2}}{\dfrac{r_{11}}{q_1} - \dfrac{r_{12}}{q_2}}$ and an intercept on the W_2-axis of

$$\frac{\dfrac{r_{22} \cdot r_{11}}{q_2 \cdot q_1} - \dfrac{r_{12} \cdot r_{21}}{q_2 \cdot q_1}}{\dfrac{r_{11}}{q_1} - \dfrac{r_{12}}{q_2}} \cdot W_o.$$

The portfolio choice problem can therefore be stated equivalently as:

$$\begin{array}{c} \text{Max} \\ W_1, W_2 \end{array} \quad p \cdot u(W_1) + (1-p) \cdot u(W_2) \qquad (2.2)$$

$$\text{subject to} \quad (2.1a).$$

The representation of the budget constraint (2.1a) in state-contingent wealth space reveals an important necessary condition for the existence of a solution to the portfolio choice problem. Note that the slope of the budget line in (2.1a) depends on the pay-offs r_{1k} and r_{2k} ($k = 1,2$) and the asset prices q_1 and q_2. Figure 2.2 illustrates the relationship.

If the budget line is upward-sloping, any consumer whose preferences increase in wealth can increase her utility infinitely by consuming even further along the budget constraint (i.e. proceeding in a north-easterly direction). This follows from the fact that

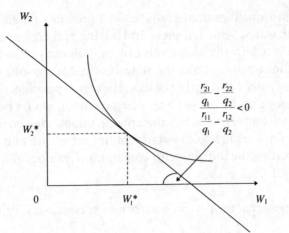

$$\frac{\dfrac{r_{21}}{q_1} - \dfrac{r_{22}}{q_2}}{\dfrac{r_{11}}{q_1} - \dfrac{r_{12}}{q_2}} < 0$$

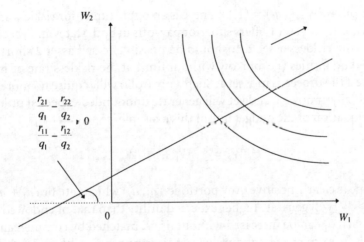

$$\frac{\dfrac{r_{21}}{q_1} - \dfrac{r_{22}}{q_2}}{\dfrac{r_{11}}{q_1} - \dfrac{r_{12}}{q_2}} > 0$$

Fig. 2.2

$$\frac{\dfrac{r_{21}}{q_1} - \dfrac{r_{22}}{q_2}}{\dfrac{r_{11}}{q_1} - \dfrac{r_{12}}{q_2}} > 0 \text{ implies:}$$

either $\quad \dfrac{r_{21}}{q_1} > \dfrac{r_{22}}{q_2}$ and $\dfrac{r_{11}}{q_1} > \dfrac{r_{12}}{q_2}$;

or $\quad \dfrac{r_{21}}{q_1} < \dfrac{r_{22}}{q_2}$ and $\dfrac{r_{11}}{q_1} < \dfrac{r_{12}}{q_2}$.

Symmetric Information: Markets

The first pair of inequalities implies that asset 1 provides a higher pay-off
than asset 2 in both states. Selling a_2 short and buying a_1 therefore allows the
consumer to achieve arbitrarily high levels of wealth in each state. Similarly,
the second pair of inequalities shows the state-contingent pay-offs of asset 2
dominating those of asset 1 and again riskless arbitrage is possible.

In short, if the slope of the budget line were positive, it would be possible
simultaneously to sell one asset and buy the other in unbounded quantities, so
as to produce ever-increasing levels of state-contingent wealth and expected
utility, without violating the initial wealth constraint. This possibility is illustrated in Example 2.1.

Example 2.1. Suppose that the pay-off matrix for the two assets is given by:

$$\begin{bmatrix} r_{11} & r_{12} \\ r_{21} & r_{22} \end{bmatrix} = \begin{bmatrix} 2 & 1 \\ \frac{3}{2} & 1 \end{bmatrix}$$

and the prices by $(q_1, q_2) = (1,1)$. There is an opportunity for riskless arbitrage
in this case, since asset 1 offers superior pay-offs in both states and yet costs the
same as the riskless asset 2. It should be possible to sell asset 2 short in unbounded quantities (i.e. borrow without limit at the riskless rate of interest)
and invest the proceeds in asset 1. Such a portfolio will require no more wealth
than initially endowed, and yet will generate unbounded expected utility.

The equation of the budget line in this example is:

$$W_2 = \frac{1}{2} \cdot W_1 + \frac{1}{2} \cdot W_o$$

The slope is clearly positive. Any portfolio (a_1, a_2) which satisfies $a_1 + a_2 = W_o$
and $a_1 > W_o$ will generate higher expected utility than that of endowed wealth
W_O. In fact, a_1 can be increased without limit, matched by commensurate re-
ductions in a_2, to create unbounded state-contingent wealth and unbounded
expected utility. ■

A necessary condition for a well-defined solution to the portfolio choice
problem whether in portfolio space (a_1, a_2) or state-contingent wealth space
(W_1, W_2) is that

$$\frac{\frac{r_{21}}{q_1} - \frac{r_{22}}{q_2}}{\frac{r_{11}}{q_1} - \frac{r_{12}}{q_2}} < 0 \text{ holds.}$$

If the budget line is downward-sloping in (W_1, W_2) space (i.e. if no arbitrage
possibilities exist), the portfolio choice yielding (W_1^*, W_2^*) is optimal so long as

the marginal rate of substitution (the slope of an indifference curve of (2.2)) equals the slope of the budget line (2.1*a*), i.e.:

$$-\frac{p \cdot u'(W_1)}{(1p) \cdot u'(W_2)} = \frac{\dfrac{r_{21}}{q_1} - \dfrac{r_{22}}{q_2}}{\dfrac{r_{11}}{q_1} - \dfrac{r_{12}}{q_2}}. \tag{2.3}$$

Since $0 \le p \le 1$ and $u'(\cdot) > 0$, the marginal rate of substitution on the left-hand side of (2.3) must be negative, and can be equal to the slope of the budget line on the right-hand side only if it is negative. This confirms the necessity of the arbitrage condition.

While the basic aim is to solve for the optimal asset demands a_1^* and a_2^*, the problem can be reduced to one in (W_1, W_2)-space, where we solve for the optimal levels of state-contingent wealth W_1^* and W_2^*. There is always a one-to-one correspondence between the portfolio space (a_1, a_2) and the state-contingent wealth space (W_1, W_2) if the asset return vectors are linearly independent. In some cases it is more convenient for expository purposes to work in one space rather than the other. We shall use both at different points in this chapter. For the present, we solve the portfolio choice problem in (W_1, W_2)-space, and use an example to derive the parallel optimum solution in $(a_1 \, a_2)$-space.

Example 2.2. Let the pay-off matrix for the two assets be as follows:

$$\begin{bmatrix} r_{11} & r_{12} \\ r_{21} & r_{22} \end{bmatrix} = \begin{bmatrix} 1 & \frac{1}{2} \\ 1 & 2 \end{bmatrix}$$

Asset 1 is clearly riskless, since its pay-off is constant across states. Furthermore, assume that the prices of the two assets are given by $(q_1, q_2) = (1, 3/4)$, the probabilities of the two states by $(p, (1 - p)) = (1/2, 1/2)$, initial wealth is $W_o = 1$, and that the expected utility index is $u(W_s) = \ln W_s$.

From the two first-order conditions (2.3) and (2.1*a*), we derive the following two equations:

$$W_2 = 5 \cdot W_1 \quad \text{and} \quad W_2 = -5 \cdot W_1 + 6 \cdot W_o.$$

These may be solved simultaneously to reveal the expected-utility-maximizing vector of state-contingent wealth:

$$(W_1^*, W_2^*) = (\tfrac{3}{5}, 3).$$

While the agent is risk-averse (indicated by the logarithmic utility index), the ratio of the prices of the two assets differs from the ratio of the probabilities of the two states, and hence the agent chooses a state-contingent wealth combination which lies off the 45°-'certainty' line, i.e. the agent chooses to bear risk in equilibrium.

The optimal portfolio choice implied by this state-contingent wealth combination is obtained by solving for a_1 and a_2 in the equations defining W_1 and W_2. This yields:

$$(a_1^*, a_2^*) = (-\tfrac{1}{5}, \tfrac{8}{5})$$

which, it can easily be checked, satisfies the initial wealth constraint given the prices of the two assets. (Check it now!) ∎

2.1.2 Exchange equilibrium

The solution to the portfolio choice problem in Section 2.1.1 yields expected-utility-maximizing values for a_1 and a_2. These will be functions of the asset pay-offs, r_{sk} $(s,k = 1,2)$, the asset prices, q_1 and q_2, and the endowed quantities of each asset, $\bar{a}_1$ and $\bar{a}_2$ (recall that $W_o = q_1 \cdot \bar{a}_1 + q_2 \cdot \bar{a}_2$). In an exchange equilibrium where there is more than a single consumer, the prices of the assets are such that the quantities demanded by each consumer in general equilibrium equal the total endowed quantities of each asset. In other words, asset markets clear at the ruling equilibrium asset prices. An example should help to clarify this point. The example shows the equilibrium price and allocation in an Edgeworth box in the asset space. Notice that individual endowments can be negative.

Example 2.3. Consider an economy with two consumers, each with identical von Neumann–Morgenstern preferences and expected utility indexes given by $u(\cdot) = \ln(\cdot)$. Assume that the pay-off matrix for two assets is as follows:

$$\begin{bmatrix} r_{11} & r_{12} \\ r_{21} & r_{22} \end{bmatrix} = \begin{bmatrix} 1 & \tfrac{1}{2} \\ 1 & 2 \end{bmatrix}$$

and that the probabilities of the two states are $p = (1 - p) = 1/2$. The endowed quantities of each asset held by the two consumers are as follows:

$$(\bar{a}_1^1, \bar{a}_2^1) = (15, 5) \text{ and } (\bar{a}_1^2, \bar{a}_2^2) = (-5, 15).$$

Since the consumers have identical preferences, they each have an expected utility function given by:

$$V(a) = \frac{1}{2} \cdot \ln(a_1 + \frac{1}{2} \cdot a_2) + \frac{1}{2} \cdot \ln(a_1 + 2 \cdot a_2),$$

where $W_1 = a_1 + \frac{1}{2} \cdot a_2$ and $W_2 = a_1 + 2 \cdot a_2$.

The general equilibrium asset allocation between these two consumers can be depicted in a 'box' diagram of the familiar Edgeworth–Bowley type. Notice, however, that the equilibrium is in portfolio space and not in the final consumption or wealth space. Thus, negative quantities of assets can be held in equilibrium (short sales are permitted) and the 'box' need not lie wholly in the positive orthant of Euclidean space. In fact, the box will not be rectangular, as in the usual Edgeworth–Bowley case, but rather trapezoidal as depicted in Figure 2.3.

The boundaries of the box in portfolio space are determined by the inequalities $W_1 \geq 0$ and $W_2 \geq 0$ in wealth space. These inequalities guarantee that final wealth, and, consequently, final consumption remain non-negative. In portfolio space, these inequalities become:

$$a_1 + \frac{1}{2} \cdot a_2 \geq 0 \quad \text{and} \quad a_1 + 2 \cdot a_2 \geq 0.$$

When these weak inequalities hold as equalities, they bound the space of feasible asset choices for each consumer.

The dimensions of the box are determined by the initial endowment (as in the usual Edgeworth–Bowley box) together with the inequalities derived from the pay-off matrix. The total endowment of the two assets is found by summing the individual endowments:

$$\bar{A}_1 = \bar{a}_1^1 + \bar{a}_1^2 = 10 \quad \text{and} \quad \bar{A}_2 = \bar{a}_2^1 + \bar{a}_2^2 = 20.$$

The point (10,20) becomes the origin for Consumer 2, as depicted in Figure 2.3.

The indifference curves for each consumer are hyperbolas which asymptote to the boundaries of the respective sides of the box. A general equilibrium occurs where the indifference curves for the two consumers share a common tangency with a price line through the endowment point marked as E in Figure 2.3.

In the present example, such a common tangency occurs at the point B in Figure 2.3. At this point, the marginal rates of substitution for each consumer are equal to the ratio of asset prices $(-14/13)$.

In the general equilibrium, the asset demands of each consumer are as follows:

$$(a_1^{*1}, a_2^{*1}) = (6.875, 13.75) \text{ and } (a_1^{*2}, a_2^{*2}) = (3.125, 6.25).$$

Note that these demands exhaust the available supply of each asset, i.e.

$$\sum_{i=1}^{2} a_1^{*i} = 10 \quad \text{and} \quad \sum_{i=1}^{2} a_2^{*i} = 20.$$

These asset demands correspond to state-contingent wealth levels of:

$$(W_1^{*1}, W_2^{*1}) = (13.75, 34, 375) \text{ and } (W_1^{*2}, W_2^{*2}) = (6.25, 15.625).$$

One can see from Figure 2.3 that arbitrage possibilities may exist for non-equilibrium prices. At a price ratio of 2, for example, consumer 1 could sell a_1 and buy a_2 in order to obtain arbitrarily high levels of utility. Consumer 2 would, of course, try to sell a_1 in exchange for a_2 as well. Hence, arbitrage possibilities cannot exist in equilibrium.

2.2 The Mean-Variance Approach and Capital Asset-Pricing

Most economists are content to note the conditions under which a general equilibrium exists and to leave it at that. At this level of generality, there is little

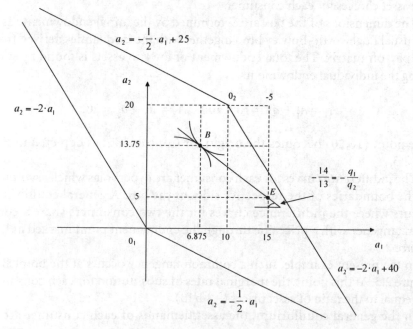

Fig. 2.3

in principle to distinguish a general equilibrium in asset markets from a general equilibrium in goods markets. Certainly interest is rarely expressed in the explicit relationship among the prices of goods in a general equilibrium.

The same cannot be said of asset markets, however. A great deal of intellectual effort was expended by finance theorists attempting to discover the explicit form of asset pricing relationships in a general equilibrium. Their work culminated in the Capital Asset-Pricing Model (CAPM). The CAPM has formed the basis of literally thousands of empirical pricing studies attempting to discover how closely actual asset prices conform to their theoretical equilibrium values.

Our interest here is not to explore the CAPM in detail but rather to show how it may be derived from the equilibrium portfolio choice problem we have been studying. The beauty of the CAPM lies in the particular form of the asset pricing relationship which emerges. A further strength is its generality, applying as it does to an arbitrary number of assets and states of the world. A major limitation, however, is that it is founded on a particularly narrow conception of preferences. This fact is rarely explained in the finance literature. Coming from the perspective of general equilibrium theory, as we do here, it should be evident that special assumptions about individual preferences are required in order to derive the CAPM pricing formula.

We begin with a discussion of the mean and variance of portfolio pay-offs since the preference relation required to generate the CAPM depends exclusively on these parameters as arguments. Finally, we derive the CAPM as the solution to a general equilibrium portfolio choice problem under the special assumptions implied by mean-variance utility.

2.2.1 Feasible combinations of mean and variance

Consider an arbitrary portfolio $a = (a_1, \ldots, a_K)$. Associated with such a portfolio is a state-contingent wealth vector

$$W_s(a) = \sum_{k=1}^{K} r_{sk} \cdot a_k, \qquad s = 1, \ldots . S.$$

For a given probability vector $p = (p_1, \ldots, p_s, \ldots, p_S)$ one can compute the expected or mean pay-off $\mu(a)$ which is achieved by this portfolio a as:

$$\mu(a) = \sum_{s=1}^{S} p_s \cdot W_s(a) = \sum_{s=1}^{S} p_s \cdot \left(\sum_{k=1}^{K} r_{sk} \cdot a_k \right) = \sum_{k=1}^{K} \sum_{s=1}^{S} p_s \cdot r_{sk} \cdot a_k = \sum_{k=1}^{K} \mu_k \cdot a_k,$$

where $\mu_k := \sum_{s=1}^{S} p_s \cdot r_{sk}$ denotes the expected or mean pay-off of asset k.

Similarly, one can compute the variance of the pay-offs from portfolio a, $\sigma^2(a)$. Let $\sigma_{jk} := \sum_{s=1}^{S} p_s \cdot (r_{sj} - \mu_j) \cdot (r_{sk} - \mu_k)$ be the covariance of the pay-offs from assets j and k. For $j = k$, $\sigma_{jj} = \sum_{s=1}^{S} p_s \cdot (r_{sj} - \mu_j)^2$ denotes the variance of the pay-off from asset j. The variance of the pay-off from portfolio a, $\sigma^2(a)$, can now be written as:

$$\sigma^2(a) = \sum_{s=1}^{S} p_s \cdot \left(W_s(a) - \mu(a) \right)^2 = \sum_{s=1}^{S} p_s \cdot \left(\sum_{k=1}^{K} (r_{sk} - \mu_k) \cdot a_k \right)^2$$

$$= \sum_{k=1}^{K} a_k \cdot \sum_{j=1}^{K} a_j \cdot \left[\sum_{s=1}^{S} p_s \cdot (r_{sj} - \mu_j) \cdot (r_{sk} - \mu_k) \right]$$

$$= \sum_{k=1}^{K} \sum_{j=1}^{K} a_k \cdot a_j \cdot \sigma_{jk}.$$

The transformations of the mean $\mu(a)$ and the variance $\sigma^2(a)$ show that the mean of a portfolio is the weighted sum of the mean pay-offs of the individual assets, where the respective asset quantities act as weights. The variance of a portfolio is the quadratic form obtained from the vector of individual asset quantities applied to the matrix of covariances of asset pay-offs, i.e.:

$$\sigma^2(a) = a \cdot \Omega \cdot a \qquad \text{where } \Omega := \begin{bmatrix} \sigma_{11} & \cdots & \sigma_{K1} \\ \vdots & \ddots & \vdots \\ \sigma_{1K} & \cdots & \sigma_{KK} \end{bmatrix}.$$

Since $\sigma^2(a)$ is a quadratic form which is non-negative for any portfolio a, it follows that the covariance matrix must be positive semi-definite. This latter property implies that the determinant of Ω must be a non-negative number.

Every portfolio a has associated with it a mean $\mu(a)$ and a variance $\sigma^2(a)$. There is, however, usually more than one portfolio for any given (μ, σ^2) combination as we demonstrate below. In particular, it is possible to determine the set of $(\mu(a), \sigma^2(a))$ combinations which are feasible for the consumer in the sense that they correspond to portfolios satisfying the budget constraint

$$\sum_{k=1}^{K} q_k \cdot a_k = W_o.$$

The feasible set of (μ, σ^2) combinations is written formally as follows:

$$\left\{ (\mu(a), \sigma^2(a)) \,\middle|\, \sum_{k=1}^{K} q_k \cdot a_k = W_o \right\}.$$

Note the dependence of the set of feasible (μ, σ^2) combinations on the asset prices q_k and the initial endowment of wealth W_o. It is possible to represent the set of feasible mean-variance combinations in a (μ, σ^2) diagram or, as is more common in the finance literature, in a mean-standard deviation diagram

((μ, σ) diagram). The set of feasible mean-standard deviation combinations has the general form displayed in Figure 2.4.

Note that, in general, all (μ, σ) combinations in the shaded arc of Figure 2.4 are feasible. If there are only two assets, however, feasible (μ, σ) combinations lie on the border of this set only and not in the interior. This latter case is studied in detail in the following sections. The restriction to two assets facilitates a neat diagrammatic derivation of the set of feasible (μ, σ) combinations and allows us to compare the (μ, σ) approach which dominates the finance literature with the microeconomic approach developed in this book.

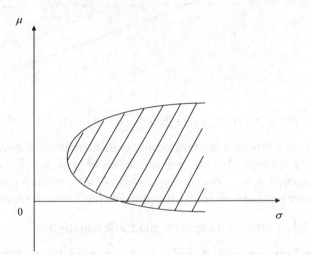

Fig. 2.4

2.2.1.1 Feasible combinations of mean and variance in a two-asset model

We begin by recognizing that it is possible to construct iso-μ and iso-σ contours in (a_1, a_2) space. Iso-μ contours represent portfolios (a_1, a_2) with the same mean, say $\bar{\mu}$. Recalling the formulation of the mean of a portfolio given above,

$$\mu(a_1, a_2) := \mu_1 \cdot a_1 + \mu_2 \cdot a_2 = \bar{\mu}.$$

Iso-μ contours are linear with slope and location parameters μ_1 and μ_2. Since $\mu_k := \sum_{s=1}^{S} p_s \cdot r_{sk}$, it is clear that iso-$\mu$ contours are drawn for a given probability distribution over states. Changing the probability distribution changes the position and slope of the iso-μ contours; however, they remain parallel linear functions in (a_1, a_2) space. Iso-μ contours are depicted in Figure 2.5.

Iso-σ contours are obtained by fixing a level of variance $\bar{\sigma}^2$ (or equivalently of standard deviation $\bar{\sigma} = \sqrt{\bar{\sigma}^2}$):

71

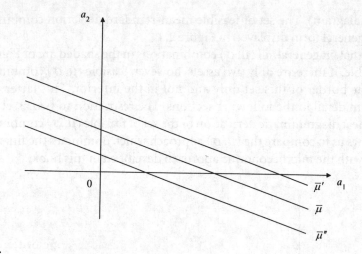

Fig. 2.5

$$\sigma^2(a_1,a_2) := \sigma_{11} \cdot a_1^2 + 2 \cdot \sigma_{12} \cdot a_1 \cdot a_2 + \sigma_{22} \cdot a_2^2 = \bar{\sigma}^2.$$

Since squaring a function is a monotonic transformation, the contour curves of $\sigma^2(a_1,a_2)$ are identical to the contour curves of $\sigma(a_1,a_2)$. The equation of a σ^2-contour, $\sigma_{11} \cdot a_1^2 + 2 \cdot \sigma_{12} \cdot a_1 \cdot a_2 + \sigma_{22} \cdot a_2^2 - \bar{\sigma}^2 = 0$, is a special case of a *general quadratic equation*. For such equations the following result applies.

LEMMA 2.1. Consider the general quadratic equation

$$\alpha_{11} \cdot x_1^2 + 2 \cdot \alpha_{12} \cdot x_1 \cdot x_2 + \alpha_{22} \cdot x_2^2 + 2 \cdot \alpha_{01} \cdot x_1 + 2 \cdot \alpha_{02} \cdot x_2 + \alpha_{00} = 0, \quad (2.7)$$

and denote by $\quad D := \det \begin{bmatrix} \alpha_{11} & \alpha_{12} & \alpha_{01} \\ \alpha_{12} & \alpha_{22} & \alpha_{02} \\ \alpha_{01} & \alpha_{02} & \alpha_{00} \end{bmatrix} \quad$ and $\quad \Delta := \det \begin{bmatrix} \alpha_{11} & \alpha_{12} \\ \alpha_{12} & \alpha_{22} \end{bmatrix}$

the determinants of two coefficient matrices of this equation. Then the following statements are true:

(i) For $D < 0$ and $\Delta > 0$, (2.7) describes an ellipse.
(ii) For $D = 0$ and $\Delta = 0$, (2.7) describes a pair of parallel lines.

In terms of the general quadratic equation (2.7), the σ^2-contour is the special case where

$$\alpha_{01} = \alpha_{02} = 0, \alpha_{00} = -\bar{\sigma}^2, \text{ and } \alpha_{ij} = \sigma_{ij} \text{ for } i,j = 1, 2$$

holds. For the case of the σ^2-contour, $\Delta = \det \Omega \geq 0$ is the determinant of the covariance matrix which we know to be non-negative since Ω is positive semi-definite. Substituting the respective parameters of the σ^2-contour into D, we discover that:

$$D = -\bar{\sigma}^2 \cdot \Delta = -\bar{\sigma}^2 \cdot \det \Omega \le 0.$$

It follows from Lemma 2.1 that there can be only two cases:

(i) if $\det \Omega > 0$, the contour of $\sigma^2(a_1, a_2)$ must be an ellipse; and
(ii) if $\det \Omega = 0$, the contour of $\sigma^2(a_1, a_2)$ must be a pair of parallel lines.

Case (i) is illustrated in Figure 2.6. As expected, the contours are ellipses in (a_1, a_2) space, centred on the origin and symmetric about a ray through the origin. Successive ellipses radiating from the origin are loci of (a_1, a_2) pairs with successively greater σ-values (i.e. standard deviations of contingent wealth levels). Once again, the position of the family of ellipses depends on the probability distribution over states. The budget line in (a_1, a_2) space, $a_2 = W_0/q_2 - (q_1/q_2) \cdot a_1$, is derived from the budget constraint of the portfolio choice problem. With positive prices for both assets, the slope of the budget line is negative. Combining the budget line with the iso-μ and iso-σ contours in a single diagram yields the upper panel of Figure 2.7.

Given the iso-μ and iso-σ contours in (a_1, a_2) space, it is easy to read off the mean and standard deviation of state-contingent wealth generated by any portfolio (a_1, a_2). In particular, each point on the budget line, representing a feasible portfolio, lies on a particular iso-μ and iso-σ contour. Thus one can view the choice of the optimal quantities of each asset to hold in a portfolio as equivalent to the choice of a particular mean and standard deviation of

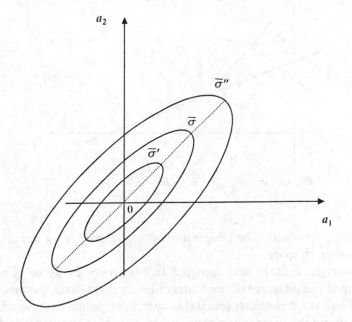

Fig. 2.6

73

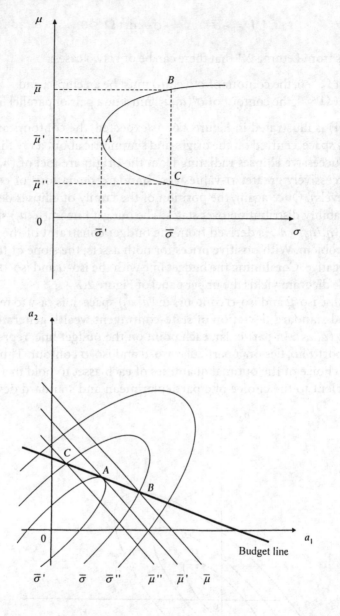

Fig. 2.7

state-contingent wealth. The budget line in (a_1, a_2) space has a unique representation in (μ, σ) space.

Consider the budget line depicted in the lower panel of Figure 2.7. Beginning at the intercept of the budget line on the a_2-axis, the positions of the iso-μ and iso-σ contours reveal that successive points downwards and to the right along the budget line have successively higher means, and at first successively lower and then successively higher standard deviations. Moving down the budget line in (a_1, a_2) space traces out a locus in (μ, σ) space of the type depicted in the right-hand panel of Figure 2.7. Note that the point of minimum standard deviation corresponds to the point at which the budget line is tangent to the lowest iso-σ contour (shown as A in both panels).

2.2.1.2 Some special cases

The portfolio which achieves minimum standard deviation is known as the *minimum variance portfolio* (MVP). In general, the standard deviation or variance of the MVP will not be zero. This is the case depicted in Figure 2.7. The variance of the MVP will be zero, however, if one or other of the assets is riskless (in which case the MVP is trivially the portfolio consisting exclusively of the riskless asset), or if it is possible to create a riskless portfolio by combining the two risky assets in appropriate proportions.

This latter possibility will only arise if there are at least as many different assets as there are states of the world, a condition we will describe in Chapter 3 as *complete markets*. Clearly, in the example we have used so far in this section, markets are *incomplete*, i.e. there are many states of the world but only two assets. It is therefore not possible to synthesize a riskless portfolio, and given that neither of the two assets available is riskless, the MVP will have positive variance.

If there is a riskless asset, or it is possible to create a riskless portfolio by combining risky assets, the iso-σ contours and the (μ, σ) frontier take on a special shape. To see this, we revert to the earlier example of two assets and two states of the world.

Case 1: Riskless asset

An asset is riskless if it pays the same amount regardless of the state of the world, i.e. if $r_{sk} = r_k$ for all $s = 1, \dots, S$. Clearly, for a riskless asset $\mu_k = r_k$ and $\sigma_{jk} = 0$ for all j, k. Hence, $\det \Omega = 0$ when there is a riskless asset and the iso-σ contours must be pairs of parallel lines. In our two-asset example, let asset 2 be the riskless asset. The determinant of the covariance matrix is:

$$\det \Omega = \det \begin{bmatrix} \sigma_{11} & 0 \\ 0 & 0 \end{bmatrix} = 0.$$

All portfolios with $a_1 = 0$ will have a variance of zero in this case. The zero iso-σ contour coincides therefore with the a_2-axis. For any positive level of variance $\bar{\sigma} > 0$, the iso-σ contours consist of two lines parallel to the a_2-axis. In general, when one of the two assets is riskless (i.e. offers the same pay-off in each state), the iso-σ contours become straight lines parallel either to the a_1-axis or the a_2-axis, depending upon which of the two assets is riskless.

Case 2: Complete markets
Two asset markets are complete if there are exactly two states of the world and the asset pay-offs are linearly independent. In this case, the iso-μ contours are given by the equation $\mu(a_1, a_2) := \mu_1 a_1 + \mu_2 a_2 = \bar{\mu}$. These are straight lines in (a_1, a_2) space.

Writing the probabilities of the two states as p and $(1 - p)$, the standard deviation can be transformed to yield:

$$\sigma(a_1, a_2) = \pm \sqrt{(p \cdot (1 - p))} \cdot \left[(r_{11} - r_{21}) \cdot a_1 + (r_{12} - r_{22}) \cdot a_2 \right].$$

The iso-σ contours, $\sigma(a_1, a_2) = \bar{\sigma}$ are therefore also linear in (a_1, a_2) space. The iso-σ contours are a set of parallel straight lines and the $(\sigma = 0)$ contour is a ray through the origin with slope equal to

$$-\frac{(r_{11} - r_{21})}{(r_{12} - r_{22})}.$$

It is easy to check that any portfolio on the $(\sigma = 0)$ contour yields the same pay-off in each state. Contours representing successively higher values of σ are straight lines parallel to the $(\sigma = 0)$ contour at equal vertical distances above and below it.

Recall that the iso-σ contours in the case of incomplete markets were ellipses centred on the origin and symmetric about a ray through the origin. In the case of complete markets, the ellipses are 'stretched out' infinitely in the direction of the longer of their two axes, and thus become a set of parallel straight lines. The $(\sigma = 0)$ contour, instead of being a single point located at the origin, becomes a ray through the origin. The higher contours, instead of being ellipses radiating from the origin, become parallel straight lines extending either side of a ray through the origin.

Figure 2.8 illustrates the case of complete markets in two assets. To deduce the shape of the (μ, σ) frontier, we note that the two linear equations for the iso-μ and iso-σ contours can be solved simultaneously to yield another linear equation relating μ and σ. This equation can in turn be solved simultaneously with the linear budget equation to obtain the equation of the (μ, σ) frontier. It is important to note that the position and slope of the (μ, σ) frontier will depend on q_1, q_2, and W_o, since these are parameters of the budget line.

In the presence either of complete markets or a riskless asset, the (μ, σ) frontier is piece-wise linear. It has the same basic shape as the (μ, σ) frontier in the case of incomplete markets except that:

(i) the positive- and negative-sloped sections of the frontier are both linear; and

(ii) the standard deviation of the minimum variance portfolio is zero (i.e. the (μ,σ) frontier meets the μ-axis at a point equal to the expected pay-off of the MVP, or the certain pay-off from the riskless asset, if there is one).

The (μ,σ) function for the case of complete markets is depicted in the lower panel of Figure 2.8.

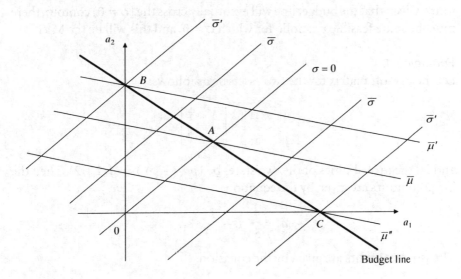

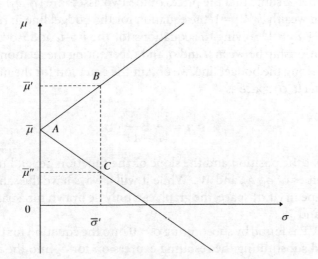

Fig. 2.8

That the standard deviation of the MVP should be zero is consistent with the fact that a negatively sloped budget line in (a_1, a_2) space *must* cross the $(\sigma = 0)$ contour. The only circumstances in which this would not be true are if the iso-σ contours and the budget line were parallel. But in this situation riskless arbitrage would be possible. In any equilibrium, the asset prices will always be such that the budget line has a slope different from that of the iso-σ contours. Given that the budget line will eventually cross the $(\sigma = 0)$ contour, there must be some feasible portfolio for which $\sigma = 0$, and this will be the MVP.

Example 2.4.
Let the pay-off matrix for the two assets be as follows:

$$\begin{bmatrix} r_{11} & r_{12} \\ r_{21} & r_{22} \end{bmatrix} = \begin{bmatrix} 1 & \frac{1}{2} \\ \frac{3}{4} & 2 \end{bmatrix}$$

and let the probabilities of the two states be $(p, (1-p)) = (1/2, 1/2)$. Then the iso-μ contours are given by the equation

$$a_2 = \frac{4}{5} \cdot \bar{\mu} - \frac{7}{10} \cdot a_1.$$

The iso-σ contours are given by the equation

$$a_2 = \pm \frac{4}{3} \cdot \bar{\sigma} + \frac{1}{6} \cdot a_1.$$

If we further assume that the prices of the two assets are $(q_1, q_2) = (3/4, 1)$ and that initial wealth is $W_o = 1$, the equation for the budget line in (a_1, a_2) space is $(3/4) \cdot a_1 + a_2 = 1$. Solving the equations for the iso-μ and iso-σ contours to find a relationship between μ and σ, and substituting the relationship between a_1 and a_2 along the budget line, we obtain the equation for the mean-variance frontier in (μ, σ) space as

$$\mu = \frac{13}{11} \pm \frac{1}{11} \cdot \sigma.$$

Notice that the position and the slope of the function depend upon the particular values of q_1, q_2, and W_o. While it will always have the same piece-wise linear shape in (μ, σ) space, the graph can only be drawn for a particular value of q_1, q_2, and W_o.

The MVP is found by substituting $\bar{\sigma} = 0$ into the equation for the iso-σ contours, and substituting the resulting expression for a_2 into the budget equation. This gives $(\bar{a}_1, \bar{a}_2) = (12/11, 2/11)$. One can check from the equation for

the iso-μ contours or the (μ,σ) frontier that the expected value of the
(the synthetic riskless pay-off) is $\bar{\mu} = 13/11$.

2.2.1.3 Portfolio choice in mean-variance space

Having established the correspondence between the budget line in (a_1, a_2)
space and the (μ,σ) frontier, we can proceed to discuss preferences and optimal
portfolio choice. As noted in Section 2.1, selection of the optimal portfolio in
(a_1, a_2) space is a matter of maximizing expected utility subject to the budget
constraint. The optimal portfolio will lie on the particular (μ,σ) frontier which
is consistent with the assumed values of q_1, q_2, and W_o.

To represent preferences in the (μ,σ) space directly, a decision-maker's preferences over risky prospects must not depend on any other characteristic of
the prospect but mean and variance, i.e. there must be a representation of the
form $V(\mu,\sigma)$. This amounts to the assumption that only its mean and variance
are relevant to the portfolio choice decision. As we show in Section 1.5, such an
assumption is generally incompatible with expected utility theory. The only
way to reconcile the assumptions of expected utility theory with a representation $V(\mu,\sigma)$ is to

- restrict decision-making to probability distributions which are completely characterized by their means and variances (this is essentially the
  class of normal distributions); or
- assume a quadratic von Neumann–Morgenstern utility index (which has
  the inconvenient property that it is not monotonically increasing in
  wealth).

Whether or not the expected utility hypothesis is adopted, assuming preferences over assets may be represented by a utility function with arguments μ
and σ, where the marginal utility of μ is positive and the marginal utility of σ
is negative, is sufficient to derive indifference curves in (μ,σ) space. They will
be upward-sloping, reflecting the assumption that an agent must be offered
additional expected wealth in order to be indifferent to the prospect of bearing
additional risk (where risk is measured by the standard deviation of state-contingent wealth).

Figure 2.9 depicts portfolio choice in the mean-variance framework with a
utility function $V(\mu,\sigma)$. The assumption that $V(\mu,\sigma)$ is increasing in μ and decreasing in σ implies positively sloped indifference curves but not the convex-
ity shown here. Utility increases in a north-westerly direction as indicated by
the arrow in Figure 2.9. It follows from the slope of the indifference curves and
the direction of increasing utility that the optimal portfolio must correspond
to a (μ,σ) combination on the upper branch of the feasible (μ,σ) set.

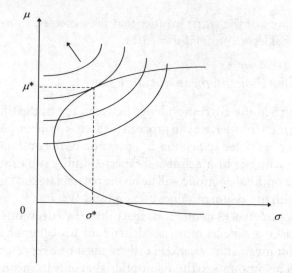

Fig. 2.9

In other words, since the consumer unambiguously prefers a portfolio with a higher expected value of wealth to one with a lower expected value *and the same standard deviation of wealth*, those points on the lower branch of the (μ,σ) frontier will never be chosen. Such points are said to be *mean-variance inefficient*. The set of *efficient* portfolios in (μ,σ) space consists of all those points on the (μ,σ) frontier which have *both a mean and a standard deviation at least as great as that of the minimum variance portfolio.*

A mean-variance utility function $V(\mu,\sigma)$ induces a ranking in the (a_1,a_2) space as well, since mean and variance depend on the portfolio chosen, i.e. $V(\mu(a_1,a_2),\sigma(a_1,a_2))$. For every preference relation over lotteries which can be represented by a mean-variance utility function $V(\mu,\sigma)$, there is an induced preference relation on the space of portfolios. The converse, however, does not generally hold, i.e. a preference relation on lotteries cannot generally be represented by a preference relation over mean and variance alone.

The following example illustrates the choice of an optimal portfolio in a case where expected utility preferences can be represented in (μ,σ) space.

Example 2.4 (*continued*). Let the quadratic expected utility index be $u(W) := 4 \cdot W - (1/2) \cdot W^2$. We solve for the expected-utility-maximizing values of a_1 and a_2 by substituting into first-order conditions (2.1) and (2.3) above. This yields the following two equations which are solved simultaneously for the optimal values of a_1 and a_2:

$$a_1 = 19 \cdot a_2 - 8 \quad \text{and} \quad a_2 = 1 - \frac{3}{4} \cdot a_1.$$

Thus $(a_1^*, a_2^*) = (44/61, 28/61)$.

We know from Section 1.5 that the expected utility function can be transformed to yield:

$$V(\mu,\sigma) = 4 \cdot \mu - \frac{1}{2} \cdot \sigma^2 - \frac{1}{2} \cdot \mu^2.$$

Therefore the slope of an indifference curve in (μ,σ) space is derived as:

$$\frac{d\mu}{d\sigma} = -\frac{\partial V(\cdot)/\partial \sigma}{\partial V(\cdot)/\partial \mu} = \frac{\sigma}{4-\mu}.$$

The slope of the (μ,σ) frontier, on the other hand, is given by the equation $\mu = 13/11 \pm (1/11) \cdot \sigma$ as $\pm 1/11$. We know that only the positive branch of this piecewise linear equation is relevant since the negative branch is dominated in the agent's preference ordering.

We solve for the optimal portfolio in (μ,σ) space by equating the slope of an arbitrary indifference curve with that of the upper branch of the (μ,σ) frontier, i.e. $\sigma/(4 - \mu) = 1/11$. This, together with the equation for the (μ,σ) efficient set, enables us to solve for the optimal values of μ and σ. Thus we obtain $(\sigma^*, \mu^*) = (31/122, 147/122)$. Substituting into the equations for μ and σ derived earlier confirms that these values correspond to the expected value and standard deviation of the expected-utility-maximizing portfolio $(a_1^*, a_2^*) = (44/61, 28/61)$.

As a final check, one can calculate the value of expected utility at the optimum by

(i) substituting $(a_1^*, a_2^*) = (44/61, 28/61)$ into the expected utility function in (a_1, a_2) space, and

(ii) substituting $(\sigma^*, \mu^*) = (31/122, 147/122)$ into the expected utility function in (μ,σ) space.

In each case, the result is approximately 4.06. ∎

Of course, dispensing with the need to represent preferences in (μ,σ) space overcomes the need to consider a restricted range of utility functions. The fundamental space in which portfolio choice takes place is (a_1,a_2) space. The tradition in finance theory of using the (μ,σ) space to tell the story of portfolio selection unnecessarily restricts the range of preferences which consumers may display. This fact is rarely, if ever, made explicit. A distinguishing feature of financial economics as opposed to finance theory is a preference for revealing the fundamental *economic* forces at work in financial decision-making.

Restricting preferences to the (μ,σ) space has the advantage, however, of enabling one to derive an explicit relationship among asset prices in an asset market equilibrium. This is the essence of the Capital Asset-Pricing Model to which we now turn.

2.2.2 The capital asset-pricing model

We consider once again the portfolio choice problem faced by individuals in a general equilibrium involving a finite number of agents and a finite number of assets. A famous result in the finance literature characterizes the relationship among the prices of assets in a general equilibrium in which there are I consumers, $(K-1)$ risky assets, and one riskless asset. Known as the *Capital Asset-Pricing Model* (CAPM), the analysis proves the surprising result that the relationship among the prices of assets in a general equilibrium (in which agents select assets so as to maximize mean-variance utility) is linear. Apart from being surprising, the result is especially convenient, since it lends itself immediately to the application of linear regression estimation techniques, as the vast literature on empirical testing of the CAPM testifies.

Our purpose here is to derive the *capital asset-pricing equation* (the general equilibrium-pricing relation) from the microeconomic foundations of portfolio choice developed in the earlier sections of this chapter.[1]

We begin by reminding ourselves of some definitions. The vector $a = (a_1,\ldots,a_K)$ represents a portfolio, where the elements correspond to quantities of each of the K assets held in portfolio. The assets have pay-offs in each of the S states denoted r_{sk} ($s = 1,\ldots,S; k = 1,\ldots,K$). The wealth derived in each state of the world depends upon the quantity of each asset held and the pay-off from each asset in the particular state, i.e.

$$W_s(a) = \sum_{k=1}^{K} r_{sk} \cdot a_k$$

for $s = 1,\ldots,S$. As shown in Section 2.2.1, the expected wealth derived from a portfolio a equals the sum of the expected pay-offs from the individual assets weighted by the quantities of the assets held in portfolio:

$$\mu(a) = \sum_{k=1}^{K} \mu_k \cdot a_k,$$

where μ_k is the expected pay-off from asset k ($k = 1,\ldots,K$). The variance of state-contingent wealth derived from holding a portfolio a is expressed as:

$$\sigma^2(a) = \sum_{k=1}^{K} a_k \cdot \sum_{j=1}^{K} a_j \cdot \sigma_{jk}.$$

If we differentiate $\mu(a)$ and $\sigma^2(a)$ with respect to a_ℓ we obtain the following:

$$\mu_\ell(a) = \mu_\ell,$$

where $\mu_\ell(a) := \partial\mu(a)/\partial a_\ell$ denotes the partial derivative of $\mu(a)$ with respect to a_ℓ, and, denoting the partial derivative of $\sigma^2(a)$ with respect to a_ℓ by $\sigma^2_\ell(a) := \partial\,\sigma^2(a)/\partial a_\ell$,

---

[1] The derivation of the CAPM follows Brennan (1989).

$$\sigma_\ell^2(a) = 2 \cdot \left[\sum_{k=1}^{K} a_k \cdot \sigma_{\ell k} \right] = 2 \cdot \sigma(a,\ell).$$

Note that $\sigma(a,\ell) := \sum_{k=1}^{K} a_k \cdot \sigma_{\ell k}$ is the covariance between the pay-off of the entire portfolio a and the pay-off of a single asset ℓ:

$$
\begin{aligned}
\sigma(a,\ell) &= \sum_{s=1}^{S} p_s \cdot (r_{s\ell} - \mu_\ell) \cdot (W_s(a) - \mu(a)) \\
&= \sum_{s=1}^{S} p_s \cdot (r_{s\ell} - \mu_\ell) \cdot \sum_{k=1}^{K} (r_{sk} - \mu_k) \cdot a_k \\
&= \sum_{k=1}^{K} a_k \cdot \sum_{s=1}^{S} p_s \cdot (r_{s\ell} - \mu_\ell) \cdot (r_{sk} - \mu_k) \\
&= \sum_{k=1}^{K} a_k \cdot \sigma_{\ell k}.
\end{aligned}
$$

Now consider the optimization problem for some consumer $i \in \{1, 2, \ldots, I\}$:

$$\underset{a}{\text{Max}} \quad V^i(\mu(a), \sigma^2(a))$$

$$\text{subject to} \quad \sum_{k=1}^{K} q_k \cdot a_k = \sum_{k=1}^{K} q_k \cdot \bar{a}_k.$$

Denoting by $V_1^i(\cdot) := \partial V^i(\cdot)/\partial \mu$ and $V_2^i(\cdot) := \partial V^i(\cdot)/\partial \sigma^2$ the partial derivatives of $V^i(\cdot)$ with respect to μ and σ^2, the first-order conditions for this problem are:

$$V_1^i(\mu(a), \sigma^2(a)) \cdot \mu_\ell(a) + V_2^i(\mu(a), \sigma^2(a)) \cdot \sigma_\ell^2(a) - \lambda \cdot q_\ell = 0 \qquad (\ast)$$

$$\text{for } \ell = 1, \ldots, K$$

and

$$\sum_{k=1}^{K} q_k \cdot a_k = \sum_{k=1}^{K} q_k \cdot \bar{a}_k,$$

where λ is the Lagrange multiplier of the budget constraint. The first-order conditions implicitly define asset demand functions of the following form

$$a_\ell^i = f_\ell^i(q_1, \ldots, q_K; \bar{a}_1^i, \ldots, \bar{a}_K^i) \text{ for all } \ell = 1, \ldots, K.$$

A general equilibrium in this exchange economy is a vector of asset prices $q^* = (q_1^*, \ldots, q_K^*)$ together with a vector of asset demands for each consumer $i = 1, 2, \ldots, I$, $a^{i*} = (a_1^{i*}, \ldots, a_K^{i*})$ such that:

$$\sum_{i=1}^{I} a_k^{i*} := \sum_{i=1}^{I} f_k^i(q_1^*, \ldots, q_K^*; \bar{a}_1^i, \ldots, \bar{a}_K^i) = \sum_{i=1}^{I} \bar{a}_k^i =: A_k,$$

where A_k denotes the aggregate quantity of the asset available in the economy. In words, the quantity of each asset demanded in equilibrium by all consumers precisely exhausts the available supply.

The capital asset-pricing equation is derived from the first-order conditions (*) given above, evaluated at equilibrium, and assuming that one of the assets is riskless.

Assuming that asset K is riskless, we know that $r_{sK} = r$ for all $s = 1, \ldots, S$. Therefore the partial derivatives of the expected pay-off and variance functions with respect to changes in the quantity of asset K held in portfolio are, respectively, $\mu_K(a) = r$ and $\sigma_K^2(a) = \sigma(a,K) = 0$. Substituting these values into the first-order conditions and choosing the riskless asset as numeraire $q_K = 1$, we solve the K-th first order condition for the Lagrange multiplier as:

$$\lambda = V_1^i(\mu(a^{i*}), \sigma^2(a^{i*})) \cdot r.$$

Substituting for λ, $\mu_\ell(a)$ and $\sigma_\ell^2(a)$, the first K-1 first order conditions (*) become:

$$V_1^i(\mu(a^{i*}), \sigma^2(a^{i*})) \cdot (\mu_\ell - q_\ell^* \cdot r) + 2 \cdot V_2^i(\mu(a^{i*}), \sigma^2(a^{i*})) \cdot \sum_{j=1}^{K} a_j^{i*} \cdot \sigma_{j\ell} = 0.$$

This equation may be rewritten as:

$$\Theta^i(a^{i*}) \cdot (\mu_\ell - q_\ell^* \cdot r) = \sum_{j=1}^{K} a_j^{i*} \cdot \sigma_{j\ell}, \qquad (2.8)$$

where $\Theta^i(a^{i*}) := -V_1^i(\mu(a^{i*}), \sigma^2(a^{i*}))/(2 \cdot V_2^i(\mu(a^{i*}), \sigma^2(a^{i*})))$ is the marginal rate of substitution along an individual agent's indifference curve in (μ, σ) space.

Summing (2.8) over all consumers, and noting that $\sum_{i=1}^{I} a_k^{i*} = A_k$ in equilibrium (market clearing), we obtain:

$$\theta(a^*) \cdot (\mu_\ell - q_\ell^* \cdot r) = \sigma(A, \ell), \qquad (2.9)$$

where $\theta(a^*) := \sum_{i=1}^{I} \Theta^i(a^{i*})$ is the sum of the agents' marginal rates of substitution and $\sigma(A, \ell) := \sum_{j=1}^{K} A_j \cdot \sigma_{j\ell}$ is the covariance of asset ℓ with the aggregate endowments, $A = (A_1, \ldots, A_K)$. Note the dependence of these marginal rates of substitution, and their summation, on the equilibrium asset allocation a^*. This reminds us that the capital asset-pricing equation is strictly true *only in a general equilibrium of the asset economy*.

Finally, multiplying equation (2.9) by A_ℓ and summing again over all risky assets $\ell = 1, \ldots K - 1$, we obtain

$$\theta(a^*) \cdot [\mu(A) - r \cdot W_o(A)] = \sigma^2(A), \qquad (2.10)$$

where $\mu(A) := \sum_{\ell=1}^{K} \mu_\ell \cdot A_\ell$ is the mean return on the aggregate endowments, i.e. the *market portfolio*, and $W_o(A) := \sum_{\ell=1}^{K} q_\ell \cdot A_\ell$ is the market value of the market portfolio. Solving equation (2.10) for $\theta(a^*)$ and substituting this

expression into equation (2.9) removes all preference-dependent term
this equation. A simple rearrangement of terms now yields the CAPM formu..
for asset units:

$$\left[\mu_\ell - r \cdot q_\ell^*\right] = \frac{\sigma(A,\ell)}{\sigma^2(A)} \cdot \left[\mu(A) - r \cdot W_o(A)\right]. \tag{2.11}$$

This formula says that the deviation of the mean return of one unit of a risky
asset ℓ from the return of an investment of the necessary amount of money, q_ℓ,
in the riskless asset is proportional to the difference between the mean return
on the aggregate endowments and the riskless return on an investment of the
market value of the aggregate endowments in the riskless asset. Moreover, the
factor of proportion is the normalized covariance of the asset with the aggregate endowment, the market portfolio. Notice that this relationship must hold
irrespective of the precise form of the utility function $V^i(\cdot)$, as long as they depend on μ and σ only.

Up to this point, we have kept with the economist's preferred mode of
operation, in which we measure asset pay-offs per unit of asset and measure
the quantities of assets held in a portfolio in absolute units. To complete the
derivation of the CAPM, we switch to the finance theorist's preferred mode of
operation, and measure asset returns as pay-offs per unit invested and asset
quantities in units of expenditure. Thus, instead of an expected pay-off, μ_k, an
asset has an expected (rate of) return in equilibrium of $\hat{\mu}_k := \mu_k/q_k^*$. Similarly,
instead of an optimal quantity of asset k in equilibrium, a_k^*, we speak of the
optimal investment share in total expenditure on asset k, $\hat{a}_k^* := a_k^* \cdot q_k^*/W_o^i$.
These equilibrium rates of return and expenditure shares clearly depend on the
set of equilibrium asset prices, q_k^*, and the initial endowment of the investor.

Thus, dividing equation (2.11) by q_ℓ and bracketing out $W_o(A)$ on the right-
hand side, one obtains:

$$\left[\hat{\mu}_\ell - r\right] = \frac{\hat{\sigma}(A,\ell)}{\hat{\sigma}^2(A)} \cdot \left[\hat{\mu}(A) - r\right], \tag{2.12}$$

where $\hat{\mu}(A) := \mu(A)/W_o(A)$ denotes the average return on the market port-
folio per unit of money invested in it and $\hat{\sigma}(A,\ell) := \sigma(A,\ell)/(q_\ell \cdot W_o(A))$ is the
covariance between the asset ℓ and the market portfolio *per unit of money*.
$\hat{\sigma}^2(A) := \sigma^2(A)/W_o(A)^2$ is the variance of the market portfolio *per unit of
money*.

Writing $\beta_\ell := \hat{\sigma}(A,\ell)/\hat{\sigma}^2(A)$ equation (2.12) becomes:

$$[\hat{\mu}_\ell - r] = \beta_\ell \cdot [\hat{\mu}(A) - r]. \tag{2.12'}$$

This is the familiar *capital asset-pricing equation*. It states that, in equilibrium, the difference between the expected rate of return on each risky asset and

85

the riskless rate of return is proportional to the difference between the expected rate of return on the market portfolio and the riskless rate of return. The factor of proportionality, β_ℓ, varies directly with the covariance of the return on the market portfolio with that on the risky asset ℓ. If the covariance of the ℓ-th risky asset with the market portfolio is greater than the covariance of the market portfolio with itself (i.e. the variance of the market portfolio), β_ℓ will be greater than one, and the risk premium required by the market in equilibrium will exceed that required on the entire portfolio of risky assets. This is illustrated in Figure 2.10.

Figure 2.10 shows why the CAPM has been so popular with finance analysts. In principle, one can observe the riskless rate of interest and the return on a market portfolio of risky assets. In practice, analysts usually take a stock-market index as the relevant 'market portfolio'. Time series of interest rates and changes in the valuation of stock-market indices are readily available and one can use familiar estimation methods to determine the β of a particular risky asset. Equipped with such an estimate, the 'risk premium required by the market' can be calculated and compared to the one implicit in the actual asset price. Purchasing an asset with an actual risk premium exceeding the one predicted by the CAPM and selling assets with CAPM risk premiums that exceed the actual one is a common decision rule for investors in financial markets. This fact makes the CAPM a useful instrument for the analysis of asset prices in financial markets.

It is important to see, however, the limitations of this approach. The reason why we can derive a 'pricing formula' which does not depend on 'individual characteristics' of the market participants is that all investors choose portfolios

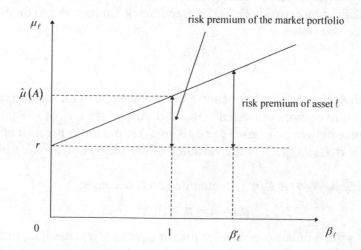

Fig. 2.10

that minimize the variance for a given mean return. This property alone ficient to establish the formula in equation (2.11) (Exercise 7). Minimization of the variance of a portfolio for a given mean return is unrelated to a consumer's preferences, though the minimizing portfolio will depend on the investor's initial endowment of assets. However, these will sum to the aggregate endowment, i.e. the market portfolio.

The CAPM is important because it was the first equilibrium model of asset-pricing under uncertainty. It spawned a vast amount of theoretical and applied literature, the former seeking to relax the strong assumptions underlying the model and the latter seeking to apply the model to actual stock-price data. The CAPM was severely criticized by Roll (1977) who undermined empirical testing of the CAPM by pointing out that the market portfolio could never be observed in practice. While the CAPM continues to be used in empirical finance, the effect of Roll's critique was to direct attention to an entirely different approach to asset pricing pioneered by Ross (1976), i.e. the Arbitrage-Pricing Theory, which justifies estimation methods similar to those used by finance analysts for the CAPM.

Notes on the Literature

The pure exchange model of asset markets is usually found in economics text books like Varian (1992). The parallel analysis of equilibrium in asset space and contingent wealth space highlights the restrictions on asset prices which follow from the need to rule out arbitrage in equilibrium. This is a novel feature of this chapter.

Mean-variance analysis is a core concept in introductory finance textbooks. A good basic treatment is that of Copeland and Weston (1988). More advanced expositions are available in Ingersoll (1987), Huang and Litzenberger (1988), and Milne (1995). The classic development of the basic framework is Markowitz (1952). The exposition in Fama and Miller (1972) has also stood the test of time. The Capital Asset-Pricing Model (CAPM) was developed by several finance theorists, among them Treynor (1961), Sharpe (1964), Lintner (1965a), and Mossin (1966). A valuable overview of the Capital Asset-Pricing Model and its place in the evolution of finance theory is contained in Brennan (1989).

Exercises

1. *Consider an economy with one commodity and two consumers, $i = 1,2$. The consumers have identical preferences which can be represented by the von Neumann–Morgenstern expected utility function $u(x) = \ln x$. There are two possible states in regard to the consumers' endowments:* (i) *either consumer 1 gets an endowment $\omega^1 = 1$ and consumer 2 obtains $\omega^2 = 3$; or consumer 1 gets an endowment $\omega^1 = 3$ and consumer 2 obtains $\omega^2 = 1$.*

(a) Derive the equilibrium allocation and the equilibrium prices in this economy for each of the two states.

(b) Suppose that consumers can trade in contingent contracts for purchases and sales before the states become revealed. Derive the equilibrium prices of these contingent contracts under the assumption that both consumers assess the likelihood of the two states with the same probability distribution.

(c) Compare the equilibrium allocation in the two states that arises from trade in contingent contracts to the allocation arising when only spot markets exist. Are both consumers better off?

(d) Suppose there are no contingent contracts possible, but consumers can trade in asset markets before the states are revealed. Assume that there is a bond that pays interest $r > 0$ and a stock that pays $r_s > 0$ in state s, $s = 1,2$. What conditions must the return rates r, r_1, r_2 satisfy to obtain the same allocation as with contingent markets? Derive the equilibrium prices of these two assets.

(e) Consider the consumers before the true state is revealed. Would the consumers want to know which state will occur? Is information about the state valuable?

2. *Consider two portfolios $a = (a_1, \ldots, a_K)$ and $a' = (a'_1, \ldots, a'_K)$ satisfying the budget constraint of a consumer.*

(a) Show that any portfolio $a^\lambda = \lambda \cdot a + (1 - \lambda) \cdot a'$, $\lambda \in \mathbb{R}$, satisfies the budget constraint as well.

(b) Let a' be a portfolio that invests all wealth in the riskless asset. Show that the mean variance combinations $(M(a^\lambda), S(a^\lambda))$ of all portfolios a^λ, $\lambda \in \mathbb{R}$, lie on a line in mean-variance space.

3. *Show that any portfolio choice problem with asset prices $q = (q_1, \ldots, q_K)$ and initial wealth W_o where the decision-maker chooses quantities of assets is equivalent to another portfolio choice problem where the decision-maker decides which proportions of her wealth to invest in the assets.*

4. *Consider an investor with mean-variance preferences represented by the utility function $V(\mu, \sigma^2)$ which is increasing in the mean μ and decreasing in the variance σ^2. The investor can choose a portfolio of K assets $a = (a_1, \ldots, a_K)$ yielding returns $r_k = (r_{1k} \ldots, r_{Sk})$, $k = 1, \ldots, K$, in S states of the world. The price of asset k is q_k, $k = 1, \ldots, K$. The probability distribution over states is given by the vector $(p_1, \ldots, p_S)$.*

(a) Derive the mean $\mu(a)$ and the variance $\sigma^2(a)$ of a portfolio a.

(b) Derive the first-order conditions for an optimal portfolio.

(c) Show that the optimal portfolio minimizes the variance over all portfolios with the same mean value that satisfy the budget constraint.

5. *Consider two portfolios of K assets, a and b, that minimize the variance given their mean returns $\mu(a)$ and $\mu(b)$ respectively.*

(a) For any $\lambda \in (0,1)$, show that $\lambda \cdot a + (1 - \lambda) \cdot b$ is a portfolio as well. For the case of two assets, draw a diagram showing the portfolios created by forming a convex combination of the portfolios a and b with some λ.

(b) Prove the following statement: 'If the portfolios a and b cost \$100, then, for any λ, the portfolio $\lambda \cdot a + (1 - \lambda) \cdot b$ costs \$100 as well.'

6. *Consider an economy with I investors, $i = 1, \ldots, I$. Each investor is endowed with a portfolio of asset holdings $\bar{a}^i = (\bar{a}^i_1, \ldots, \bar{a}^i_K)$. Investors trade assets at given market prices $(q_1, \ldots, q_K)$. Assets pay returns $r_s = (r_{s1}, \ldots, r_{sK})$ in each of S states that occur with probabilities $(p_1, \ldots, p_S)$.*

(a) Write down the definition of an asset-market equilibrium for this economy.

(b) Show that, in equilibrium, the (per capita) aggregate endowments of assets form a convex combination of the optimally chosen (per capita) portfolios of the investors.

7. *Consider an economy with trade in K assets at market prices $(q_1, \ldots, q_K)$. Assets pay returns $r_s = (r_{s1}, \ldots, r_{sK})$ in each of S states that occur with probabilities $(p_1, \ldots, p_S)$.*

(a) Write down the optimization problem for the choice of a portfolio that minimizes the variance subject to the constraint that it satisfies the budget constraint and that it achieves a certain level of mean return.

(b) Derive the first-order conditions for the variance-minimizing portfolio. Are these conditions sufficient as well?

(c) Assume that asset K is riskless with return R and price $q_K \equiv 1$. Show that the first-order conditions for the $K - 1$ risky assets can be written in the following form:

$$[\mu_k - q_k \cdot R] = \frac{\sigma(k, a)}{\sigma^2(a)} \cdot [\mu(a) - R \cdot \sum_{k=1}^{K} q_k \cdot a_k].$$

SYSTEMS OF FINANCIAL MARKETS

The central theme of this chapter is the structure of financial markets. The first section reminds us why efficiency of trade fails if there are no financial markets. We then consider two extreme forms of financial assets: (i) financial assets where each asset specifies the delivery of one particular good under well-specified conditions; and (ii) financial assets where each asset specifies the delivery of a numeraire good (money) in just one spot market. Both systems of financial markets can provide trading opportunities that allow agents to achieve a Pareto-optimal allocation in competitive markets. An important insight of the analysis is the observation that a minimum number of sufficiently distinct securities is necessary for efficiency of trade.

....

3.1 Some Preliminary Considerations and Definitions

....

The history of the world can be conceptualized as one of infinitely many possible paths through an event-tree of the type depicted in Figure 3.1. Each node of the event-tree is a date–state pair and represents a unique historical conjunction of time and the resolution of uncertainty. Each state is a complete description of all aspects of the exogenous environment that traders consider relevant for their decisions. This may include weather conditions, the configuration of political parties in power, or social conditions.

At each date–state pair, consumption of goods and services takes place and consumers may trade in *spot markets*. Commodities are indexed by a pair, indicating the particular date and state of the world in which they will be consumed. Even if the underlying good or service is physically identical, appending a date–state index creates commodities which are analytically distinct. Wheat consumed at node a at time 0 is conceptually different from wheat

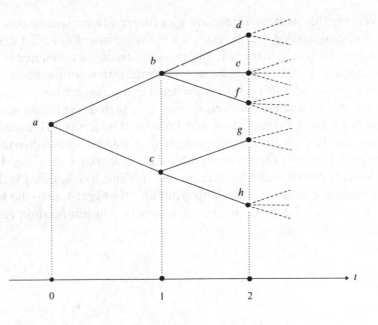

Fig. 3.1

consumed at node f at time 2. This distinction is not simply a matter of theory; in real-world futures markets, traders distinguish between 'spot wheat', which is available for immediate delivery, and, say, 'July wheat', which is available for delivery next July. They are distinct commodities (in this case, indexed only by time and not also by the state of the world) and can be expected to trade at different prices. Similarly, there is trade in insurance contracts that promise payments or replacement of goods under certain specified contingencies. Insuring a replacement car against damage in a road accident may be priced differently from insuring the same car against theft. A commodity that is created by indexing an underlying good or service by the date and state in which it becomes available is known as a *contingent commodity*. Since each contingent commodity is a separate entity, regardless of whether the underlying good or service is the same, it has a distinct price.

An event-tree as in Figure 3.1 not only describes all possible states and dates of the world but, by the sequential nature of time, also describes the evolution of information about these states. As the history of the world unfolds, whole sections of the tree become irrelevant. For example, if, at date 1, state b eventuates, states c, g, and h at date 2 (and states to which they lead at later points in time) fall out of consideration. Thus a trader knows at date 2 whether states in the upper part of the tree (following b) or in the lower part of the tree (following c) can be disregarded in further planning.

Whether this sequential revelation of information matters for a trader's decision-making depends crucially on the structure of financial markets. If there are no financial markets in the economy, traders are confined to trade in spot markets. In this case, information about states cannot affect their decisions. We consider this case in more detail in the next section.

Alternatively, financial markets may open in period 0 only, and never again thereafter. If this is the case, the gradual release of information is once again irrelevant for the decision-making process. All that agents know when they trade in financial assets is the set of possible date–state pairs. One can therefore equivalently drop the reference to time-periods and, by relabelling states, consider each date-state as a state. This simplifies the event-tree to the form depicted in Figure 3.2, since the dynamic structure of information revelation about states has vanished.

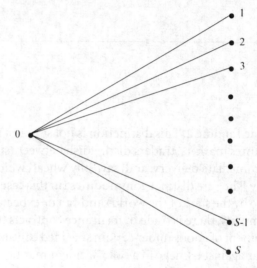

Fig. 3.2

Note that there is a finite number of states in the tree of Figure 3.2. This corresponds to the case where the event-tree in Figure 3.1 ends in terminal nodes. If the tree grows forever, the set of states would be countably infinite. Such a case is no different conceptually from the finite case but demands more sophisticated mathematics.

In line with the literature, most of this chapter deals with the case where trade in financial assets occurs once only in period 0. Without loss of generality, we assume throughout that the set of states is finite. Indeed, the portfolio choice model treated in Chapter 2 can be viewed as a special case of this approach. Though we consider a set of spot markets for commodities in period 0 together with a set of financial markets, it will become clear that trade in commodities in period 0 is irrelevant. The crucial assumption is that trade in assets is impossible after date 0.

It is only in Chapter 4, where we deal with option-pricing, that sequential trade in securities is considered. Though in a very much simplified version, we consider the case where trade in securities is possible in an infinite sequence of periods. The main consequence of sequential trade in securities is the fact that a smaller number of assets, i.e. a simpler structure of financial markets, may suffice for an equilibrium in securities markets to be Pareto optimal.

Before beginning to analyse the structure of financial markets, it is useful to introduce some notation for the case where trade in financial assets takes place in period 0 only.

Let $I = \{1, \ldots, I\}$ be the set of consumers, $L = \{1, \ldots, L\}$ be the set of underlying goods and services and $S = \{1, \ldots, S\}$ be the set of states at date 1. Using the subscript 0 to signify the single state at date 0, a typical consumption bundle consumed by consumer i is written as:

$$x^i \equiv (x_0^i, \ldots, x_S^i) \equiv (x_{01}^i, \ldots, x_{0L}^i; x_{11}^i, \ldots, x_{1L}^i; \ldots; x_{S1}^i, \ldots, x_{SL}^i),$$

where $x_{s\ell}^i$ represents the quantity of commodity ℓ which consumer i plans to consume should state s occur. Similarly, a typical endowment bundle for consumer i is written as:

$$\omega^i \equiv (\omega_0^i, \ldots, \omega_S^i) \equiv (\omega_{01}^i, \ldots, \omega_{0L}^i; \omega_{11}^i, \ldots, \omega_{1L}^i; \ldots; \omega_{S1}^i, \ldots, \omega_{SL}^i),$$

where $\omega_{s\ell}^i$ represents the quantity of commodity ℓ which consumer i owns in state s. Finally, we assume a utility function $V^i(x^i)$ exists on the space of contingent commodity bundles representing the preferences of consumer i over those bundles.

3.2 Spot Markets

We begin by considering a hypothetical market structure in which it is not possible to trade goods and services until the prevailing state of the world is known, i.e. uncertainty is resolved. This is equivalent to the assumption that it is not possible to trade contingent commodities *with different state indexes* before these states actually eventuate. Thus it is possible to exchange x_{11} for x_{12} but not x_{11} for x_{21}. In other words, it is possible to trade commodities which are available in a particular state but trade between different states, whether in the same underlying good or not, is not possible. Such an economy is referred to as a *spot market economy*. The term 'spot market' refers to a goods market system in which all trade takes place in the same state.

A consumer in such an economy faces a choice problem of the following type:

$$\underset{x^i}{Max}\ V^i(x^i) \qquad \text{s.t.}$$

$$p_0 \cdot x_0^i \le p_0 \cdot \omega_0^i$$

$$p_s \cdot x_s^i \le p_s \cdot \omega_s^i \qquad\qquad \text{for all } s \in S$$

$$x^i \ge 0,$$

where p_0 is the vector of spot prices of the L underlying commodities in state (date) 0 and $p_1, \ldots, p_S$ are the spot price vectors of the L underlying commodities in each of the S states.

Note that there are as many budget constraints as there are states. In each state, consumers are constrained to consume a bundle of goods whose value at prices ruling in that state does not exceed the value of their endowment in that state. They cannot augment their consumption in one state by sacrificing consumption in another state. In other words, they can neither save (exchange goods between dates) nor insure (exchange goods between states).

Equilibrium in a spot market economy is an allocation plus a set of prices which clear spot markets in each state. This allocation will be Pareto optimal within the confines of the spot market economy, i.e. 'constrained' Pareto optimal. Pareto improvements are not possible so long as the constraints imposed by the spot market structure of the economy are observed. Relaxing those constraints, for example, by allowing trade between different states, will create opportunities for Pareto improvements in the consumption allocation.

Example 3.1. Suppose there is just one underlying good, i.e. $L = \{1\}$ and that there is no uncertainty, i.e. $S = \{1\}$. The ith consumer's choice set is depicted in Figure 3.3 as a single point. It is not possible for the consumer to exploit gains from trade between dates (by saving/dissaving) within the constraints imposed by the spot market economy.

Suppose instead that there is just one underlying good, i.e. $L = \{1\}$, two states of the world, i.e. $S = \{1, 2\}$ and no trade at date 0. The ith consumer's choice set is again a single point as depicted in Figure 3.4. This time, however, the commodities measured on the axes are contingent commodities. In this case, the structure of the spot market economy prevents trade between states (i.e. forbids insurance). ∎

The distinctive feature of the spot market economy is that the prices attaching to contingent commodities in equilibrium are the same as the spot prices which would apply were that particular state to materialize. The prices which clear the various contingent commodities markets are the prices which will clear the spot markets upon the resolution of uncertainty and the realization

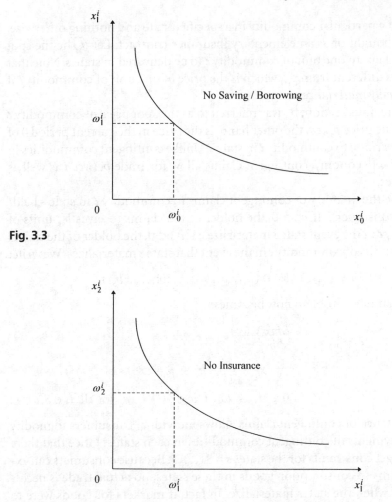

Fig. 3.3

Fig. 3.4

of one of the S states. In effect, there are $S + 1$ different configurations of the L spot commodities markets, one at date 0 and one each for the S possible states of the world, and it is not possible to rearrange the endowments in each of these configurations by exchanging commodities between them.

3.3 Contingent Claims Markets

Consider now the situation where consumers can trade in period 0 financial assets called *contingent claims*. A contingent claim is a firm promise to deliver

95

one unit of a particular commodity in a specified state and nothing otherwise. It can be thought of as an elementary insurance contract. Let $\hat{p}_{s\ell}$ be the spot price of a claim to one unit of commodity ℓ to be delivered in state s. Note that this price is different from $p_{s\ell}$, which is the price of one unit of commodity ℓ if state s *actually materializes*.

In the previous section, $p_{s\ell}$ was referred to as the spot price of commodity ℓ in state s. The price $\hat{p}_{s\ell}$, on the other hand, is the price in the current period 0 of a *contingent claim* to commodity ℓ in state s. Unlike contingent commodities in a spot market economy, contingent claims allow for trade *between* as well as *within* states.

Let $b^i_{s\ell}$ be the quantity of contingent claims to commodity ℓ in state s held/ issued by consumer i. If $b^i_{s\ell} > 0$, the holder of the claims receives $b^i_{s\ell}$ units of commodity ℓ in the event state s materializes; if $b^i_{s\ell} < 0$, the holder of the claims delivers $b^i_{s\ell}$ units of commodity ℓ in the event that state s materializes. We write:

$$b^i \equiv (b^i_1, \ldots, b^i_S) \equiv (b^i_{11}, \ldots, b^i_{1L}; \ldots; b^i_{S1}, \ldots, b^i_{SL})$$

The consumer's problem now becomes:

$$\underset{x^i, b^i}{Max\ } V^i(x^i) \qquad \text{s.t.}$$

$$\hat{p}_0 \cdot x^i_0 + \sum_{s \in S} \hat{p}_s \cdot b^i_s \leq \hat{p}_0 \cdot \omega^i_0$$

$$0 \leq x^i_{s\ell} \leq \omega^i_{s\ell} + b^i_{s\ell} \qquad\qquad \text{for all } s \in S, \ell \in L.$$

The existence of contingent claims allows individual consumers to modify their endowments of contingent commodities in each state. Notice that there are no budget constraints for the states $s = 1, \ldots, S$. Because consumers can exchange claims to consumption goods in these states, no actual trade is necessary if and when the states materialize. In fact, if markets for goods were to open in any state, no trade would occur. Note, however, that the feasibility constraints, $0 \leq x^i_{s\ell} \leq \omega^i_{s\ell} + b^i_{s\ell}$, imply that $b^i_{s\ell} \geq -\omega^i_{s\ell}$ holds. Thus, a consumer cannot promise to deliver more than all of her endowment of any good in any state. It is now possible for trade between date 0 and date 1, and between different states, to occur, i.e. for consumers to save and/or to purchase insurance.

Rather than the multiple budget constraints of the spot market economy, the contingent claims market economy faces consumers with a single budget constraint. This can be verified by substituting $b^i_s = x^i_s - \omega^i_s$ into the budget constraint and re-expressing the consumer's problem as:

$$\underset{x^i}{Max\ } V^i(x^i) \qquad \text{s.t.}$$

$$\hat{p}_0 \cdot x^i_0 + \sum_{s \in S} \hat{p}_s \cdot x^i_s \leq \hat{p}_0 \cdot \omega^i_0 + \sum_{s \in S} \hat{p}_s \cdot \omega^i_s.$$

In the contingent claims market economy, trade takes place in contingent claims at date 0 and no retrading is necessary at date 1 when the state of the world is resolved. At that time, contracts are simply fulfilled and goods exchanged in the ratios agreed at date 0, a result reflected in the following definition.

DEFINITION 3.1. A competitive equilibrium of the contingent claims economy is a price vector: $\hat{p} \equiv (\hat{p}_0, \hat{p}_1, \ldots, \hat{p}_S) \equiv (\hat{p}_{01}, \ldots, \hat{p}_{0L}; \hat{p}_{11}, \ldots, \hat{p}_{1L}; \ldots;$ $\hat{p}_{S1}, \ldots, \hat{p}_{SL})$ and an allocation of state contingent consumption $x^1, \ldots, x^I$ such that:

$$x^i \in \text{argmax}\left\{ V^i(x^i) \;\middle|\; x^i \geq 0, \hat{p}_0 \cdot x^i_0 + \sum_{s \in S} \hat{p}_s \cdot x^i_s \leq \hat{p}_0 \cdot \omega^i_0 + \sum_{s \in S} \hat{p}_s \cdot \omega^i_s \right\} \text{ for all } i \in I$$

and

$$\sum_{i \in I} x^i_{s\ell} = \sum_{i \in I} \omega^i_{s\ell} \qquad \text{for all } s = 0, 1, \ldots, S \text{ and all } \ell = 1, \ldots, L.$$

This definition is identical to that which obtains in a pure exchange economy under certainty. A contingent claims economy is in fact identical to a pure exchange economy in all respects, except that the objects of trade are claims to commodities contingent upon particular states of the world occurring at particular dates in time.

An immediate implication is that such an equilibrium is Pareto optimal (by the First Fundamental Theorem of welfare economics). Strictly speaking, the optimality is *ex ante*, since it refers to the trading of contingent claims before the resolution of uncertainty. Nevertheless, no further trade takes place *ex post*, i.e. on spot markets. The exchange of goods upon the realization of the state merely represents the fulfilment of prior contingent contracts.

Example 3.2. Let $L = \{1\}$, $I = \{A, B\}$, and $S = \{1, 2\}$. Figure 3.5 depicts an exchange equilibrium in which consumer A trades claims to the consumption good contingent on state 1 against claims to the consumption good contingent on state 2. Consumer B performs the opposite exchange. Note that the aggregate endowment of the consumption good is larger in state 1 than in state 2. This represents aggregate uncertainty or social risk. By exchanging contingent claims to consumption, i.e. engaging in mutual insurance, each consumer has reduced his exposure to uncertainty and improved his welfare.

In the special case where the aggregate endowment of the consumption good in each state is the same (Figure 3.6), so that there is no aggregate uncertainty, risk-averse consumers with von Neumann–Morgenstern expected utility functions will fully insure. The exchange equilibrium will lie on the diagonal of the (square) Edgeworth box diagram and the prices of contingent claims will be proportional to the probabilities of the two states, π_1 and π_2, i.e.:

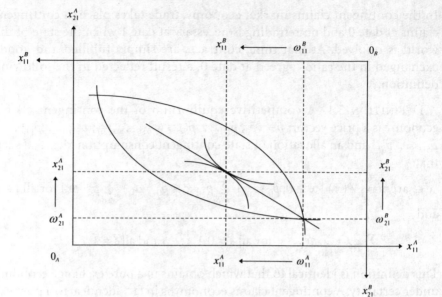

Fig. 3.5

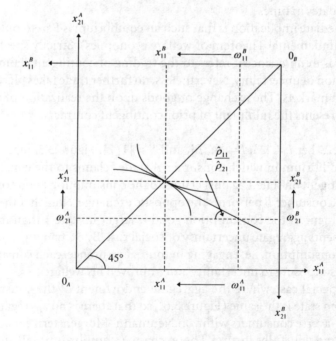

Fig. 3.6

$$\frac{\hat{p}_1}{\hat{p}_2} = \frac{\pi_1}{\pi_2}$$

This result will·be proved in Exercise 2. ∎

It is not difficult to confirm that a contingent claims equilibrium is optimal *ex post* as well as *ex ante*. In other words, if spot markets were opened upon the resolution of uncertainty, no agent would desire to engage in further trade. Assuming an interior optimum,[1] the following equality holds for all $k, \ell \in L$ and all $s, t \in S$:

$$\frac{\hat{p}_{s\ell}}{\hat{p}_{tk}} = \frac{\partial V^i(x^i)}{\partial x^i_{s\ell}} \Bigg/ \frac{\partial V^i(x^i)}{\partial x^i_{tk}} .$$

In particular, when $s = t$, we have:

$$\frac{\hat{p}_{s\ell}}{\hat{p}_{sk}} = \frac{\partial V^i(x^i)}{\partial x^i_{s\ell}} \Bigg/ \frac{\partial V^i(x^i)}{\partial x^i_{sk}} ,$$

which indicates that marginal rates of substitution between any two commodities are equal in equilibrium, even after the resolution of uncertainty, i.e. within any single state. Thus there are no gains to be reaped from engaging in further trade.

Contingent claims markets allow consumers to attain optimal allocations under conditions of uncertainty but at the expense of the need for a vast number of financial assets to be traded. In addition to the L spot markets for commodities at date 0, $S \cdot L$ financial markets for contingent claims are required, making a total of $L + (S \cdot L)$ markets in all. Of course, this is not a problem if markets are costless to operate and if consumers are fully informed about all trading opportunities.

Before turning to more realistic financial assets, another artificial type of security is introduced in the following section. Arrow (1964) showed that economies with a complete set of such assets, called *Arrow securities*, provide the same trading possibilities for consumers as economies with contingent claims markets.

3.4 Arrow Securities

Unlike a contingent claim which promises to deliver one unit of a physical commodity in a specified state, an Arrow security promises to deliver one unit

---

[1] The proof that this claim holds, even if consumers choose a corner solution, is left as an exercise.

of purchasing power in the specified state. This quantity of purchasing power is then used to purchase physical commodities on spot markets once the state of the world has been resolved. By construction, there can be at most S Arrow securities.

Let $\hat{a}_k^i$ be the quantity of Arrow security k bought (sold) by consumer i if $\hat{a}_k^i > 0 \, (< 0)$. A portfolio of Arrow securities is a vector:

$$\hat{a}^i \equiv (\hat{a}_1^i, \dots, \hat{a}_K^i),$$

where security $k \in \{1, \dots, K\}$ pays one unit of purchasing power in state $k \in S$ and nothing in any other state. The index of an Arrow security is identical to the state in which it pays off. The possibility that there might be fewer Arrow securities than states of the world gives rise to the following definition:

DEFINITION 3.2. A set of Arrow securities is said to be *complete* if $K = S$ and *incomplete* if $K < S$.

An economy with a complete set of Arrow securities markets, i.e. exactly $K = S$ securities, can achieve the same trading possibilities as an economy with a complete set of contingent claims markets.

Let $\hat{q} \equiv (\hat{q}_1, \dots, \hat{q}_K)$ be the vector of Arrow securities prices. The consumer's problem is written as follows:

$$\underset{x^i, \hat{a}^i}{Max} \; V^i(x^i) \qquad \text{s.t.}$$

$$p_0 \cdot x_0^i + \hat{q} \cdot \hat{a}^i \le p_0 \cdot \omega_0^i$$

$$p_s \cdot x_s^i \le p_s \cdot \omega_s^i + \hat{a}_s^i \qquad \text{for all } s \in S$$

$$x^i \ge 0.$$

Notice that there are budget constraints for spot markets in the states $s = 1, \dots, S$. Since Arrow securities do not require direct delivery of goods, trade in goods and services must occur once the true state becomes known and transfers of purchasing power according to the Arrow securities, $\hat{a}_s^i$ have been carried out. Note that Arrow securities do not pay off in terms of a particular good but pay some amount of purchasing power. One might wonder whether the choice of a numeraire commodity in each state would affect the allocations of goods that a consumer can achieve. As the following argument shows, this is not the case if there is a *complete* set of Arrow securities. As will be discussed at some length in Section 3.6, the independence of the equilibrium allocation from the choice of a numeraire no longer holds if Arrow securities markets are *incomplete*.

To see that the economy with a complete set of Arrow securities is in fact identical to an economy with a system of contingent claims markets, multiply the budget constraint in each state by the price of the respective Arrow security, $\hat{q}_s$, and sum over all budget constraints to yield:

$$\underset{x^i}{Max}\ V^i(x^i) \quad \text{s.t.}$$

$$p_0 \cdot x_0^i + \sum_{s \in S} \hat{q}_s \cdot p_s \cdot x_s^i \leq p_0 \cdot \omega_0^i + \sum_{s \in S} \hat{q}_s \cdot p_s \cdot \omega_s^i$$

$$x_s^i \geq 0.$$

This is identical to the consumer's problem in the contingent claims economy when we note that $p_{0\ell} = \hat{p}_{0\ell}$ and $\hat{q}_s \cdot p_{s\ell} = \hat{p}_{s\ell}$ for $\ell = 1,\ldots,L$.

In equilibrium, the price of a contingent claim to one unit of commodity ℓ in state s is equal to the price of a bundle of Arrow securities which pay off in aggregate an amount sufficient to purchase one unit of commodity ℓ on the spot market should state s materialize. Such an amount is the spot price of commodity ℓ in state s expressed in units of the numeraire.

We can draw further inferences. Since $\hat{q}_s \cdot p_{s\ell} = \hat{p}_{s\ell}$ for all $s \in S$ and $\ell \in L$, we have:

$$\frac{\hat{p}_{s1}}{p_{sk}} = \frac{\hat{q}_s \cdot p_{s1}}{\hat{q}_s \cdot p_{sk}} = \frac{p_{s1}}{p_{sk}}.$$

In other words, relative prices between any two commodities within a given state (i.e. relative 'spot' prices) are equal to the relative contingent claims prices and to the relative prices of the appropriate bundles of Arrow securities. Furthermore, for $s, t \in S$:

$$\frac{\hat{p}_{s1}}{\hat{p}_{t1}} = \frac{\hat{q}_s \cdot p_{s1}}{\hat{q}_t \cdot p_{t1}}.$$

The relative price of the same commodity in different states equals the ratio of the spot-market price of the commodity in each state multiplied by the Arrow security price for that state.

Choosing a numeraire commodity in each state by normalizing the price of a commodity to one, say, for commodity 1 in states s and t (i.e. $p_{s1} = 1$ and $p_{t1} = 1$), the equilibrium state–price ratio of this commodity 1 will determine the Arrow security price ratio $\hat{q}_s/\hat{q}_t$. The choice of numeraire does not disturb consumer's choices amongst state-contingent commodities and, therefore, has no effect on the equilibrium allocation.

A complete set of Arrow (or 'pure') securities markets is sufficient to replicate the equilibrium allocation in an economy with a full set of contingent claims markets. Summing the L spot markets at date 0, the L spot markets in the state which eventuates and the S markets for Arrow securities gives a total of $2 \cdot L + S$ markets required for optimality rather than the $L \cdot (S + 1)$ markets required with contingent claims. Thus the number of markets required for optimality can be reduced substantially via the device of Arrow securities.

The two financial market systems studied so far provide benchmarks for the study of ordinary securities in the following section. A system of contingent claims markets creates a pure exchange economy in contingent commodities. This is the most extensive system of financial markets that one can imagine. A complete system of Arrow securities provides the same trading opportunities for consumers as the contingent claims system of financial markets but with the smallest possible set of financial markets. Section 3.5 investigates whether systems of ordinary securities are capable of achieving the same trading opportunities.

3.5 Ordinary Securities Markets

Ordinary securities, the type of asset studied in Chapter 2, pay off units of purchasing power in more than just a single state. An ordinary security k is characterized by its state-contingent pay-off vector

$$r_k = (r_{1k}, \ldots, r_{sk}, \ldots, r_{Sk}),$$

where r_{sk} denotes the number of units of purchasing power that a holder of one unit of asset k receives if state s occurs. If there are K ordinary securities, their pay-off vectors, written as column vectors, can be combined in a pay-off matrix as follows:

$$R = \begin{bmatrix} r_{11} & \cdots & r_{1K} \\ \vdots & \ddots & \vdots \\ r_{S1} & \cdots & r_{SK} \end{bmatrix}$$

Note that columns indicate the pay-off vectors of the K assets, while rows give the pay-offs of the assets in the various states,

$$r_s = (r_{s1}, \ldots, r_{sK}).$$

An ordinary security k is traded in period 0 at price q_k and the vector of security prices is written

$$q = (q_1, \ldots, q_K).$$

Denoting by a_k^i the quantity of asset k bought ($a_k^i > 0$) or sold ($a_k^i < 0$) by consumer i, her portfolio of securities can be written as

$$a^i = (a_1^i, \ldots, a_K^i).$$

The portfolio a^i costs $q \cdot a^i = \sum_{k=1}^{K} q_k \cdot a_k^i$ in period 0 and returns $r_s \cdot a^i = \sum_{k=1}^{K} r_{sk} \cdot a_k^i$ in state s.

In a financial market system with K ordinary securities, a consumer's choice problem takes the following form:

$$Max\ V(x^i) \qquad s.t.$$
$$x^i, a^i$$

$$p_0 \cdot x_0^i + q \cdot a^i \le p_0 \cdot \omega_0^i$$

$$p_s \cdot x_s^i \le p_s \cdot \omega_s^i + r_s \cdot a^i \qquad\qquad \text{for all } s \in S$$

$$x^i \ge 0.$$

The consumer's problem in a financial market system with ordinary securities is similar to the problem in a system with a complete set of Arrow securities. The only obvious difference is the fact that the pay-off of a portfolio of Arrow securities in state s was given by a_s^i, the quantity of the single Arrow security that paid off in state s, while with ordinary securities, the pay-off of the portfolio is $r_s \cdot a^i = \sum_{k=1}^{K} r_{sk} \cdot a_k^i$ since all securities may pay off a positive amount in state s. In both cases, the return on the portfolio determines the total amount of purchasing power transferred in favour of the consumer ($r_s \cdot a^i > 0$) or away from the consumer ($r_s \cdot a^i < 0$).

The similarity of the two problems suggests that the two systems may be equivalent, in the sense that both provide the same trading opportunities for consumers. We now investigate conditions under which such an equivalence holds.

For an asset market system of ordinary securities to provide the same trading opportunities as a financial market system with a complete set of Arrow securities, it must be possible to find for each portfolio of Arrow securities $\hat{a} = (\hat{a}_1, \ldots, \hat{a}_S)$ a portfolio of ordinary securities that yields the same vector of state-contingent pay-offs as the portfolio $\hat{a}$. Clearly, it suffices to show that, for each Arrow security s, there is a portfolio of ordinary securities $a(s)$ that pays off one unit in state s and nothing otherwise. Then, to reproduce the pay-off of the portfolio $\hat{a}$, the consumer needs to buy $\hat{a}_s$ units of the portfolio $a(s)$ for $s = 1, \ldots, S$.

To find the portfolio $a(s) = (a_1(s), \ldots, a_K(s))$, one needs to solve the equation system:

$$r_1 \cdot a\,(s) = 0,$$
$$\vdots \qquad \vdots$$
$$r_s \cdot a\,(s) = 1,$$
$$\vdots \qquad \vdots$$
$$r_S \cdot a\,(s) = 0.$$

Whether or not a solution exists to this linear equation system depends on the return matrix R whose row vectors are the coefficients of the equation system. A necessary condition is that there are at least as many assets as there are states of the world, $K \geq S$, because the number of assets determines the number of unknowns in the equation system and the number of states determines the number of equations.

If there are S Arrow securities, one has to solve S equation systems of this type to determine the S pay-off-replicating portfolios $a(s)$. The following well-known lemma from linear algebra gives the necessary and sufficient conditions for the solution of all these equation systems and, as a result, for the equivalence of a system of ordinary security markets and a complete set of Arrow securities. Note that Arrow securities are the special case of ordinary securities where $r_{sk} = 1$ for $k = s$ and $r_{sk} = 0$ for $k \neq s$ holds. The return matrix for S Arrow securities is therefore the $S \times S$-identity matrix:

$$\hat{R} = \begin{bmatrix} 1 & \cdots & 0 \\ \vdots & \ddots & \vdots \\ 0 & \cdots & 1 \end{bmatrix}.$$

LEMMA 3.1. Suppose R is an $S \times S$ matrix of full rank. Then there exists an inverse matrix R^{-1} such that $R \cdot R^{-1} = \hat{R}$.

Lemma 3.1 is a standard result from linear algebra. The 'full-rank condition' tells us that, if there are at least as many ordinary securities with linearly independent pay-off vectors as there are states, it is possible to combine the pay-offs of ordinary securities so as to synthesize a set of S Arrow securities. Each column of the matrix R^{-1} is one of the portfolios $a(s)$ which, given the pay-offs of the K securities in the matrix R, generates pay-offs identical to one of the S Arrow securities. This condition provides us with a characterization of *completeness* in a system of *ordinary* securities markets.

DEFINITION 3.3. A set of ordinary securities is said to be *complete* if there are at least as many ordinary securities whose pay-off vectors are linearly independent as there are states, i.e. $K \geq S$ where K is the number of linearly independent securities.

The following example shows how one can construct portfolios of ordinary securities that replicate the Arrow securities.

Example 3.3. Let there be two states and two ordinary securities with contingent pay-offs as given in the following matrix:

$$R = \begin{bmatrix} 2 & 3 \\ 5 & 1 \end{bmatrix}.$$

Since the determinant of R is non-zero, the inverse matrix exists:

$$R^{-1} = \begin{bmatrix} \dfrac{-1}{13} & \dfrac{3}{13} \\ \dfrac{5}{13} & \dfrac{-2}{13} \end{bmatrix}.$$

Thus a portfolio $(a_1, a_2) = (-1/13, 5/13)$ synthesizes the pay-off vector from the Arrow security $(1, 0)$. Similarly, a portfolio $(\tilde{a}_1, \tilde{a}_2) = (3/13, -2/13)$ synthesizes the pay-off vector from the Arrow security $(0, 1)$. Figure 3.7 illustrates this result. ∎

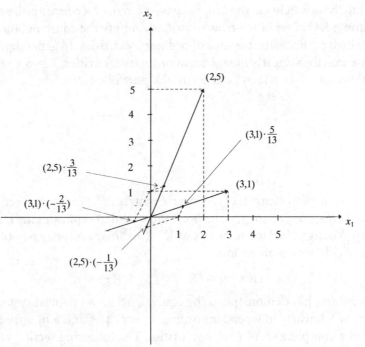

Fig. 3.7

Since it is possible to synthesize both Arrow securities by combining the two ordinary securities in appropriate proportions, it must also be possible to create any pattern of pay-offs across states that can be created by combining Arrow securities. This is illustrated in the following example which resumes Example 3.3.

Example 3.4. To obtain the contingent pay-off vector $(5,2)$, one purchases 5 units of Arrow security $(1,0)$ and 2 units of Arrow security $(0,1)$. Since the Arrow securities are not traded, one must purchase portfolios of ordinary securities instead.

Since the portfolio $(a_1, a_2) = (-1/13, 5/13)$ produces Arrow security $(1, 0)$ and portfolio $(\tilde{a}_1, \tilde{a}_2) = (3/13, -2/13)$ produces Arrow security $(0, 1)$, to obtain the pay-off vector $(5, 2)$, one forms the compound portfolio:

$$
\begin{aligned}
(\mathring{a}_1, \mathring{a}_2) &= 5 \cdot (a_1, a_2) + 2 \cdot (\tilde{a}_1, \tilde{a}_2) \\
&= (5 \cdot a_1 + 2 \cdot \tilde{a}_1, 5 \cdot a_2 + 2 \cdot \tilde{a}_2) \\
&= \left(\frac{1}{13}, \frac{21}{13} \right).
\end{aligned}
$$

Applying these weights to the original pay-off matrix R confirms the result. ■

Example 3.4 shows how Arrow securities simplify the construction of portfolios which replicate the pay-offs of ordinary securities. In general, whenever there are exactly S linearly independent ordinary securities, $K = S$, to achieve a pay-off vector $r = (r_1, \ldots, r_S)$, one forms the portfolio

$$
R^{-1} \cdot r = \begin{bmatrix} \sum\limits_{k=1}^{S} \tilde{a}_{1k} \cdot r_k \\ \vdots \\ \sum\limits_{k=1}^{S} \tilde{a}_{Sk} \cdot r_k \end{bmatrix},
$$

where $\tilde{a}_{sk}$ is the skth element of the inverse matrix R^{-1}. Notice that a column of the matrix R^{-1}, $(\tilde{a}_{1k}, \ldots, \tilde{a}_{Sk})$, is the portfolio $a(k)$ that replicates the kth Arrow security. When applied to the matrix of $K = S$ ordinary security pay-offs, these weights yield the pay-off vector:

$$
R \cdot (R^{-1} \cdot r) = (R \cdot R^{-1}) \cdot r = \hat{R} \cdot r = r.
$$

This section has demonstrated the equivalence of a financial system based on a set of S linearly independent ordinary securities and a financial system based on a complete set of Arrow securities. The following section considers the case where there are fewer ordinary securities than states $K < S$. In Chapter 4, we study the case of redundant securities $K > S$. The latter case provides the background for many asset pricing results in modern finance.

3.6 Incomplete Markets

The previous sections have shown that, when there exists a set of $K = S$ Arrow securities or $K = S$ ordinary securities with linearly independent return vectors, financial markets are *complete*, in the sense that trades between any two date–state pairs at appropriate rates of exchange are possible. With complete financial markets, competitive equilibria are Pareto optimal. In this section, we consider the consequences of *incompleteness* of financial markets, i.e. where $K < S$.

The analysis of this case is complicated by the fact that diagrammatic analysis is nearly impossible because the smallest economy in which one can discuss incompleteness of markets in a meaningful way comprises two states in addition to the asset trading period 0. Thus, even if one considers a single consumption good in each state only, a consumer's choice will be amongst three variables. A general analysis of incomplete market systems therefore requires rather abstract methods. The exposition in this section draws heavily on an example to illustrate the two most important aspects of incomplete market systems.

If financial markets are incomplete, then:

(i) trade between some date–states is not possible, there are 'missing' markets, and Pareto optimality of an equilibrium fails to hold; and

(ii) market equilibria are indeterminate, in the sense that the equilibrium allocation depends on prices which can be chosen arbitrarily.

Example 3.5. Consider an economy with two states and one consumption good, i.e. $S = \{1,2\}$ and $L = \{1\}$. Suppose that there is just one asset in this economy which pays (r_1, r_2) in the two states, respectively. Consumers are endowed with $(\omega_0^i, \omega_1^i, \omega_2^i)$ of the consumption good in period 0 and states 1 and 2, respectively, and their preferences are represented by a utility function $V^i(x_0^i, x_1^i, x_2^i)$.

Denote by a^i the quantity of the asset bought or sold by consumer i and let q be the unit price of the asset. The consumer's choice problem then becomes:

Choose $(x_0^i, x_1^i, x_2^i, a^i)$ to maximize

$$V^i(x_0^i, x_1^i, x_2^i)$$

subject to:
$$p_0 \cdot x_0^i + q \cdot a^i = p_0 \cdot \omega_0^i,$$
$$p_1 \cdot x_1^i = p_1 \cdot \omega_1^i + r_1 \cdot a^i,$$
$$p_2 \cdot x_2^i = p_2 \cdot \omega_2^i + r_2 \cdot a^i,$$
$$x_0^i \geq 0, \, x_1^i \geq 0, \, x_2^i \geq 0.$$

In writing the budget constraints as equalities it is been assumed that the consumer has monotonic preferences in the single consumption good in each period. Notice that markets are incomplete because there is one asset but two states.

Solving the first budget constraint for a^i, and substituting the result into the second and third budget constraints (dropping the superscript i for convenience), leads to the following description of all possible choices of state contingent consumption:

$$p_1 \cdot x_1 + \left(\frac{r_1}{q}\right) \cdot p_0 \cdot x_0 = p_1 \cdot \omega_1 + \left(\frac{r_1}{q}\right) \cdot p_0 \cdot \omega_0$$

$$p_2 \cdot x_2 + \left(\frac{r_2}{q}\right) \cdot p_0 \cdot x_0 = p_2 \cdot \omega_2 + \left(\frac{r_2}{q}\right) \cdot p_0 \cdot \omega_0$$

$$x_0 \geq 0, x_1 \geq 0, x_2 \geq 0.$$

We can express the relative price of consumption in state s in terms of period 0 consumption as $P_s = (p_s/p_0) \cdot (q/r_s)$. Now the set of feasible consumption bundles (x_0, x_1, x_2) can be written more compactly as:

$$P_1 \cdot x_1 + x_0 = P_1 \cdot \omega_1 + \omega_0,$$

$$P_2 \cdot x_2 + x_0 = P_2 \cdot \omega_2 + \omega_0,$$

$$x_0 \geq 0, x_1 \geq 0, x_2 \geq 0.$$

Unlike the case of complete markets, it is not possible to collapse multiple budget constraints into a single budget constraint by substitution. The set of feasible consumption allocations is therefore more heavily constrained in the case of incomplete markets than in the case of complete markets. In particular, it is not possible to exchange state 1 claims for state 2 claims directly; the market is 'missing'. State 1 claims and state 2 claims can be exchanged for period 0 claims separately, but not directly for each other, since the market does not exist.

The upper panel of Figure 3.8 depicts the two budget constraints as separate planes in the non-negative orthant of (x_0, x_1, x_2) space. Only allocations which lie in the intersection of these two planes, illustrated separately in the lower panel, are feasible.

To see how the incompleteness of markets constrains the consumer's choice set, consider the feasible set for the same example when asset markets are complete. For this purpose, let us assume that there are two assets with return vectors (r_{11}, r_{21}) and (r_{12}, r_{22}), respectively. The following budget constraints determine the consumer's feasible consumption allocation in this case:

$$p_0 \cdot x_0 + q_1 \cdot a_1 + q_2 \cdot a_2 = p_0 \cdot \omega_0,$$

$$p_1 \cdot x_1 = p_1 \cdot \omega_1 + r_{11} \cdot a_1 + r_{12} \cdot a_2,$$

$$p_2 \cdot x_2 = p_2 \cdot \omega_2 + r_{21} \cdot a_1 + r_{22} \cdot a_2,$$

$$x_0 \geq 0, x_1 \geq 0, x_2 \geq 0.$$

Using any two of these three equations to solve for a_1 and a_2, one can reduce the system to a single budget constraint as follows:

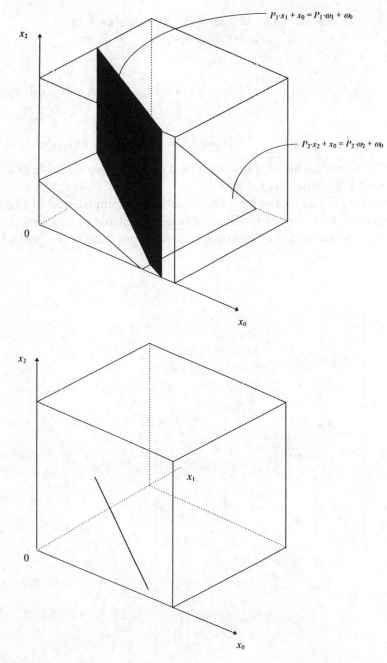

$P_1 \cdot x_1 + x_0 = P_1 \cdot \omega_1 + \omega_0$

$P_2 \cdot x_2 + x_0 = P_2 \cdot \omega_2 + \omega_0$

Fig. 3.8

$$Q_1 \cdot x_1 + Q_2 \cdot x_2 + x_0 = Q_1 \cdot \omega_1 + Q_2 \cdot \omega_2 + \omega_0$$
$$x_0 \geq 0, x_1 \geq 0, x_2 \geq 0,$$

where

$$Q_1 \equiv \left\{ \left[r_{21}/q_1 - r_{22}/q_2 \right] \cdot p_1 \right\} / \left\{ \left[(r_{21}/q_1) \cdot (r_{12}/q_2) - (r_{11}/q_1) \cdot (r_{22}/q_2) \right] \cdot p_0 \right\}$$

and

$$Q_2 \equiv \left\{ \left[r_{12}/q_2 - r_{11}/q_1 \right] \cdot p_2 \right\} / \left\{ \left[(r_{21}/q_1) \cdot (r_{12}/q_2) - (r_{11}/q_1) \cdot (r_{22}/q_2) \right] \cdot p_0 \right\}.$$

Figure 3.9 shows the set of state-contingent commodities available to a consumer under this budget constraint.

Comparing Figures 3.8 and 3.9 illustrates how incompleteness of financial markets reduces the set of feasible exchanges available to consumers. In a world of complete markets, consumers can exchange claims contingent on any

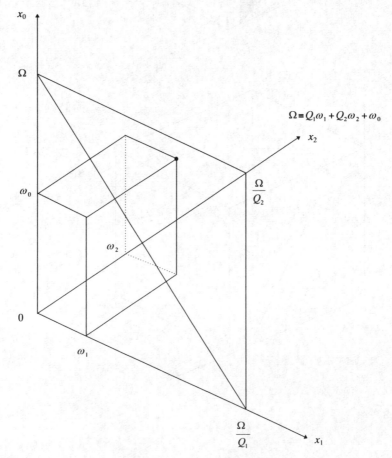

Fig. 3.9

one state for those contingent on any other at a fixed market-determined rate. There are no 'missing' markets.

To see that a competitive equilibrium with incomplete markets is not Pareto optimal, note that, for any two consumers i, j, the following two relationships hold in equilibrium:

$$MRS_{0,1}^i = P_1^* = MRS_{0,1}^j \text{ and } MRS_{0,2}^i = P_2^* = MRS_{0,2}^j,$$

where $MRS_{0,s}^i$ denotes the marginal rate of substitution for consumer i between consumption in state s and consumption in period 0. Since the marginal rates of substitution between states 1 and 2 are not equalized in this equilibrium, there is scope for potential Pareto-welfare improvement.

By contrast, an economy with complete markets will exhibit the following relationship in competitive equilibrium for all consumers i, j:

$$MRS_{0,1}^i = Q_1^* = MRS_{0,1}^j \text{ and } MRS_{0,2}^i = Q_2^* = MRS_{0,2}^j \text{ and}$$
$$MRS_{1,2}^i = Q_1^*/Q_2^* = MRS_{1,2}^j.$$

With relative prices and marginal rates of substitution equalized in all markets for all consumers, there is no room for further welfare improvement and a Pareto optimum is achieved. ∎

The fact that incompleteness of markets rules out certain types of exchanges plays havoc with the determination of competitive equilibrium. In particular, there is insufficient information to pin down a unique set of relative prices. An equilibrium allocation can generally be found but will depend on the choice of numeraire. Hence, the equilibrium allocation will not be determined uniquely.

In general, there are L goods markets in each of the S states and in period 0. Hence there are $(S + 1) \cdot L$ commodity markets and K asset markets that must clear in a general equilibrium. There are accordingly $(S + 1) \cdot L$ commodity prices, $(p_{01}, \ldots, p_{0L}, \ldots, p_{S1}, \ldots, p_{SL})$, and K asset prices, $(q_1, \ldots, q_K)$, which must be determined in equilibrium. However, given that there are $(S + 1)$ budget constraints faced by each consumer, there are only $\{[(S + 1) \cdot L + K] - (S + 1)\}$ independent market-clearing conditions to determine $[(S + 1) \cdot L + K]$ prices. This leaves $(S + 1)$ prices indeterminate.

Note that even in a pure exchange equilibrium without uncertainty, where consumers face a single budget constraint, there are only $L - 1$ independent market-clearing conditions to determine L commodity prices. One can however normalize any one price to any number without affecting the equilibrium trades. This raises the question of how many prices can be normalized in the incomplete market economy without affecting the equilibrium allocation of goods.

Example 3.5 (*continued*). Take the case of incomplete markets, and suppose there is an equilibrium price system $(p_0^*, p_1^*, p_2^*, q^*)$ and, for each consumer i, a corresponding allocation $(x_0^{*i}, x_1^{*i}, x_2^{*i}, a^{*i})$.

Let $P_1^* = (p_1^*/p_0^*) \cdot (q^*/r_1)$ and $P_2^* = (p_2^*/p_0^*) \cdot (q^*/r_2)$ be the relative price ratios which determine consumers' budget sets in (x_0, x_1, x_2) space. As long as these ratios remain unchanged, each consumer demands the same real allocation $(x_0^{*i}, x_1^{*i}, x_2^{*i})$ in equilibrium. Hence, any system of nominal prices which leaves P_1^* and P_2^* unchanged is also an equilibrium price system.

For given (r_1, r_2), one can choose arbitrary prices (p_0, q) and find an alternative equilibrium price system (p_0, p_1, p_2, q) without changing P_1^* and P_2^*. Given equilibrium values of P_1^* and P_2^*, the system

$$[p_0, (P_1^* \cdot p_0 \cdot r_1/q), (P_2^* \cdot p_0 \cdot r_2/q), q]$$

is an equilibrium price system for any (p_0, q). Thus two of the four prices can be normalized without affecting the equilibrium consumption allocation. Any further normalization will affect the consumer's budget planes, however.

To see that further normalization is required, note that there are *three* budget constraints and *four* market-clearing conditions. This leaves only one independent market-clearing condition to determine the equilibrium values of the two remaining prices. One can choose either p_1 or p_2 arbitrarily, and solve for equilibrium by choosing the other price appropriately. But different choices of p_1 (or p_2) lead to different equilibrium consumption allocations. ∎

In general, one can normalize the prices of assets $(q_1, \ldots, q_K)$ and the price of one commodity, for example, commodity 1 in period 0, p_{01}, without changing the equilibrium allocation. This leaves $[(S+1) \cdot L - 1]$ prices to be determined by $\{[(S+1) \cdot L + K] - (S+1)\}$ independent market-clearing conditions.

The number $n \equiv [(S+1) \cdot L - 1] - \{[(S+1) \cdot L + K] - (S+1)\} = (S-K)$ is called the *degree of indeterminacy* of the incomplete markets system. It indicates the number of prices which cannot be determined by the equilibrium conditions and which must be chosen arbitrarily, thereby affecting the equilibrium allocation. In Example 3.5, $S = 2$ and $K = 1$ and hence $n = 1$; either p_1 or p_2 must be chosen arbitrarily, and the equilibrium allocation influenced accordingly.

If financial markets are complete, S equals K, and the degree of indeterminancy, n, is zero. In this case, there are as many independent market-clearing conditions as there are relative price ratios determining the slopes of consumers' budget planes.

Example 3.5 (*continued*). Take the case of complete markets and suppose there is an equilibrium price system $(p_0^*, p_1^*, p_2^*, q_1^*, q_2^*)$ and a corresponding allocation $(x_0^{*i}, x_1^{*i}, x_2^{*i}, a_1^{*i}, a_2^{*i})$ for each consumer i.

As long as the relative price ratios Q_1^* and Q_2^* defined by these prices remain unchanged, consumers will find their allocation $(x_0^{*i}, x_1^{*i}, x_2^{*i})$ optimal. Hence, any price system that maintains Q_1^* and Q_2^* is an equilibrium price system for an appropriately chosen asset allocation (a_1^{*i}, a_2^{*i}).

A brief inspection of the defining equations for Q_1^* and Q_2^* reveals that one can choose the asset prices q_1 and q_2 and one of the goods prices, say p_0, arbitrarily and still find prices p_1 and p_2 that leave Q_1^* and Q_2^* unchanged. No further normalization is necessary. Since there are five markets in this case, and three budget constraints, two independent market-clearing conditions remain to determine the two equilibrium price ratios Q_1^* and Q_2^*, and there is no indeterminacy. ∎

The reason why incompleteness of financial markets leads to some arbitrariness of the equilibrium exchange ratios is the assumption that financial securities pay off in purchasing power rather than in a numeraire good. Thus securities do not specify the good in terms of which settlement of promised transfers must take place.

Choosing a numeraire commodity in each state if assets pay off in purchasing power is equivalent to determining the good in which settlement of transfers must occur. To see this, assume for example that securities pay off in a particular good in each state, say commodity 1. Budget constraints in the states $s = 1, \ldots, S$, then have the following form:

$$p_s \cdot x_s^i \leq p_s \cdot \omega_s^i + p_{s1} \cdot (r_s \cdot a^i). \tag{3.1}$$

On the other hand, if securities pay off in purchasing power, as we have assumed throughout this chapter, and one normalizes the price of commodity 1 in each state to 1, then the budget constraint in state s would take the following form:

$$x_{s1}^i + \sum_{\ell=2}^{L} p_{s\ell} \cdot x_{s\ell}^i \leq \omega_{s1} + \sum_{\ell=2}^{L} p_{s\ell} \cdot \omega_{s\ell}^i + r_s \cdot a^i. \tag{3.2}$$

Clearly, the consumption possibilities in each state s are identical whether assets pay off in commodity 1 (budget constraint (3.1)) or whether they pay off in purchasing power and with commodity 1 as numeraire (budget constraint (3.2)). To convince yourself of this fact, just draw a diagram of the two budget constraints for the case of $L = 2$.

Choosing a numeraire in each state makes the equilibrium allocation determinate. Such a choice fixes one price in each state plus one price in period 0 and, therefore, reduces the number of prices to be determined in equilibrium to $(S + 1) \cdot L + K - (S + 1)$ which is equal to the number of independent market equilibrium conditions. Thus, if assets pay off in a numeraire commodity rather than in purchasing power, or equivalently if a numeraire is chosen in each state, then all relative prices will be determined in equilibrium, with the consequence of a determinate equilibrium allocation, even if markets are incomplete. The importance of the choice of asset pay-offs for the determinacy of equilibrium is discussed extensively in the literature under the heading of 'nominal' versus 'real' assets (Magill and Shafer (1991), 1565–73).

By choosing a numeraire in each state, prices and allocations are determinate in equilibrium whether markets are complete or incomplete. It should be clear, however, that specifying the commodity in which assets have to pay off or choosing a numeraire in each state $s = 1, \ldots, S$, is not without consequence for the equilibrium allocation. If markets are incomplete, choosing commodity 2 rather than 1 as the good in which assets pay off leads to different consumption possibilities for consumers in equilibrium. This would not be true if markets were complete.

The choice of numeraire matters if markets are incomplete but is irrelevant if markets are complete. This is the most important message to emerge from the analysis. Thus specifying that a security should pay off in US dollars rather than Australian dollars will affect the insurance possibilities provided by the financial market system if markets are incomplete but would have no effect if markets were complete.

Notes on the Literature

Classic statements of the theory of contingent claims may be found in Debreu (1959, ch. 7) and Hirshleifer (1970, ch. 9). The original paper in which the notion of Arrow securities was proposed is Arrow (1964), an English translation of an article first published in French. A comprehensive though highly technical discussion of incomplete markets is found in Magill and Shafer (1991).

Exercises

1. *Consider an economy with one commodity in each state and two consumers,* $i = 1,2$, *with preferences satisfying the expected utility hypothesis. Consumer 1 is risk-neutral and consumer 2 is risk-averse.*

There are two possible states in regard to the consumers' endowments: either consumer 1 gets an endowment $\omega^1 = 6$ *and consumer 2 obtains* $\omega^2 = 4$, *or consumer 1 gets an endowment* $\omega^1 = 3$ *and consumer 2 obtains* $\omega^2 = 2$. *Both* consumers agree that the probability of the state with an aggregate endowment of 10 is 0.25.

(a) Draw an Edgeworth-box diagram of this economy. Is there aggregate uncertainty? Would consumers want to insure each other?

(b) Explain what contingent contracts are and derive the equilibrium price ratio of these contingent contracts in this economy.

(c) Will there be complete insurance in an equilibrium of the contingent contract economy? Explain under what conditions complete insurance results in a contingent contract economy.

(d) Give an example of an asset market system that would allow consumers to obtain the same trading opportunities as they have with contingent markets.

(e) Discuss the importance of information about the states in an economy for the feasibility and Pareto optimality of trade.

2. *For an economy with* $I = 2, L = 1, S = 2$ *and no aggregate uncertainty, show the following propositions. Support your formal argument with a diagram.*

(a) If both agents have preferences that satisfy the expected utility hypothesis and if the players hold identical beliefs about the probability of the states, then the equilibrium prices will be proportional to the probabilities of the two states.

(b) If agents have utility functions of the type

$$u^i(x_1, x_2) = \min\{x_1, x_2\},$$

where x_s, $s = 1,2$, denotes the state-contingent consumption, then they will insure each other completely, irrespective of their beliefs about the probabilities of the states.

(c) If the players have von Neumann–Morgenstern utility functions but player i believes that state 1 occurs with probability π_i with $\pi_1 > \pi_2$, then the equilibrium price ratio p_1/p_2 will satisfy

$$\pi_1/(1 - \pi_1) > p_1/p_2 > \pi_2/(1 - \pi_2).$$

3. *If agents can trade in contingent contracts, then, in equilibrium, the endowments in every state plus the contracted trades form a Pareto-optimal allocation. Show that this statement is true. Draw a diagram to illustrate the argument.*

4. *Suppose that a consumer with a utility function* $u(x_0, x_1, \ldots, x_S)$ *on state-contingent consumption vectors* x_s, $s = 0,1,\ldots,S$, *faces* $S + 1$ *budget constraints which require her expenditures on consumption goods in each state to be less or equal to her wealth available in state* $s = 0,1,\ldots,S$, $(W_0, W_1, \ldots, W_S)$.

115

(a) Derive the indirect utility function $v(W_0, W_1, \ldots, W_S)$ of this consumer which shows the maximum utility she can get given her endowments and her wealth transfers.

(b) Show that the indirect utility function is strictly increasing in the wealth variable W_s, $s = 0, 1, \ldots, S$, if the consumer's direct utility function $u(x_0, x_1, \ldots, x_S)$ is strictly increasing in at least one consumption good in each state.

5. *Consider an economy with $L = 1$, $S = 2$.*

(a) For $K = 2$, show that a consumer's budget constraints,

$$p_0 \cdot x_0 + q_1 \cdot a_1 + q_2 \cdot a_2 = p_0 \cdot \bar{x}_0,$$

$$p_1 \cdot x_1 = p_1 \cdot \bar{x}_1 + r_{11} \cdot a_1 + r_{12} \cdot a_2, \, p_2 \cdot x_2 = p_2 \cdot \bar{x}_2 + r_{21} \cdot a_1 + r_{22} \cdot a_2,$$

can be collapsed into one budget constraint,

$$Q_1 \cdot x_1 + Q_2 \cdot x_2 + x_0 = Q_1 \cdot \bar{x}_1 + Q_2 \cdot \bar{x}_2 + \bar{x}_0.$$

Determine Q_1 and Q_2.

(b) For $K = 1$, show that the consumer's budget constraints,

$$p_0 \cdot x_0 + q_1 \cdot a_1 = p_0 \cdot \bar{x}_0, \, p_1 \cdot x_1 = p_1 \cdot \bar{x}_1 + r_{11} \cdot a_1, \, p_2 \cdot x_2 = p_2 \cdot \bar{x}_2 + r_{21} \cdot a_1,$$

can be collapsed into two budget constraints,

$$P_1 \cdot x_1 + x_0 = P_1 \cdot \bar{x}_1 + \bar{x}_0, \, P_2 \cdot x_2 + x_0 = P_2 \cdot \bar{x}_2 + \bar{x}_0.$$

Determine P_1 and P_2.

ARBITRAGE AND OPTION PRICING

This chapter deals with two fundamental insights about the relationship among asset returns. First, an asset may have state-contingent pay-offs that can also be obtained by forming an appropriate portfolio of other assets. Indeed, if markets are complete, then the state-contingent returns of any additional asset can be synthesized by a portfolio of the existing assets. Since perfect substitutes must command the same price, the price of any asset must equal the price of a portfolio that replicates its returns.

The possibility of arbitrage imposes constraints on asset prices. In particular, as the first section of this chapter will show, the requirement that prices must not allow for arbitrage possibilities imposes constraints on state-contingent discount prices. If markets are complete, then these constraints will determine the state-contingent discount prices uniquely. In this case, state-contingent discount prices are the prices of the Arrow securities.

A second important insight concerns the fact that repeated trading of an asset creates a larger set of possible returns. If states are identified with the different possible returns an asset may have at a date, then a much larger number of returns, i.e. states, will emerge once the asset is traded repeatedly. To replicate the large number of pay-offs after several rounds of trading, one needs a portfolio with no more securities than the asset has pay-offs in the base period. A combination of this idea and the arbitrage principle has been applied extensively to price derivative securities, including, for example, stock options. Section 2 introduces this method.

4.1 Arbitrage

The last section of Chapter 3 studied the case of incomplete financial market systems. In this section we turn to the case where there is a greater number of assets than there are states, $K > S$. In this case, some assets are redundant in the sense that they provide the same pay-offs across states as one could obtain from combining other assets into an appropriate portfolio. One of the fundamental principles in economics is the so-called *law of one price* which states that two homogeneous goods must sell at the same price. Hence, one would expect an asset with state-contingent pay-offs equal to the state-contingent pay-offs of a portfolio to be traded at the same price as the portfolio. If this were not the case, a consumer could buy the cheaper of the portfolio or asset and sell the more expensive of the two in exchange. Since the asset has the same pay-off as the portfolio in every state, payments from this transaction would cancel each other in every state. The difference between the price of the asset and the price of the portfolio would therefore represent a riskless *arbitrage* gain. The *arbitrage principle* is the application of the law of one price to financial assets.

The possibility or impossibility of arbitrage depends on the relative prices of assets. Arrow securities play a special role. If there are more ordinary securities than states, one can find portfolios that replicate the Arrow securities and the prices of Arrow securities are determined uniquely. Hence one can use Arrow security prices to price any other asset in the economy. This feature of a financial market system is a mainstay of theoretical asset pricing in finance.

As the previous chapter has shown, if asset markets are complete, that is, if there are at least as many linearly independent ordinary securities as there are states, it does not matter in which form the assets actually pay off. For the exposition of the arbitrage principle in this section, one can therefore abstract from trade in the spot markets of each state and of period 0 by simplifying the consumer's problem. The idea is to split the consumer's choice problem into two parts:

1. Given goods price vectors in the various states $(p_0, p_1, \ldots, p_S)$, the optimal consumption plan is determined for arbitrary nominal wealth levels W_0, $W_1, \ldots, W_S$ by solving the following problem:

$$\text{Choose} \quad x^i \equiv (x_0^i, x_1^i, \ldots, x_S^i) \text{ to maximize } V^i(x^i)$$
$$\text{s.t.} \quad p_0 \cdot x_0^i + W_0 \leq p_0 \cdot \omega_0^i$$
$$p_s \cdot x_s^i \leq p_s \cdot \omega_s^i + W_s \quad \text{for all } s = 1, \ldots, S$$
$$x_0^i \geq 0, x_1^i \geq 0, \ldots, x_S^i \geq 0.$$

The solution to this problem yields an indirect utility function

$$\tilde{V}(W_0, W_1, \ldots, W_S; p_0, p_1, \ldots, p_S)$$

which depends on the wealth variables $(W_0, W_1, \ldots, W_S)$ and the goods prices $(p_0, p_1, \ldots, p_S)$. It is not difficult to show that this indirect utility function is strictly increasing in W_s, $s = 1, \ldots, S$, and strictly decreasing in W_0, if the original utility function $V(\cdot)$ is strictly increasing in at least one good in each state and at date 0. The wealth variables $(W_0, W_1, \ldots, W_S)$ can be interpreted as nominal wealth which is available for consumption in addition to the wealth from initial endowments if $W_s > 0$. Otherwise it represents a liability that must be settled out of the wealth from the initial endowment in the respective state.

2. In the second stage, the portfolio choice problem can be considered separately, by studying the following problem:

$$\text{Choose} \quad a^i \equiv (a^i_1, \ldots, a^i_k) \text{ to maximize}$$

$$\tilde{V}(W_0, W_1, \ldots, W_S; p_0, p_1, \ldots, p_S)$$

$$\text{s.t.} \qquad q \cdot a^i = W_0 \quad \text{and}$$

$$W_s = r_s \cdot a^i \qquad \text{for all } s = 1, \ldots, S.$$

The analysis can now be carried out easily in terms of the second-stage problem of pure portfolio choice. To facilitate diagrammatic exposition, we consider only two states $S = \{1,2\}$ and take W_0 as fixed.

Example 4.1. Assume that there are only two states and two ordinary securities with contingent pay-offs (in 'purchasing power' or 'wealth') as given in the following matrix:

$$R = \begin{bmatrix} r_{11} & r_{12} \\ r_{21} & r_{22} \end{bmatrix}.$$

Taking W_0 as given, a portfolio $a = (a_1, a_2)$ must satisfy the constraint

$$q_1 \cdot a_1 + q_2 \cdot a_2 = W_0,$$

and will yield the wealth levels

$$W_1 = r_{11} \cdot a_1 + r_{12} \cdot a_2,$$

$$W_2 = r_{21} \cdot a_1 + r_{22} \cdot a_2.$$

Figure 4.1 shows the state-contingent wealth combinations that can be achieved by choosing portfolios with value W_0 in period 0. Point A is the wealth combination achieved if all of W_0 is spent on asset 1. Point B is obtained by spending all of W_0 on asset 2. It is not difficult to check that points on the line between A and B correspond to portfolios with positive quantities of both assets, while points to the left of A imply short selling of asset 2 and points to the right of B have a_1 negative. The equation of the line through A and B is obtained by solving the last two equations for a_1 and a_2 and substituting these values into the first equation:

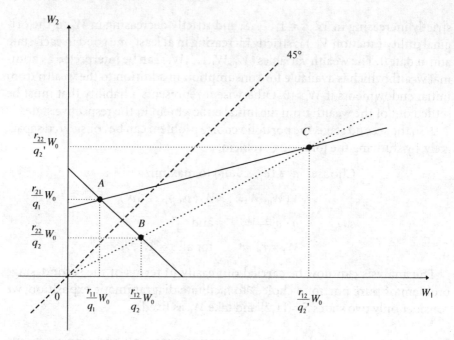

Fig. 4.1

$$W_2 = \left[\frac{r_{21}}{q_1} - \zeta\,\frac{r_{11}}{q_1}\right] \cdot W_0 + \zeta \cdot W_1,$$

where

$$\zeta = \left[\frac{r_{12}}{q_2} - \frac{r_{11}}{q_1}\right]^{-1} \cdot \left[\frac{r_{22}}{q_2} - \frac{r_{21}}{q_1}\right].$$

The line through A and B illustrates the case where $\zeta < 0$ since

$$\left[\frac{r_{12}}{q_2} - \frac{r_{11}}{q_1}\right] > 0 \text{ and } \left[\frac{r_{22}}{q_2} - \frac{r_{21}}{q_1}\right] < 0.$$

If $\zeta < 0$, an agent must trade off contingent consumption in state 1 against contingent consumption in state 2 at a fixed rate in order to remain within the feasible set of state-contingent wealth combinations. Note that complete insurance is possible since there is a portfolio, where the 45°-line intersects the line through A and B, which yields the same wealth in both states, $W_1 = W_2$.

If asset prices change, the position of the line of feasible state-contingent wealth combinations changes too. Assume, for example, that the price of asset 2 falls to q_2', while the price of asset 1 remains unchanged. If all of W_0 were invested in asset 2, the state-contingent wealth combination C in Figure 4.1

would be realized. Note that this wealth combination lies on a ray from the origin through point B. Thus, changes in the price of asset 2 will move the wealth combination obtained from holding all wealth in asset 2 up and down this ray. Since we keep the price of asset 1 constant, the wealth combination obtainable from investing exclusively in asset 1 will remain unchanged at A.

By forming portfolios with wealth W_0, state-contingent wealth combinations on the line through A and C can be obtained. Notice that the slope of this line is positive now, $\zeta > 0$, since asset 2 offers a higher pay-off per unit of wealth invested than asset 1 in both states, i.e.

$$\left[\frac{r_{12}}{q_2'} - \frac{r_{11}}{q_1}\right] > 0 \text{ and } \left[\frac{r_{22}}{q_2'} - \frac{r_{21}}{q_1}\right] > 0.$$

In these circumstances, an agent with preferences monotonically increasing in wealth would seek to take an unbounded position by short-selling asset 1 in order to increase without bound his or her position in asset 2. In other words, the agent would seek to obtain a wealth combination at a point as far to the 'north-east' along the feasible line as possible.

The process of selling asset 1 in order to purchase asset 2 and increase wealth in both states is an example of *arbitrage*. Since wealth is higher in all states as a result, i.e. a gain of some sort is guaranteed irrespective of the state, the arbitrage is described as 'riskless'. Note that whether or not an opportunity exists to make unbounded profit through arbitrage depends upon asset prices, i.e. the slope of the feasible line.

Clearly a set of asset markets in which riskless arbitrage is possible cannot achieve equilibrium so long as consumers remain unsated. Furthermore, if an equilibrium exists in an economy with unsated consumers, arbitrage cannot be possible. If a riskless arbitrage opportunity were to exist, all unsated consumers would demand unlimited wealth by all offering to sell the same assets in order to buy the other assets.

The absence of arbitrage (existence of equilibrium) requires $\zeta < 0$ which holds if and only if

$$\text{either} \quad \frac{r_{11}}{q_1} - \frac{r_{12}}{q_2} > 0 \quad \text{and} \quad \frac{r_{21}}{q_1} - \frac{r_{22}}{q_2} < 0,$$

$$\text{or} \quad \frac{r_{11}}{q_1} - \frac{r_{12}}{q_2} < 0 \quad \text{and} \quad \frac{r_{21}}{q_1} - \frac{r_{22}}{q_2} > 0. \qquad \blacksquare$$

In Example 4.1, asset prices that do not allow for arbitrage could be characterized by a downward-sloping line of feasible state-contingent wealth combinations. This geometric characterization of 'no arbitrage' prices fails, however, if there are more than two states. The following definition applies to economies with an arbitrary number of asset markets and states. Notice that this definition can be used whether or not asset markets are complete. Recall that

$$\begin{pmatrix} W_1 \\ \vdots \\ W_S \end{pmatrix} = R \cdot a.$$

DEFINITION 4.1.[1] A price vector for securities $q = (q_1, \ldots, q_S)$ does not permit arbitrage if, for all portfolios $a = (a_1, \ldots, a_S)$ with $R \cdot a > 0$, it is true that $q \cdot a > 0$.

This definition may be interpreted in the following way. For asset prices to be 'no arbitrage' prices, a portfolio which yields a non-negative return in each state (and a positive return in at least one state) must have a positive cost when priced using the 'no arbitrage' prices.

For the case where the number of assets with linearly independent return vectors equals the number of states, Definition 4.1 imposes a constraint on asset prices only. If there are more assets than states, the return vectors cannot be linearly independent. Definition 4.1 allows us to determine the asset prices of the redundant assets completely. Example 4.1 can be used to illustrate this point. In particular, it can be seen that the prices of the two Arrow securities are completely determined by the prices and returns of the two ordinary assets.

Example 4.1 (*continued*). First note that, for any R of full rank, there is a portfolio $a = (a_1, a_2)$ such that

$$r_{11} \cdot a_1 + r_{12} \cdot a_2 = 1 \text{ and } r_{21} \cdot a_1 + r_{22} \cdot a_2 = 0.$$

The portfolio a, therefore, creates the same return vector as the Arrow security 1. Assume for the sake of argument that, in addition to the two ordinary securities, there is an Arrow security 1 priced arbitrarily at $\tilde{q}_1$. Figure 4.2 shows the state-contingent wealth pair that a consumer could obtain by putting all her initial wealth into the Arrow security as point C. Notice that, at a price of $\tilde{q}_1$, the state-contingent wealth pair does not lie on the line of portfolios of ordinary securities through A and B. In terms of the ordinary assets, the portfolio (a_1, a_2) which creates the return pattern $(1,0)$ of Arrow security 1 costs

$$\hat{q}_1 = q_1 \cdot a_1 + q_2 \cdot a_2.$$

Thus, by investing W_0 in this portfolio a, the consumer can realize the state-contingent wealth pair $(W_0/\hat{q}_1, 0)$ which lies on the line through A and B at D.

Consider now the following portfolio of the two ordinary assets and the Arrow security 1,

---

[1] When dealing with vectors, like portfolio returns across states $R \cdot a = (r_1 \cdot a, \cdots, r_S \cdot a)$, $R \cdot a > 0$ means $r_s \cdot a \geq 0$ for all $s = 1, \ldots, S$ and $r_s \cdot a > 0$ for some s.

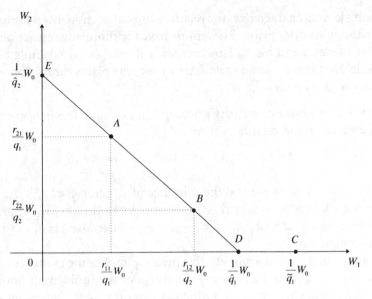

Fig. 4.2

$$(-a_1,-a_2,b) \quad \text{with} \quad b = (q_1 \cdot a_1 + q_2 \cdot a_2)/\tilde{q}_1,$$

which sells one unit of the portfolio (a_1,a_2) to spend the proceeds on the Arrow security. By construction, this portfolio costs nothing, yields no return in state 2, but returns $(q_1 \cdot a_1 + q_2 \cdot a_2)/\tilde{q}_1 - 1 > 0$ in state 1. The strict inequality follows because

$$\hat{q}_1 = q_1 \cdot a_1 + q_2 \cdot a_2 > \tilde{q}_1,$$

i.e. C lies to the right of D in Figure 4.2. The portfolio $(-a_1,-a_2,b)$ creates non-negative wealth in each state and positive wealth in state 1, but costs nothing (is *self-financing* in finance parlance). The asset price system $(q_1,q_2,\tilde{q}_1)$ does not satisfy Definition 4.1 and is therefore not arbitrage-free. In fact, it is easy to see that the only arbitrage-free asset price system is $(q_1,q_2,\hat{q}_1)$. Thus, arbitrage-free pricing determines the price of the Arrow security.

In general, any third asset (Arrow security or ordinary security) must be priced such that the state-contingent wealth pair obtained from investing W_0 in it lies on the feasible line through A and B. As a further example, the price of the second Arrow security $\hat{q}_2$ is determined in Figure 4.2 by the requirement that the wealth pair created by spending W_0 on the second Arrow security lies on the line through A and B at E. ∎

Example 4.1 demonstrates that any redundant security has a price determined by the non-arbitrage condition. In particular, in a complete market system the prices of the Arrow securities will be uniquely determined. The following lemma characterizes the relationship between Arrow security prices and ordinary security prices. The lemma holds without any restriction on the number of states and assets. However, only if markets are complete can we conclude that there is a *unique* set of Arrow security prices compatible with the ordinary security prices.

LEMMA 4.1. *A vector of security prices* $q \equiv (q_1,\ldots,q_K)$ *does not permit arbitrage if and only if there exists a vector*

$$\hat{q} \equiv (\hat{q}_1,\ldots,\hat{q}_S) >> 0 \text{ such that } q = \hat{q} \cdot R.$$

PROOF. (i) It is easy to see that the existence of a vector $\hat{q} \equiv (\hat{q}_1,\ldots,\hat{q}_S) >> 0$ with $q = \hat{q} \cdot R$ precludes arbitrage, since any portfolio $a \equiv (a_1,\ldots,a_K)$ with $R \cdot a > 0$ implies $q \cdot a = (\hat{q} \cdot R) \cdot a = \hat{q} \cdot (R \cdot a) > 0$ because $\hat{q}$ is strictly positive in each component.

(ii) To see that a set of arbitrage-free prices q implies the existence of a vector $\hat{q} \equiv (\hat{q}_1,\ldots,\hat{q}_S) >> 0$ with $q = \hat{q} \cdot R$, consider the problem of finding the cheapest portfolio $a \equiv (a_1,\ldots,a_K)$ which satisfies $R \cdot a \geq 0$. The cheapest portfolio is obtained as the solution to the following optimization problem:

Choose $a \equiv (a_1,\ldots,a_K)$ *to minimize* $q \cdot a$ *subject to* $R \cdot a \geq 0$.

This optimization problem will have a solution if and only if asset prices q do not permit arbitrage. Furthermore, it is a convex optimization problem because the objective function and all constraints are linear. Hence, a solution to the first-order conditions of the associated Kuhn–Tucker problem will be a solution of this optimization problem.

By the Kuhn–Tucker theorem, a solution of this optimization problem is characterized by a vector of non-negative Lagrange multipliers for the S constraints $R \cdot a \geq 0$, say $\hat{q} \equiv (\hat{q}_1,\ldots,\hat{q}_S)$, such that the Lagrangian

$$L(a,\hat{q}) \equiv -q \cdot a + \hat{q} \cdot R \cdot a = -\sum_{k=1}^{K} q_k \cdot a_k + \sum_{s=1}^{S} \hat{q}_s \cdot [\sum_{k=1}^{K} r_{sk} \cdot a_k]$$

is maximized with respect to a. This Lagrangian function is differentiable. Hence, at the optimum, the following first-order conditions must hold:

$$\frac{\partial L(a,\hat{q})}{\partial a_k} = -q_k + \sum_{s=1}^{S} \hat{q}_s \cdot r_{sk} = 0 \quad \text{for all } k = 1,\ldots,K.$$

The vector of non-negative Lagrange multipliers $\hat{q} \equiv (\hat{q}_1,\ldots,\hat{q}_S)$ satisfies $q_k = \sum_{s=1}^{S} \hat{q}_s \cdot r_{sk}$ for all $k = 1,\ldots,K$, or equivalently $q = \hat{q} \cdot R$. Hence, existence of a vector $\hat{q}$ follows from applying the Kuhn–Tucker theorem to the problem of finding the cheapest portfolio with non-negative pay-offs in each state.

It remains to show that arbitrage-free prices imply that $\hat{q}_s > 0$ for all $s = 1,\ldots,S$.

If markets are complete, i.e. $K \geq S$ and there are at least S assets with independent pay-off vectors, then, for any state s, one can find a portfolio $a(s)$ of the K ordinary securities which replicates the state-contingent pay-off vector of the Arrow security s, i.e.

$$R \cdot a(s) = (0, \ldots, 0, 1, 0, \ldots 0).$$
$$\uparrow$$
$$s\text{-th position}$$

At asset prices that are arbitrage-free, this portfolio $a(s)$ must be valued as strictly positive. Hence,

$$0 < q \cdot a(s) = \hat{q} \cdot R \cdot a(s) = \hat{q} \cdot (0, \ldots, 0, 1, 0, \ldots, 0) = \hat{q}_s.$$

Since this is true for all states s, $\hat{q} >> 0$ follows, for complete markets.

If markets are incomplete, rank $R = K < S$, then there are at least K of the Lagrangian multipliers $\hat{q} = (\hat{q}_1, \ldots, \hat{q}_S)$ strictly greater than zero. Without loss of generality, assume that the first K multipliers are positive. Let R_K be the submatrix of the first K rows and columns of R. Then

$$(\hat{q}_1, \ldots, \hat{q}_K) = R_K^{-1} \cdot \left(q_1 - \sum_{s=K+1}^{S} \hat{q}_s \cdot r_{s1}, \ldots, q_K - \sum_{s=K+1}^{S} \hat{q}_s \cdot r_{sK} \right) := f(\hat{q}_{K+1}, \ldots, \hat{q}_S)$$

is a linear and continuous function. Since $f(\hat{q}_{K+1}, \ldots, \hat{q}_S) >> 0$, there must be $(\hat{q}'_{K+1}, \ldots, \hat{q}'_S) >> 0$ such that $f(\hat{q}'_{K+1}, \ldots, \hat{q}'_S) >> 0$. Hence, there also exists $\hat{q} >> 0$, if markets are incomplete. ∎

The logic of this lemma is particularly easy to follow in the case of complete markets. As illustrated in Example 4.1, with complete markets, one can form portfolios that have the same pay-off as the S Arrow securities and, hence, must have the same price as these securities. To render arbitrage impossible, these portfolios must command positive prices. Moreover, as Lemma 4.1 shows, there is a *unique* vector of Arrow security prices $\hat{q}$. Though one may be able to choose different sets of S linearly independent assets from the K securities in order to construct the Arrow securities, each choice will lead to the same Arrow security prices $\hat{q}$.

The Arrow security prices, whose general existence is guaranteed for arbitrage-free asset prices, allow us to price vectors of state-contingent pay-offs and, therefore, any security or portfolio of securities. Thus, any asset with return vector $r \equiv (r_1, \ldots, r_S)$ must cost

$$\hat{q} \cdot r \equiv \sum_{s=1}^{S} \hat{q}_s \cdot r_s.$$

This fact enables us to price 'new' securities by examining the pattern of their pay-offs across states. The pricing formulae so derived are known as 'arbitrage pricing' results since they apply the principle of 'no arbitrage' in order to deduce the equilibrium prices of complex securities. The following example illustrates how one can apply this method.

Example 4.2. Let $S = \{1,2\}$ and let there be two assets with contingent pay-offs as follows:

$$R = \begin{bmatrix} r & r_{12} \\ r & r_{22} \end{bmatrix}.$$

Security 1 has a certain (i.e. non-stochastic) pay-off of r while security 2 has a state-dependent pay-off. Note that the set of two markets is complete. Suppose a third security is developed which is an option to buy one unit of security 2 at a strike price of k (a 'call' option). Since the option will be exercised only if $r_{s2} > k$, it has a pay-off vector given by:

$$r_{so} = \max \{0, (r_{s2} - k)\} \qquad s = 1,2.$$

We use the 'no arbitrage' principle to deduce that the price of the option, q_o, must obey the following relationship:

$$\sum_{s=1}^{2} \hat{q}_s \cdot r_{so} = q_o.$$

Let $R = \begin{bmatrix} 1 & 4 \\ 1 & 0 \end{bmatrix}$ and $k = 2$, then $r_{so} = \begin{bmatrix} 2 \\ 0 \end{bmatrix}$.

The portfolio $a = (0, 1/4)$ produces the pay-off vector of the Arrow security for state 1 while the portfolio $\tilde{a} = (1, -1/4)$ synthesizes Arrow security 2. Hence:

$$\hat{q}_1 = q_1 a_1 + q_2 a_2 = \frac{q_2}{4} \quad \text{and} \quad \hat{q}_2 = q_1 \tilde{a}_1 + q_2 \tilde{a}_2 = q_1 - \frac{q_2}{4} > 0,$$

since (q_1, q_2) is arbitrage free only if $4/q_2 > 1/q_1$ holds. Thus:

$$q_o = r_{1o} \cdot \hat{q}_1 + r_{2o} \cdot \hat{q}_2 = 2 \cdot \frac{q_2}{4} + 0 \cdot (q_1 - \frac{q_2}{4}) = \frac{q_2}{2}.$$

The price of the option is exactly one half of the price of security 2. ∎

We conclude this section with the observation that even for incomplete markets Lemma 4.1 shows the existence of some set of prices $\hat{q}$ that value the pay-offs of the states. These prices are, however, no longer unique. Still they are useful to determine whether a 'new security' can be priced by arbitrage or not. For example, suppose that there are two states and one asset with returns (r_1, r_2) that is traded at the price of q. By Lemma 4.1, there are strictly positive prices $(\hat{q}_1, \hat{q}_2)$ such that

$$q = \hat{q}_1 \cdot r_1 + q_2 \cdot r_2.$$

If a new asset with returns $(\lambda \cdot r_1, \lambda \cdot r_2)$ were introduced, its price would have to be

$$\hat{q} = \hat{q}_1 \cdot (\lambda \cdot r_1) + \hat{q}_2 \cdot (\lambda \cdot r_2) = \lambda \cdot [\hat{q}_1 \cdot r_1 + \hat{q}_2 \cdot r_2] = \lambda \cdot q,$$

if arbitrage is supposed to be impossible. Figure 4.3 illustrates this case.

Notice that, for incomplete markets $S = 2 > 1 = K$, there is an infinite number of pairs of positive prices $(\hat{q}_1, \hat{q}_2)$. Two pairs $(\hat{q}_1, \hat{q}_2)$ and $(\hat{q}_1', \hat{q}_2')$ are indicated in the figure. This shows that there are many different possibilities to put positive prices on state-contingent pay-offs, all of which will make arbitrage impossible.

4.2 Option-Pricing

The no-arbitrage principle forms the basis of the theory of asset-pricing used to price derivative securities, including options. An option is a contract that

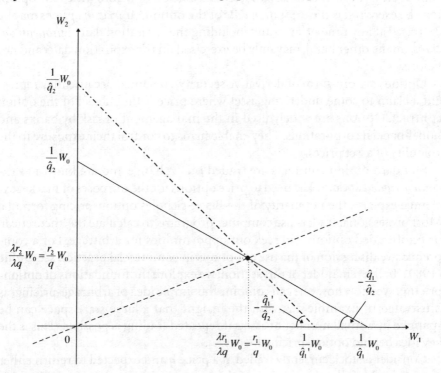

Fig. 4.3

allows one to buy or sell an object, usually a security, at a future date for a guaranteed price. Trade in such contracts allows individuals to insure against the risk of future price movements. In contrast to futures contracts, options need not be exercised.

With the increasing number of financial contracts and associated derivatives traded in modern stock markets, the demand for rules to gauge whether the current price of an asset over- or under-values the future pay-offs associated with the asset has grown considerably. An important formula for pricing derivative securities was derived by Black and Scholes (1973). They used an arbitrage argument to relate the option price to a small number of 'observable' variables like the variance of the asset on which the option was written, the riskless interest rate, and, of course, the characteristics of the option.

There are two types of option contract: calls and puts. A call option grants the holder the right to *buy* a specified quantity of an asset at a designated price on or before a nominated date. A put option grants the holder the right to *sell* a specified quantity of an asset at a designated price on or before a nominated date.

The price agreed between the writer (or seller) of the option and its holder (or buyer) is known as the *strike price*. The date on or before which the option may be exercised is the *expiration date* of the option. *American options* may be exercised at any time prior to and including the expiration date. *European options*, on the other hand, may only be exercised on the expiration date, and not before.

Options are one form of derivative security, so named because they represent a claim to some underlying asset where price is the subject of the option contract. Options are widely used in the management of risk by banks and non-financial corporations. They enable firms to control their exposure to the volatility of asset prices.

Standard option contracts are traded on exchange and are known as *exchange traded options*. The need to price options for the purposes of market exchange explains the popularity of the Black–Scholes option-pricing formula. Most professional traders use computer programs to calculate the 'theoretical' price of traded options and seek out opportunities for arbitrage. For a comprehensive discussion of the use of options in commercial practice, see Duffie (1989). In the remainder of this section, we explore the foundations of option-pricing. We show how one can combine the simple idea of arbitrage-pricing, as illustrated in Example 4.2, with the insight that a large state space can be spanned by a small number of assets if repeated trading is possible. This is the key idea behind option-pricing theory.

Consider a stock currently traded at a price q and expected to return either r_1 or r_2 in the following period. If there are no dividends paid during this period, r_s will equal the future price of this stock. Hence, r_s may be viewed as the state-contingent future price of the stock. Suppose there is, in addition, a riskless bond trading at a price of 1 and yielding a pay-off r, satisfying

$$r_1 > r \cdot q > r_2.$$

These two assets are sufficient to create a complete set of markets if one considers only two states as relevant, namely the state where the stock has a high pay-off r_1 and the state where it has a low pay-off r_2. Hence, any other asset where pay-offs depend only on these two states can be priced by arbitrage.

Consider a European call option that allows the holder to buy one unit of the stock in the next trading period at the guaranteed price K. Clearly, the option will only be exercised if the market price of the stock next period exceeds the strike price. Hence, the option will pay off

$$r_{so} = max\{r_s - K, 0\} \quad \text{for } s = 1,2.$$

Notice the special feature of derivative securities that their pay-offs depend only on the pay-off of the underlying asset.

By arbitrage-free pricing, this option must trade at the same price as a *hedging portfolio*, that is, a portfolio with the same state-contingent pay-offs as the option. One computes the hedging portfolio by solving the following two equations for the required units of stock a and of bonds b,

$$r_{1o} = r_1 \cdot a + r \cdot b \quad \text{and} \quad r_{2o} = r_2 \cdot a + r \cdot b.$$

One obtains

$$a = \frac{(r_{1o} - r_{2o})}{(r_1 - r_2)} \quad \text{and} \quad b = \frac{1}{r} \cdot \left[\frac{(r_{2o} \cdot r_1 - r_{1o} \cdot r_2)}{(r_1 - r_2)} \right]$$

as the hedging portfolio (a,b). The option price q_o must be equal to the price of this hedging portfolio and can be determined therefore as

$$q_o = q \cdot a + b = q \cdot \frac{(r_{1o} - r_{2o})}{(r_1 - r_2)} + \frac{1}{r} \cdot \left[\frac{(r_{2o} \cdot r_1 - r_{1o} \cdot r_2)}{(r_1 - r_2)} \right]$$

$$= \frac{1}{r} \cdot \left[\frac{r_{1o} \cdot (r \cdot q - r_2) + r_{2o} \cdot (r_1 - r \cdot q)}{(r_1 - r_2)} \right].$$

An alternative way to determine the option price is to derive the prices of the Arrow securities first and, then, use the Arrow securities to price the state-contingent pay-offs of the option. By choosing the respective replicating portfolios for the Arrow securities, one can easily determine their prices as

$$\hat{q}_1 = \frac{1}{r} \cdot \frac{(r \cdot q - r_2)}{(r_1 - r_2)} \quad \text{and} \quad \hat{q}_2 = \frac{1}{r} \cdot \frac{(r_1 - r \cdot q)}{(r_1 - r_2)}.$$

The option price can be obtained alternatively as

$$q_o = \hat{q}_1 \cdot r_{1o} + \hat{q}_2 \cdot r_{2o} = \frac{1}{r} \cdot \frac{(r \cdot q - r_2)}{(r_1 - r_2)} \cdot r_{1o} + \frac{1}{r} \cdot \frac{(r_1 - r \cdot q)}{(r_1 - r_2)} \cdot r_{2o}$$

$$= \frac{1}{r} \cdot \left[\frac{r_{1o} \cdot (r \cdot q - r_2) + r_{2o} \cdot (r_1 - r \cdot q)}{(r_1 - r_2)} \right].$$

Deriving the option price in this way is particularly helpful for the following analysis. Note that, for $r_1 > K > r_2$,

$$r_{2o} = 0 \text{ and } r_{1o} = r_1 - K.$$

Hence,

$$q_o = \frac{1}{r} \cdot \frac{(r \cdot q - r_2)}{(r_1 - r_2)} \cdot (r - K).$$

For the numerical values of Example 4.2, one easily confirms that $q_o = q/2$.

4.2.1 The binomial option-pricing formula

A fundamental insight, used extensively in the derivative pricing literature, is that repeated trading of the same asset with the same basic pay-offs increases the number of possible different pay-offs and states, provided one considers states that are distinguished only by the different pay-offs of the asset. If, in each trading period, an asset has essentially the same returns, then one can span the much larger state-contingent pay-off space of the repeatedly traded asset with the same number of assets that are necessary to span the state-contingent pay-offs in a single period. The important assumption is that all trading periods offer essentially the same returns.

Consider the case where the stock and the bond are traded in two consecutive periods and where the stock has a return that can take one of only two values after each trading period. To make sure that trading periods are identical, assume that no dividends are paid. The return to a unit of stock is just the future stock price. Furthermore, assume that the stock price after each trading period will be proportional to the original stock price with two proportionality factors u and d, $u > d$, that do not change over time. Thus, in any trading period, if the stock trades at price q, the traders know that it will trade in the next period at either $u \cdot q$ or $d \cdot q$. With just one period of asset trading, the return on the stock would be

$$r_1 = u \cdot q \quad \text{or} \quad r_2 = d \cdot q.$$

The assumption $r_1 > r \cdot q > r_2$ is in this case equivalent to the assumption $u > r > d$. Figure 4.4 illustrates the cases where the asset markets open twice and three times.

Figure 4.4 shows how the number of possible state-contingent pay-offs r_s increases as the number of trading periods grows. Because each market period has the same return structure, one needs only two assets, the stock and the bond, to replicate the state-contingent pay-offs of any derivative asset. Note that derivative assets have pay-offs related to the pay-offs of the underlying asset which are therefore conditional on the same state-space. We now show how one can derive Arrow security prices for these extended state spaces which will allow us to price derivative assets.

The Arrow securities of the state-space created by repeated trading have prices that are simple products of the Arrow security prices in a single trading period. If trade takes place only once, there are just two possible return states. We can use the pricing formula derived above to obtain

$$\hat{q}_1 = \frac{1}{r} \cdot \frac{(r-d)}{(u-d)} \quad \text{and} \quad \hat{q}_2 = \frac{1}{r} \cdot \frac{(u-r)}{(u-d)}$$

after substituting $r_1 = u \cdot q$ and $r_2 = d \cdot q$.

Consider now two trading periods and, with reference to the left tree in Figure 4.4, Arrow security 3 which pays off one unit in the state where the stock has the return r_3. The following trading strategy will create this return pattern:

(i) If the price of the stock rises after the first trading period, no investment is necessary in the second trading period because Arrow security 3 has a pay-off of 0 in this case.

(ii) If the price of the stock falls after the first trading period, then, in the second trading period, one has to buy a portfolio of stock and bonds yielding a return of 1 if the stock price increases and a return of 0 if the stock price falls.

The portfolio that must be bought following a fall of the stock price is the portfolio that synthesizes Arrow security 1 for a single trading period. Since prices in the second period must be arbitrage-free, such a portfolio must be priced at $\hat{q}_1$. Thus an investment of $\hat{q}_1$ is necessary in the second trading period after a fall in the stock price, while no investment is necessary following a price rise.

In the first trading period, one must buy a portfolio of stock and bonds yielding a return of 0 if the stock price rises and a return of $\hat{q}_1$ if the stock price falls. From the derivation of the Arrow security prices in the one-period-trading case, we know that a portfolio that pays 0 after a stock price increase and 1 after a stock price fall must be priced at $\hat{q}_2$. Hence, buying $\hat{q}_1$ units of this

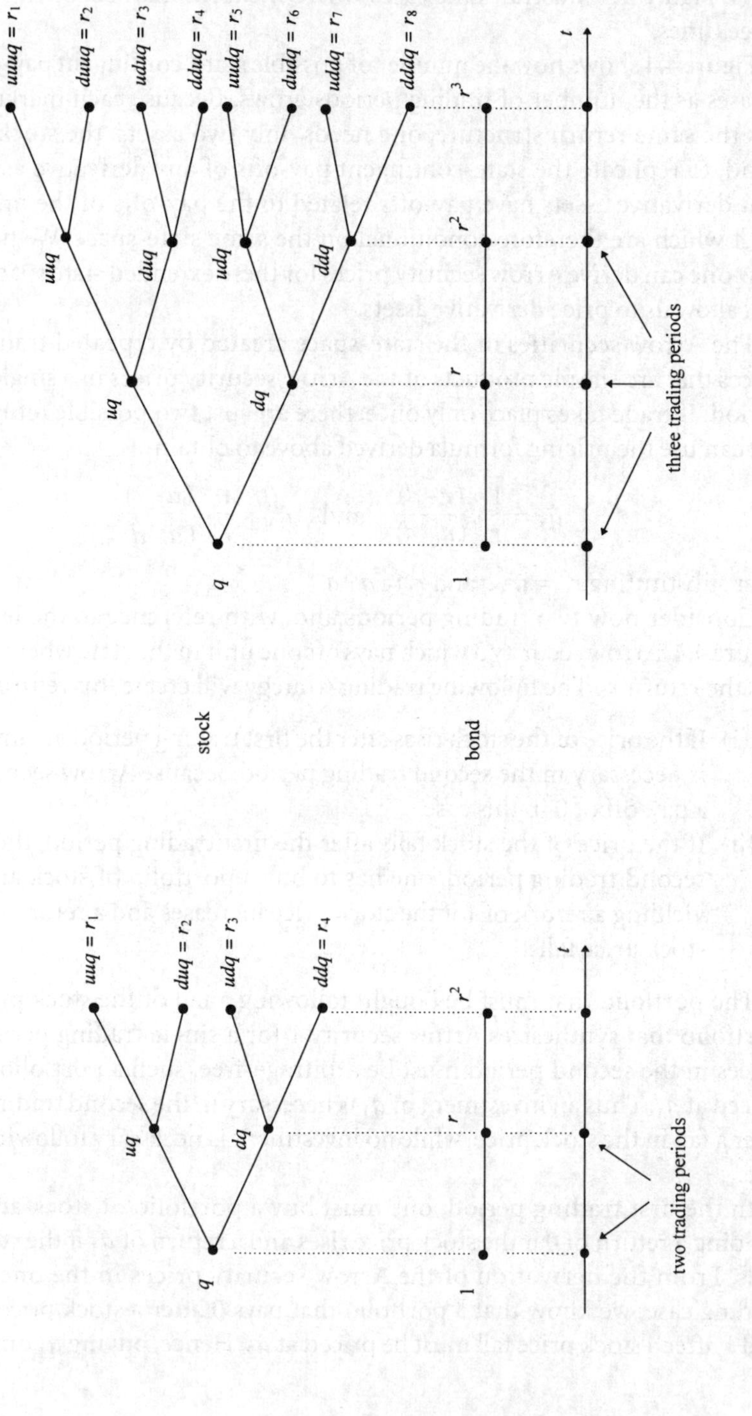
stock
bond
q
uq
dq
uuq = r1
duq = r2
udq = r3
ddq = r4
1
r
r2
t
two trading periods
uuq
duq
udq
ddq
uuuq = r1
duuq = r2
uduq = r3
dduq = r4
uudq = r5
dudq = r6
uddq = r7
dddq = r8
r3
three trading periods

Fig. 4.4

portfolio costs $\hat{q}_2 \cdot \hat{q}_1$ and will create a return of $\hat{q}_1$ if the stock price falls and nothing otherwise, as is required for the investment strategy yielding the return pattern of Arrow security 3. Denote by $\hat{q}_s(n)$ the price of Arrow security s in the case of n trading periods. Our argument shows that $\hat{q}_3(2) = \hat{q}_2 \cdot \hat{q}_1$ must hold for prices to be arbitrage-free. A similar argument shows that the price of Arrow security 5 must be $\hat{q}_5(3) = \hat{q}_2 \cdot \hat{q}_1 \cdot \hat{q}_1$. Figure 4.5 illustrates the pricing of the Arrow securities for these two cases.

Returning to Figure 4.4, it is clear that not all state-contingent returns of the stock are different. For two trading periods, $r_2 = r_3$ holds and, for three trading periods, $r_2 = r_3 = r_5$ and $r_4 = r_6 = r_7$ holds. This is a consequence of the assumption that trading in each period must have the same proportional

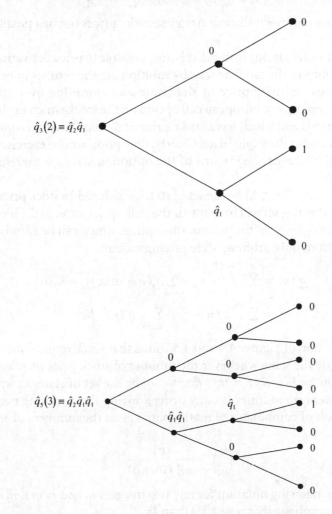

Fig. 4.5

returns. Thus, trading twice leads to three rather than four distinct pay-offs and trading three times induces four rather than eight distinct pay-offs. In general, with n trading periods, one obtains $n + 1$ distinct pay-offs out of 2^n possible pay-offs.

Similarly, from Figure 4.5, it easy to see that states with the same stock returns have identical Arrow security prices, i.e. $\hat{q}_2(2) = \hat{q}_3(2) = \hat{q}_2 \cdot \hat{q}_1$ for two trading periods and, for three trading periods,

$$\hat{q}_2(3) = \hat{q}_3(3) = \hat{q}_5(3) = \hat{q}_2 \cdot \hat{q}_1 \cdot \hat{q}_1$$

and

$$\hat{q}_4(3) = \hat{q}_6(3) = \hat{q}_7(3) = \hat{q}_2 \cdot \hat{q}_2 \cdot \hat{q}_1.$$

Thus, there are only $n + 1$ distinct Arrow security prices out of a possible total of 2^n.

With these observations in mind, it is now possible to price derivative securities like options in the familiar way, by multiplying the returns in each state with the Arrow security price of that state and summing over all states. Consider, for example, a European call option on the stock which expires after n trading periods and which has a strike price of K. Recall that this option can only be exercised at the expiry date. Clearly, the option will be exercised if and only if $r_s - K \geq 0$ holds. The return of the option in state s is therefore $r_{so} = max\{r_s - K, 0\}$.

Let $S(K) := \{s \in S|\ r_s \geq K\}$ be the set of states which yield a stock price higher than K. Note that this set will be empty if the strike price exceeds the highest return r_s. Denoting by $q_o(n)$ the price of this option, which can be exercised after n trading periods only, arbitrage-free pricing requires

$$q_o(n) = \sum_{s=1}^{S} \hat{q}_s(n) \cdot r_{so} = \sum_{s=1}^{S} \hat{q}_s(n) \cdot max\{r_s - K, 0\}$$

$$= \sum_{s \in S(K)} \hat{q}_s(n) \cdot r_s - \sum_{s \in S(K)} \hat{q}_s(n) \cdot K.$$

A brief inspection of Figures 4.4 and 4.5 shows that stock returns after n trading periods are the same whenever the number of stock price increases is the same. Let $S(m) := \{s \in S |\ r_s = u^m \cdot d^{(n-m)} \cdot q\}$ be the set of states in which the stock price went up m times (in any order) during the n trading periods. A standard result of combinatorial mathematics gives the numbers of elements in $S(m)$ as

$$\binom{n}{m} = \frac{n!}{m!\ (n-m)!}$$

Consider the following notation for any two integers m and n, $m \leq n$, and any positive real number p that is smaller than 1:

$$B(m \mid n, p) := \binom{n}{m} \cdot p^m \cdot (1 - p)^{n - m}.$$

If p were the probability of drawing a red ball out of an urn containing only red and blue balls, then $B(m \mid n, p)$ gives the probability that m red balls will be drawn in n independent trials. In probability theory $B(m \mid n, p)$ is called the *binomial distribution*. The expected value of this distribution, i.e. the expected number of red balls, is $\mu(n, p) = n \cdot p$ and the variance is $\sigma^2(n, p) = n \cdot p \cdot (1 - p)$.

With this notation, one can simplify the formula for the option price as follows:

$$q_o(n) = \sum_{s \in S(K)} \hat{q}_s(n) \cdot r_s - \sum_{s \in S(K)} \hat{q}_s(n) \cdot K$$

$$= \sum_{m \geq \delta(K/q)} \binom{n}{m} \cdot [(\hat{q}_1)^m \cdot (\hat{q}_2)^{n-m}] \cdot [u^m \cdot d^{n-m} \cdot q]$$

$$- K \cdot \sum_{m \geq \delta(K/q)} \binom{n}{m} \cdot [(\hat{q}_1)^m \cdot (\hat{q}_2)^{n-m}],$$

where $\delta(K/q) := min\{m \mid u^m \cdot d^{n-m} \geq (K/q)\} = [\ln u - \ln d]^{-1} \cdot [\ln (K/q) - n \cdot \ln d]$ denotes the smallest number of price increases that will make it worth while for a buyer to exercise the option. Recalling the Arrow security prices in the one-period trade environment,

$$\hat{q}_1 = \frac{1}{r} \cdot \frac{(r - d)}{(u - d)} \quad \text{and} \quad \hat{q}_2 = \frac{1}{r} \cdot \frac{(u - r)}{(u - d)},$$

it is easy to check that

$$\hat{q}_1 \cdot r + \hat{q}_2 \cdot r = 1 \quad \text{and} \quad \hat{q}_1 \cdot u + \hat{q}_2 \cdot d = 1$$

holds. One can, therefore, treat $p := \hat{q}_1 \cdot u$ and $p' := \hat{q}_1 \cdot r$ as probabilities and write the option-pricing formula as

$$q_o(n) = q \cdot [\sum_{m \geq \delta(K/q)} B(m \mid n, p)] - \frac{K}{r^n} \cdot [\sum_{m \geq \delta(K/q)} B(m \mid n, p')].$$

This is the so-called *binomial option-pricing formula* as derived by Cox, Ross, and Rubinstein (1979). If p and p' were probabilities, then the expressions in square brackets would give the probability of the event that the stock will experience more than $\delta(K/q)$ price increases. $\delta(K/q)$ is the smallest number of stock price increases for the option to be 'in the money' at the exercise date n. Denoting by

$$\beta(x \mid n, p) := \sum_{m \geq x} B(m \mid n, p)$$

the decumulative binomial distribution function, one may write the option-pricing formula as

$$q_o(n) = q \cdot \beta \left(\delta \left(\frac{K}{q} \right) \mid n, p \right) - \frac{K}{r^n} \cdot \beta \left(\delta \left(\frac{K}{q} \right) \mid n, p' \right).$$

The parameters p and p' are, however, not probabilities but Arrow security prices, normalized such that summing them over all states will equal 1. No assumption about the actual probabilities of price increases has been made. Note that this formula is true only for a European option and for return processes of the stock and the riskless asset with the following properties: the riskless asset pays off r after each trading period, and the stock pays off either $u \cdot q$ or $d \cdot q$ after each trading period.

It is a well-known property of the binomial distribution that, as the number of trials increases, it converges to the normal distribution. More precisely, as $n \to \infty$,

$$\beta(x \mid n, p) \to 1 - \Phi(x) = \Phi(x),$$

where $\Phi(x)$ denotes the standard normal distribution:

$$\Phi(x) := [\sqrt{2} \cdot \pi]^{-1} \cdot \int_{-\infty}^{x} e^{-\frac{1}{2} \cdot y^2} dy.$$

Using this fact allows one, with some further assumptions, to show that the binomial option pricing formula converges to the Black–Scholes option-pricing formula

$$q_o = q \cdot \Phi \left[\frac{\ln (q / K) + (\rho + \frac{1}{2} \cdot \sigma^2)}{\sigma} \right] - \frac{K}{e^{\rho}} \cdot \Phi \left[\frac{\ln (q / K) - (\rho + \frac{1}{2} \cdot \sigma^2)}{\sigma} \right].$$

Note that ρ is the interest rate on the riskless asset over the period from the option purchase to the exercise date. Similarly σ^2 denotes the variance of the stock over this period.[2]

Notes on the Literature

A survey article covering the whole field of security valuation is Duffie (1991). Dybvig and Ross (1989) discuss arbitrage in detail while the classic articles on option-pricing are Black and Scholes (1973) and Cox, Ross, and Rubinstein (1979). Duffie (1989) contains helpful applied material relating to the commercial use of options. Intuitive explanations of the Black–Scholes formula can be found in most finance textbooks (e.g. Copeland and Weston 1988).

----

[2] Most of the literature uses $\rho \cdot T$ as the interest rate to the exercise date and $\sigma^2 \cdot T$ for the variance of the stock. Substituting these values for ρ and σ^2, respectively, yields the formula in its usual form.

Exercises

1. *Consider an economy under certainty. A firm produces a cash flow X over one period and there is a single financial asset, a bond, that pays off R.*

(a) How much of the bond must a consumer buy to obtain the same cash flow as she would obtain from owning the firm?

(b) Show that the single Arrow security price of this economy is the discount factor.

2. *A 'forward contract' is a commitment between two agents to make a particular exchange at a particular future date. Suppose that g_t is the forward price at time t for delivery of one unit of a particular asset at a given time T. This means that the buyer of such a forward contract agrees at time t to receive one unit of the asset at time T from the seller of the contract in exchange for g_t dollars paid at time T* (quoted from Duffie (1989), p.129).

(a) Suppose you can buy the asset at date t in the spot market for the price of $100 per unit. A loan can be obtained at an interest rate of 10 per cent per period. Funds can be saved at an interest rate of 5 per cent. Determine the arbitrage-free price range for the forward contact.

(b) Suppose that there is a common borrowing and lending rate of 10 per cent. How many Arrow securities are there in this economy and what are the prices of the Arrow securities?

3. *A 'European call option' for the purchase of an asset in period 1 at a strike of K is traded for a price of q_0 in period 0. The asset can be bought at a price of s_0 in period 0 and will have a price of s_H or s_L, $s_H > K > s_L$, in period 1. Borrowing and lending is possible at an interest rate r.*

(a) Determine the *hedging portfolio* for the European call option.

(b) What price must the option have in period 0 to make arbitrage impossible? How could an agent make arbitrary riskless profits if the option price q_0 was less than the arbitrage-free price.

(c) Determine the price of the Arrow securities in this economy.

4. *A 'European call option' for the purchase of a stock in period 1 at a strike price of $75 is traded at a price of q_0 in period 0. This stock can be bought or sold at a price of $40 in period 0 and is expected to have a price of either $100 or $50 in period 1. Borrowing and lending is possible at an interest rate r.*

(a) Show that markets are complete by deriving the unique price vector of the Arrow securities.

(b) Draw a diagram showing the per-dollar returns of the stock, the riskless asset, and the Arrow securities.

(c) Determine the *hedging portfolio* for the call option and indicate it in the diagram derived in (b).

(d) Give a formal definition of an 'arbitrage-free price system' and derive the arbitrage-free price of the option.

(e) Show that for any other price of the option arbitrage would allow an investor to obtain an arbitrarily high riskless return.

5. *Reconsider the two-states two-assets model of example 4.1.*

(a) Determine the replicating portfolio for the second Arrow security.

(b) Assume that asset 1 is safe. Write down the no-arbitrage conditions for the asset prices.

(c) Using the Arrow security prices compute the price of an option on the risky asset 2.

(d) Derive the Arrow security prices for the case where the assets are traded repeatedly for two and three periods.

5
...

FIRMS AND FINANCIAL MARKETS

Models of contingent consumption, such as those discussed in Chapter 3, skirt around problems that arise with production in such a framework. In this chapter, we introduce the notion of a firm. In an economy with financial markets where shares of ownership in a firm can be traded, a firm's decision about its production plan is at one and the same time a decision about the pay-offs to an asset, viz. the firm's equity or stock.

The first part of this chapter investigates issues arising from the dual role of a firm's production decision, i.e. creating return streams for its owners (profits, dividends) in different states of the world and altering the set of available securities in the economy. With firms whose stock can be traded, we introduce assets with 'endogenous' returns.

There are two main issues which financial economists study in the context of the firm. The first is the goal or objective function of the firm. In modern economies, where production decisions in large firms are no longer made by the firm's owners directly but rather by managers appointed to run the firm, two important questions concern: (i) the objective that owners should give these managers, and (ii) whether the owners can agree on a single objective for the firm's management. Shareholder unanimity about the objective function of the firm is important because, without it, there can be no effective separation of ownership and control. In economies with a complete set of markets, delegating authority to a group of managers whose instructions are to maximize the firm's profit is consistent with shareholder expected utility maximization. This result is known as the Fisher Separation Theorem after Irving Fisher, a famous financial economist.[1] With incomplete financial markets, as we shall see, shareholders will give a common objective for the firm only under very restrictive assumptions.

The second major issue is the existence of an optimal financial structure for the firm. Modigliani and Miller (1958) shocked the community of financial economists at the

---

[1] Amongst numerous other works, Fisher wrote *The Theory of Interest* (1930) which laid the foundations of much of the modern theory of intertemporal choice.

time with their 'proof' of the irrelevance of the firm's financial structure, i.e. the mix of debt and equity claims a firm sells to finance its purchase of inputs. Much of the literature prior to the appearance of the Modigliani–Miller paper had been devoted to the various principles according to which one might determine the optimal mix of debt and equity for particular firms. To be told that none of the arguments was valid was shocking indeed! In this chapter, we present the original Modigliani–Miller result in a form which relates to the framework we have developed. In doing so, we again encounter the fundamental role played by the assumption of complete markets.

5.1 Firms and Stock Market Equilibrium

The firm is the basic production unit. It buys goods as inputs and produces other goods as outputs for sale, both in period 0 ('the present') and in period 1 ('the future'). Investments are input purchases in period 0 which lead to outputs in period 1. Production, like preferences or endowments, can be subject to uncertainty. Thus the description of states of the world now includes contingencies which are relevant to production, e.g. machine failures, labour shortages, technical improvements, etc.

A production plan for firm j specifies input–output vectors $y_s^j \in \mathbb{R}^L$ for each state $s \in S$, including 'the present' as 'state 0'. Each firm is characterized by a production set $Y^j \subset \mathbb{R}^{(S+1) \cdot L}$ which contains all state-dependent input–output vectors that are technologically feasible. To simplify notation, we introduce the convention that inputs are represented by negative numbers and outputs by positive numbers, e.g. the production plan of a firm that uses

- 5 units of commodity 1 in period 0,
- 3 units of commodity 3 in state 1, and
- 1 unit of commodity 3 in state 2

to produce

- 2 units of commodity 2 in state 1, and
- 1 unit of commodity 4 in state 2

is written as (omitting the superscript indicating the firm)

$$y := (y_0, y_1, y_2) = ((y_{01}, y_{02}, y_{03}, y_{04}), (y_{11}, y_{12}, y_{13}, y_{14}), (y_{21}, y_{22}, y_{23}, y_{24}))$$
$$= ((-5, 0, 0, 0), (0, 2, -3, 0), (0, 0, -1, 1)).$$

This convention allows us to write the net pay-out for each input–output vector given state-contingent prices simply as $p_s \cdot y_s$ for all states s in S including the present state/date 0. As in Chapter 3, price vectors may be expressed in terms of a predetermined numeraire, say commodity 1. Thus, in the previous example, for a given price vector

$$p := (p_0, p_1, p_2) = ((p_{01}, p_{02}, p_{03}, p_{04}), (p_{11}, p_{12}, p_{13}, p_{14}), (p_{21}, p_{22}, p_{23}, p_{24}))$$
$$= ((1,3,2,4), (1,5,7,3), (1,9,2,3)),$$

the following state-dependent pay-outs are associated with the production plan y:

$$p_0 \cdot y_0 = 1 \cdot (-5) = -5, \; p_1 \cdot y_1 = 2 \cdot 5 + 7 \cdot (-3) = -11,$$
$$p_2 \cdot y_2 = 3 \cdot 1 + 2 \cdot (-1) = 1.$$

For given state-contingent prices, the owner of a firm can be viewed as holding a set of securities with state-contingent returns

$$\{(p_0 \cdot y_0, p_1 \cdot y_1, \ldots, p_S \cdot y_S) \in \mathbb{R}^{S+1} \mid y := (y_0, y_1, \ldots, y_S) \in Y^j\}.$$

Choosing a particular production plan $\hat{y} \in Y^j$ introduces a security into the economy with state-contingent pay-offs

$$(p_0 \cdot \hat{y}_0, p_1 \cdot \hat{y}_1, \ldots, p_S \cdot \hat{y}_S).$$

Firms are assumed to be owned by consumers. Denote by σ_j^i the share of firm $j \in J$ held by consumer i. Shares are percentages of ownership, rather than nominal claims to a nominal amount. The shares of any firm held by consumers therefore sum to one, $\sum_{i \in I} \sigma_j^i = 1$. Clearly, some consumers might have no shareholding in firm j, $\sigma_j^i = 0$, or there may be a particular consumer i' who is the single owner (shareholder) of firm j, $\sigma_j^{i'} = 1$. The market price of firm j is denoted by e^j. Notice that the market price of a firm's share capital equals the value of the firm, i.e. for the price e^j one can buy the firm. Of course, buying half of the firm, $\sigma_j = 0.5$, costs $0.5 \cdot e^j$.

There are K financial asset markets, $k = 1, \ldots, K$. As in Chapter 3, assets are characterized by a return matrix.

$$R := \begin{pmatrix} r_1 \\ \vdots \\ r_s \\ \vdots \\ r_S \end{pmatrix} := \begin{pmatrix} r_{11} \cdots\cdots r_{1K} \\ \vdots \quad\quad \vdots \\ r_{s1} \cdots\cdots r_{sK} \\ \vdots \quad\quad \vdots \\ r_{S1} \cdots\cdots r_{SK} \end{pmatrix}$$

and can be bought and sold at prices $q = (q_1, \ldots, q_K)$ in period 0. Firms may finance their input purchases in period 0, $p_0 \cdot y_0^j$ by selling β_k^j units of asset k at price q_k, thus raising $q_k \cdot \beta_k^j$ units of the numeraire in period 0. In exchange, firm j has to repay $r_{sk} \cdot \beta_k^j$ units of the numeraire in every state $s \in S$. Notice that the quantities of assets sold by a firm are denoted by positive numbers $\beta_k^j > 0$, while purchases of assets are represented by negative numbers.[2] Firm j's financial structure is therefore given by the portfolio of its asset holdings $\beta^j :=$ $(\beta_1^j, \ldots, \beta_K^j)$ which might include debt but not equity. Equity is the right to participate in a residual surplus or deficit after all other claims on the firm have been met. A firm's production and financial plan is thus completely described by (y^j, β^j), a production vector and a portfolio financing it.

Any expenditures in period 0 that are not covered by the proceeds of the firm's asset sales, $p_0 \cdot y_0^j + q \cdot \beta^j$, must be financed by the owners of the firm. Similarly, a surplus in any state s, $p_s \cdot y_s - r_s \cdot \beta^j$, will be distributed to the existing shareholders. This cash flow from the firm's operations is denoted by $\delta^j :=$ $(\delta_0^j, \delta_1^j, \ldots, \delta_s^j, \ldots, \delta_S^j)$ with

$$\delta_0^j := p_0 \cdot y_0^j + q \cdot \beta^j \quad \text{and} \quad \delta_s^j := p_s \cdot y_s - r_s \cdot \beta^j \quad \text{for all} \quad s \in S.$$

As in Chapter 3, consumers are characterized by preferences represented by a utility function over state-contingent consumption bundles

$$V^i(x^i) := V^i(x_0^i, x_1^i, \ldots, x_S^i), \quad \text{with} \quad x_0^i, x_s^i \in \mathbb{R}_+^L \quad \text{for all} \quad s \in S,$$

by a state-contingent initial endowment

$$\omega^i := (\omega_0^i, \omega_1^i, \ldots, \omega_S^i), \quad \text{with} \quad \omega_0^i, \omega_s^i \in \mathbb{R}_+^L \quad \text{for all} \quad s \in S,$$

and initial shareholdings

$$\bar{\sigma}^i := (\bar{\sigma}_1^i, \ldots, \bar{\sigma}_j^i, \ldots, \bar{\sigma}_J^i).$$

These initial shareholdings represent the ownership structure of the economy before trading of shares begins. By trading shares in period 0, this ownership structure can be changed.

Finally, consumers can buy, $a_k^i > 0$, or sell, $a_k^i < 0$, assets on the same conditions as firms. A portfolio of the assets $a^i := (a_1^i, \ldots, a_K^i)$ and choice of shareholdings $\sigma^i := (\sigma_1^i, \ldots, \sigma_J^i)$ which gives a consumer a share of the firms' cash flows $(\delta^1, \ldots, \delta^j, \ldots, \delta^J)$ provide the consumer with opportunities to transfer purchasing power across time and states of the world. The following budget constraints for consumer i summarize the implications of asset and share transactions for final consumption:

$$p_0 \cdot x_0^i + q \cdot a^i + \sum_{j \in J} \sigma_j^i \cdot e^j \leq p_0 \cdot \omega_0^i + \sum_{j \in J} \bar{\sigma}_j^i \cdot (e^j + \delta_0^j). \tag{5.1}$$

$$p_s \cdot x_s^i \leq p_s \cdot \omega_s^i + \sum_{j \in J} \sigma_j^i \cdot \delta_s^j + r_s \cdot a^i \quad \text{for all } s \in S. \tag{5.2}$$

---

[2] This is opposite to the convention adopted for asset holdings by consumers.

To complete the description of this economy with firms and a stock market we need a definition of a 'stock-market equilibrium'. While our focus will rest on the appropriate objective function for the firm, at this state, so as to avoid pre-empting the result, we define a stock-market equilibrium assuming that the *production and financing decisions of firms* are given.

DEFINITION 5.1 (*stock-market equilibrium*). Consider an economy with consumers $(V^i, \omega^i, (\bar{\sigma}^j_i)_{j \in J})_{i \in I}$ and a set of financial assets R. Given a production-finance plan for each firm $(y^j, \beta^j)_{j \in J}$, a list of prices $(\hat{p}, \hat{q}, \hat{e})$ and an allocation $(\hat{x}^i, \hat{a}^i, \hat{\sigma}^i)_{i \in I}$ constitutes a *stock-market equilibrium* if

(1) *consumers choose optimal consumption and portfolio plans*, i.e. for all consumers $i \in I$

$$(\hat{x}^i, \hat{a}^i, \hat{\sigma}^i) \in argmax\{ V^i(x^i_0, x^i_1, \ldots, x^i_S) \mid$$

$$\hat{p}_0 \cdot x^i_0 + \hat{q} \cdot a^i + \sum_{j \in J} \sigma^i_j \cdot \hat{e}^j \le \hat{p}_0 \cdot \omega^i_0 + \sum_{j \in J} \bar{\sigma}^i_j \cdot (\hat{e}^j + \delta^j_0),$$

$$\hat{p}_s \cdot x^i_s \le \hat{p}_s \cdot \omega^i_s + \sum_{j \in J} \sigma^i_j \cdot \delta^j_s + r_s \cdot a^i \quad \text{for all } s \in S\},$$

and if

(2) *all markets clear*, i.e.

$$\sum_{i \in I} \hat{x}^i = \sum_{j \in J} y^j + \sum_{i \in I} \omega^i, \quad \sum_{i \in I} \hat{\sigma}^i_j = 1, \quad \sum_{j \in J} \beta^j = \sum_{i \in I} \hat{a}^i.$$

According to this definition of equilibrium, consumers maximize their utility by choosing a consumption plan financed by a portfolio of assets and share-holdings such that the spot markets for commodities, the asset markets, and the share markets clear for a given commodity price vector, a given asset price vector, and a given share price vector. The equilibrium prices and allocations depend, however, on the production and financial decisions of all firms.

In the following section, we investigate whether shareholders can agree on an objective function for the firm. In order to see how the owners of a firm evaluate their firm's activities, we wish to determine the effect of a small change in production and financing plans on a shareholder's utility. As in Chapter 4, we define the *indirect utility function* of a consumer for a given financial wealth pattern across states and dates.

Notice, however, that the wealth level of period 0 appears on the right-hand side of the budget constraint. Thus, in contrast to the indirect utility function in Section 4.1, the indirect utility function here will be increasing in wealth of period 0. In order to distinguish the indirect utility function of this chapter from the one of Chapter 4, we will denote it by v^i. Let W^i_s be the wealth of consumer i in state s. The indirect utility function $v^i(W^i_0, W^i_1, \ldots, W^i_S)$ associates the maximum utility that consumer i can achieve from purchases of commodities with a given financial wealth pattern $(W_0^i, W_1^i, \ldots, W_S^i)$ over states and dates. Formally,

$$v^i(W_0^i, W_1^i, \ldots, W_S^i) = \max\{V^i(x_0^i, x_1^i, \ldots, x_S^i) \mid p_s \cdot x_s^i \le$$
$$p_s \cdot \omega_s^i + W_s^i, s = 0, 1, \ldots S\}.$$

In this problem, the consumer is restricted to consume out of the wealth available in each date and state. No savings or insurance possibilities exist. This indirect utility function $v^i(W_0^i, W_1^i, \ldots, W_S^i)$ depends of course on the state-contingent commodity prices p_s as well. Since changes in the commodity prices are not considered in this context, they have been suppressed here. It is easy to check that the indirect utility function $v^i(W_0^i, W_1^i, \ldots, W_S^i)$ is strictly increasing in state-dependent wealth if the direct utility function $V^i(x^i)$ is strictly increasing in at least one commodity in each state, and differentiable if the direct utility function $V^i(x^i)$ is differentiable.

In the stock market economy presented above, wealth transfer between states and dates is possible by trading in financial assets and equities. The wealth in different states and dates is therefore linked by the following equations:

$$W_0^i = \sum_{j \in J} \bar{\sigma}_j^i \cdot (e^j + \delta_0^j) - \sum_{k \in K} q_k \cdot a_k^i - \sum_{j \in J} \sigma_j^i \cdot e^j, \quad \text{and} \tag{5.3}$$

$$W_s^i = \sum_{j \in J} \sigma_j^i \cdot \delta_s^j + \sum_{k \in K} r_{sk} \cdot a_k^i \qquad \text{for all } s \in S. \tag{5.4}$$

Maximizing $v^i(W_0^i, W_1^i, \ldots, W_S^i)$ subject to the constraints (5.3) and (5.4), by choosing a portfolio of financial assets a^i and shares σ^i, is equivalent to the original consumer problem. In this form, however, it is easier to see how the firms' production and financing decisions affect the welfare of a consumer.

A firm's production and financing decision (y^j, β^j) determines the dividend stream $(\delta_0^j, \delta_1^j, \ldots, \delta_S^j)$ directly. Changing the production and financing decision of firm j by some small amount $(\Delta y^j, \Delta \beta^j)$ induces a change in dividends equal to:

$$\Delta \delta_0^j (\Delta y^j, \Delta \beta^j) := p_0 \cdot \Delta y_0^j + q \cdot \Delta \beta^j \quad \text{and}$$
$$\Delta \delta_s^j (\Delta y^j, \Delta \beta^j) := p_s \cdot \Delta y_s - r_s \cdot \Delta \beta^j \qquad \text{for all } s \in S.$$

Neglecting the impact that a change of a firm's production and financing decision may have on equilibrium prices other than its own stock price, a consumer's evaluation of such a change will mainly depend on the presumed effect on this firm's own equity price $\Delta e^j(\Delta y^j, \Delta \beta^j)$. For small changes of the production and financing decision of firm j, evaluated at a stock-market equilibrium, the approximate impact on consumer i's welfare can be calculated as:

$$\Delta v^i \approx \frac{\partial v^i (\cdot)}{\partial W_0^i} \cdot \{\bar{\sigma}_j^i \cdot [\Delta e^j(\Delta y^j, \Delta \beta^j) + \Delta \delta_0^j(\Delta y^j, \Delta \beta^j)]$$

$$+ \, \bar{\sigma}_j^i \cdot [\sum_{s \in S} MRS_{s,0}^i \cdot \Delta \delta_s^j(\Delta y^j, \Delta \beta^j) - \Delta e^j(\Delta y^j, \Delta \beta^j)]\}, \qquad (5.5)$$

where $MRS_{s,0}^i \equiv (\partial v^i (\cdot) / \partial W_s^i) / (\partial v^i (\cdot) / \partial W_0^i)$ denotes the marginal rate of substitution of consumer i between a unit of wealth in state s and in date 0.

The first square bracket within the braces shows that the old shareholder who is affected by the changed cash flow in period 0, δ_0^j, gains or loses due to the induced change in equity value. The second square bracket gives the net gain to the consumer from holding a share of the firm in period 1, that is the value of the changes in the cash flows across states in period 1, evaluated with the marginal rate of substitution $MRS_{s,0}^i$, minus the induced change in equity value. This formulation stresses the importance of the stock price change $\Delta e^j(\Delta y^j, \Delta \beta^j)$ for a consumer's evaluation of a firm's activities. Equation (5.5), which shows the impact on a consumer's utility of a small change in firm j's production and financing decision, is used below to gauge the desirability of the firm's decision for its owners.

5.2 Separation of Ownership and Control

Standard microeconomic models of the firm simply assume that the firm aims to maximize profit. The relationship between the objective function of the firm and that of its owners, the shareholder-consumers, is not made explicit. The same is not true of financial economics, however, in which this issue is tackled directly.

A famous result in economics, known as the *Fisher Separation Theorem*, specifies conditions under which utility-maximizing shareholders agree on profit maximization as the appropriate objective function for the firm. Thus, notwithstanding the differing preferences and endowments of shareholders as consumers, each achieves maximum utility when the firm adopts its profit-maximizing production plan. When the Fisher Separation Theorem holds, it is possible for shareholders to delegate control of the firm to managers whose goal is to implement the profit-maximizing production plan on behalf of the shareholders. Fisher separation holds under conditions of certainty and, in appropriate circumstances, also under uncertainty.

Considering the case of certainty first, assume there is only one state, say state 1, in period 1. Consumers choose optimal consumption and portfolio plans to maximize utility $V^i(x^i)$ subject to only two budget constraints:

$$p_0 \cdot x_0^i + \sum_{k \in K} q_k \cdot a_k^i + \sum_{j \in J} \sigma_j^i \cdot e^j \leq p_0 \cdot \omega_0^i + \sum_{j \in J} \bar{\sigma}_j^i \cdot (e^j + \delta_0^j) \qquad \text{for period 0, and}$$

$$p_1 \cdot x_1^i \leq p_1 \cdot \omega_1^i + \sum_{j \in J} \sigma_j^i \cdot \delta_1^j + \sum_{k \in K} r_{1k} \cdot a_k^i \qquad \text{for the only state in period 1.}$$

Notice that consumers have K financial assets and J stocks available to transfer wealth between period 0 and the single state of period 1. Though dividends of a firm j, δ_1^j, depend on the production-finance decision of the firm, from the point of view of consumers, they are fixed like the returns on a financial asset k, r_{1k}. Hence, there are $K + J$ assets available in this economy. Since there is just one state in period 1, only one trading ratio, the terms of trade between wealth in period 0 and wealth in the single state of period 1, needs to be determined in equilibrium. Therefore, to be free of arbitrage, the prices of the financial assets, q_k, and of the stock, e^j, must be such that the rates of return on all assets equal this trading ratio.

Denote by $\bar{r}$ the terms of trade between wealth in period 0 and wealth in the single state of period 1. This rate will be determined in equilibrium. Then all financial assets, $k = 1, \ldots, K$, must have a price q_k such that $r_{1k}/q_k = \bar{r}$ holds and stock prices e^j, $j = 1, \ldots, J$, must satisfy $\delta_1^j/e^j = \bar{r}$. If, for any two assets k and ℓ, prices were such that $r_{1k}/q_k > r_{1\ell}/q_\ell$, then the consumers could sell asset ℓ short and buy asset k, earning a riskless profit of $(r_{1k}/q_k) - (r_{1\ell}/q_\ell)$ for every unit of this portfolio. Thus, because there can be no arbitrage in equilibrium,

$$r_{1k}/q_k = r_{1\ell}/q_\ell = \delta_1^j/e^j \equiv \bar{r}$$

for all financial assets k and ℓ and all stocks j.

Substituting $q_k = r_{1k}/\bar{r}$ for all asset prices and $e^j = \delta_1^j/\bar{r}$ for all stock prices, multiplying the budget constraint of period 1 by $1/\bar{r}$, and summing the two budget constraints yields:

$$p_0 \cdot (x_0^i - \omega_0^i) + \frac{1}{\bar{r}} \cdot p_1 \cdot (x_1^i - \omega_1^i) \leq \sum_{j \in J} \bar{\sigma}_j^i \cdot (\frac{1}{\bar{r}} \cdot \delta_1^j + \delta_0^j).$$

This inequality is the intertemporal budget constraint which requires the sum of the discounted net trade values (the left side of the inequality) to be less than or equal to the value of the discounted dividend stream earned from the initial shareholdings. Because it allows a consumer more consumption, it is desirable for any consumer with monotonic preferences that the discounted dividend stream $\sum_{j \in J} \bar{\sigma}_j^i \cdot ((1/\bar{r}) \cdot \delta_1^j + \delta_0^j)$ be maximized. This is the case, however, if and only if each firm $j \in J$ maximizes discounted dividends $((1/\bar{r}) \cdot \delta_1^j + \delta_0^j)$. Therefore, all consumers, no matter how diverse their preferences, will agree to instruct a firm's manager to maximize discounted dividends, i.e. the present value of the firm.

It is worth reconsidering formula (5.5) which shows the effect of a change in a firm's production-finance plan on consumer's utility. In a stock-market equilibrium, the transformation rate between wealth in period 0 and wealth in period 1, $\tilde{r}$, is determined by the endowments and the consumers' marginal rates of substitution:

$$MRS^i_{1,0} \equiv \frac{\partial v^i(\cdot)}{\partial W^i_1} \Big/ \frac{\partial v^i(\cdot)}{\partial W^i_0} = \frac{1}{\tilde{r}}, \qquad \text{for all } i \in I.$$

Note that, in equilibrium, all consumers face the same intertemporal market rate of transformation for wealth $\tilde{r}$. The stock price must therefore equal the present value of dividends in period 1, $e^j = (1/\tilde{r}) \cdot \delta^j_1$ for all firms j, or arbitrage opportunities would exist. It follows immediately that a change in a firm's production-finance plan, $(\Delta y^j, \Delta \beta^j)$, leads to a change in the firm's stock price which equals the discounted value of the changes in dividends,

$$\Delta e^j(\Delta y^j, \Delta \beta^j) = \frac{1}{\tilde{r}} \cdot \Delta \delta^j_1(\Delta y^j, \Delta \beta^j).$$

The second square bracket in (5.5) therefore vanishes and the total effect on a consumer's welfare becomes

$$\Delta v^i \approx \frac{\partial v^i(\cdot)}{\partial W^i_0} \cdot \bar{\sigma}^i_j \cdot \left[\Delta e^j(\Delta y^j, \Delta \beta^j) + \Delta \delta^j_0(\Delta y^j, \Delta \beta^j) \right]$$

$$= \frac{\partial v^i(\cdot)}{\partial W^i_0} \cdot \bar{\sigma}^i_j \cdot \left[\frac{1}{\tilde{r}} \cdot \Delta \delta^j_1(\Delta y^j, \Delta \beta^j) + \Delta \delta^j_0(\Delta y^j, \Delta \beta^j) \right].$$

If the marginal utility of wealth is positive, as we assume throughout, then Δv^i of a stockholder will increase or decrease as the present value of the firm's cash flows rises or falls:

$$\Delta v^i \gtreqless 0 \Leftrightarrow \left[\frac{1}{\tilde{r}} \cdot \Delta \delta^j_1(\Delta y^j, \Delta \beta^j) + \Delta \delta^j_0(\Delta y^j, \Delta \beta^j) \right] \gtreqless 0.$$

The utility of a firm's owner will therefore be maximized if the present values of the firm's cash flows are maximized.

Hence, in a world of certainty where there exists at least one firm (and hence, one asset, the stock of this firm), ownership of the firm can be separated from control since all owners will agree that managers should maximize the present value of the firm. This is the Fisher Separation Theorem. The following example illustrates the result.

Example 5.1. Consider a two-period economy without uncertainty and with one commodity in each period. Suppose that there is just one consumer, one firm and no financial asset. The technology of the firm is described by a strictly increasing production function f,

$$Y \equiv \{(y_0, y_1) \in \mathbb{R}^2 \mid f(-y_0) = y_1\}.$$

Since there is just one commodity in each date, one can normalize the commodity prices, $p_0 = p_1 = 1$. The firm's production choice (y_0, y_1) determines the firm's dividend stream directly, because there are no financial assets in this economy: $\delta_0 = y_0$, $\delta_1 = y_1$.

Figure 5.1 shows the production possibilities of this economy and indifference curves representing the preferences of the single consumer. It shows an interest rate $\tilde{r}$ for which demand and supply of the single commodity are equalized in both periods. The stock market is trivially in equilibrium because there is just one consumer who owns the firm. Note however that the consumer could delegate the production decision to a manager by instructing her to maximize the present value of the firm $((1/\tilde{r}) \cdot \delta_1 + \delta_0)$. In Figure 5.1, it is easy to see that the consumer's intertemporal budget line is further to the right of the endowment point (ω_0, ω_1) the larger the present value of the firm. Increasing the present value of the firm therefore has a pure wealth effect, shifting the budget line to the right and thereby allowing the consumer increased consumption. ∎

Example 5.1 shows that the consumption decision can be separate from the firm's production decision if there is a single state in period 1, i.e. no uncertainty. Separation of ownership and control is possible in this case because transfers between dates are feasible independently of the production decision

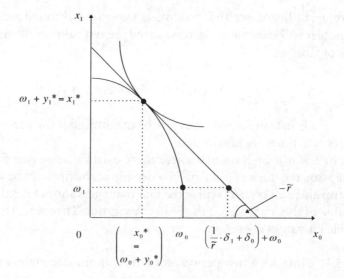

Fig. 5.1

made by the firm. The following two subsections investigate qualifications to this standard result when the assumption of certainty is relaxed.

5.2.1 Complete markets and shareholder unanimity about value maximization

Up to this point, we have neglected uncertainty. We now consider whether unanimous agreement amongst shareholders about the objective function of the firm can be expected if there is more than one state in period 1. We will see that the answer to this question is closely linked to the completeness of the system of securities markets. If there are at least as many assets with independent return vectors, stocks, or financial assets, as there are states of the world, then our analysis remains essentially the same as that in the case of certainty.

Consider first the case where there is a complete set of financial markets, i.e. where there are $K = S$ linearly independent assets. Note that a larger number of assets than states simply requires some assets to be perfect substitutes for portfolios of others. Arbitrage ensures that the prices of these redundant assets equal the prices of those assets (or combinations of assets) to which they are equivalent. The same is true for the shares of firms. With a complete set of assets, they can and must be priced by arbitrage.

If one has a complete set of financial assets, as we assume here, then the production-finance decisions of firms do not affect the completeness of the asset market system. If there are fewer financial assets than states but a sufficient number of firms and stocks, $K < S < K + J$, then completeness or incompleteness of the market system depends, in general, upon the decisions of these firms. Because dividend streams are not exogenous, unlike return vectors of financial assets, a firm's production and financing decision may produce a dividend stream which is linearly dependent on the other assets. Of course, for $K + J < S$, the system of financial markets cannot be complete. This case is treated in Subsection 5.2.2 below.

Consider, once again, an arbitrary consumer i with the following budget constraints:

$$p_0 \cdot x_0^i + \sum_{k \in K} q_k \cdot a_k^i + \sum_{j \in J} \sigma_j^i \cdot e^j \leq p_0 \cdot \omega_0^i + \sum_{j \in J} \bar{\sigma}_j^i \cdot (e^j + \delta_0^j) \quad \text{for period 0, and}$$

$$p_s \cdot x_s^i \leq p_s \cdot \omega_s^i + \sum_{j \in J} \sigma_j^i \cdot \delta_s^j + \sum_{k \in K} r_{sk} \cdot a_k^i \quad \text{for all states } s \in S.$$

We saw in Chapter 4 (Lemma 4.1) that, for an arbitrage-free asset price system, there exist Arrow security prices $\hat{q} = (\hat{q}_1, \ldots, \hat{q}_s, \ldots, \hat{q}_S)$, i.e. prices for delivery of a unit of wealth in the different states of the world. In fact, if markets are complete, this Arrow security price vector $\hat{q}$ is unique. Since a financial asset k yields returns $r_k \equiv (r_{1k}, \dots, r_{sk} \dots, r_{Sk})$, its price must satisfy the equation $q_k = \sum_{s \in S} \hat{q}_s \cdot r_s$. Similarly, a stock j with dividend stream $\delta^j \equiv (\delta^j_1, \dots, \delta^j_s, \dots, \delta^j_S)$ must be priced at $e^j = \sum_{s \in S} \hat{q}_s \cdot \delta^j_s$. Substituting these evaluations into the budget constraint of period 0, then multiplying the budget constraints of all states $s \in S$ by the respective state-price $\hat{q}_s$ and summing, yields the following intertemporal budget constraint:

$$p_0 \cdot x^i_0 + \sum_{s \in S} \hat{q}_s \cdot p_s \cdot x^i_s \leq p_0 \cdot \omega^i_0 + \sum_{s \in S} \hat{q}_s \cdot p_s \cdot \omega^i_s + \sum_{j \in J} \bar{\sigma}^i_j \cdot \left(\sum_{s \in S} \hat{q}_s \cdot \delta^j_s + \delta^j_0 \right).$$

These transformations of the consumer's budget constraints reflect the fact that, in a complete system of financial markets, any state-contingent pay-off can be replicated by an appropriate portfolio. Thus shareholdings and the production-finance decision of a firm matter only to the extent that they modify the overall wealth of consumers. With a complete set of financial markets, it is possible to achieve any distribution of wealth across states.

From the intertemporal budget constraint, it is obvious that each consumer wishes the firm to maximize the value $\sum_{j \in J} \bar{\sigma}^i_j \cdot \left(\sum_{s \in S} \hat{q}_s \cdot \delta^j_s + \delta^j_0 \right)$. Thus all stockholders, irrespective of their risk-preferences and their beliefs about the likelihood of the states, will support a policy requiring the firm to maximize $\sum_{s \in S} \hat{q}_s \cdot \delta^j_s + \delta^j_0$, i.e. the value of the firm in period 0.

Recall that an Arrow security price $\hat{q}_s$ represents the market rate of transformation between wealth in period 0 and wealth in state s of period 1. If the system of asset markets is complete, then all consumers face the same unique market rate of wealth transformation. Hence, consumers will choose a financial investment policy such that their marginal rates of substitution between wealth in period 0 and wealth in state s period 1 equal this common market rate of transformation:

$$MRS^i_{s,0} \equiv \frac{\partial v^i(\cdot)}{\partial W^i_s} \Big/ \frac{\partial v^i(\cdot)}{\partial W^i_0} = \hat{q}_s, \qquad \text{for all } s \in S \text{ and all } i \in I.$$

As argued above, arbitrage-free pricing in a complete market system requires $e^j = \sum_{s \in S} \hat{q}_s \cdot \delta^j_s$. Any change in a firm's production-finance decision $(\Delta y^j, \Delta \beta^j)$ will therefore be evaluated by all consumers $i \in I$ as

$$\Delta e^j(\Delta y^j, \Delta \beta^j) = \sum_{s \in S} \hat{q}_s \cdot \Delta \delta^j_s(\Delta y^j, \Delta \beta^j) = \sum_{s \in S} MRS^i_{s,0} \cdot \Delta \delta^j_s(\Delta y^j, \Delta \beta^j).$$

As in the case of certainty, with complete markets, the second square bracket in equation (5.5) vanishes. A consumer's utility change is therefore again proportional to the net present value of the changes in the firm's dividend stream:

$$\Delta v^i \gtreqless 0 \iff \left[\sum_{s \in S} \hat{q}_s \cdot \Delta \delta^j_s(\Delta y^j, \Delta \beta^j) + \Delta \delta^j_0(\Delta y^j, \Delta \beta^j) \right] \gtreqless 0.$$

This is the familiar result which once again allows separation of ownership and control to occur. Hence, Fisher separation holds under uncertainty, at least so long as securities markets are complete.

5.2.2 Incomplete markets and shareholder unanimity about value maximization

Even if there are fewer financial assets than states of the world, $K < S$, the market system may still be complete if there are sufficiently many different firms, and therefore different types of shares, to fill the gap. For this to occur, firms must choose production plans which yield state-contingent returns that cannot be replicated by existing assets. The shares of a firm may not provide a dividend vector that is linearly independent of the return vectors of the other assets. The following example should clarify this point.

Example 5.2. Consider the case of two states, $S = 2$, and one commodity in each state, $L = 1$. Suppose there is one asset with return vector $r = (r_1, r_2)$, and one firm with a technology described by the (implicit) state-contingent production function $f(y_0, y_1, y_2) := (y_1)^2 + y_2 + y_0$. The spot market price of the single commodity can be normalized to unity in each date and state. To simplify the argument, it is assumed that the firm raises all funds for input purchases from its equity holders. Note that, with these assumptions, a firm's cash flow is simply $(\delta_0, \delta_1, \delta_2) = (y_0, y_1, y_2)$.

Figure 5.2 illustrates that the production choice of the firm determines whether there are one or two independent securities in this economy. With two

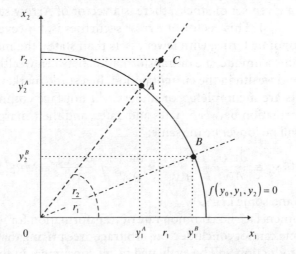

Fig. 5.2

securities, the set of financial markets is complete, while with one, it is incomplete. The figure shows the transformation curve of the firm's technology for a given input vector. The firm's production plan must lie on the production possibility frontier $(y_1)^2 + y_2 + y_0 = 0$. The diagram indicates the return vector of the financial asset. One unit of the asset yields (r_1, r_2), i.e. point C in the diagram.

It is easy to see from Figure 5.2 that the firm's production decision will determine whether markets are complete or not. If the firm chooses production plan A, it creates a cash flow which can be achieved by holding an appropriate amount of the financial asset, i.e. there is a' such that $r_1 \cdot a' = y_1^A$ and $r_2 \cdot a' = y_2^A$. Arbitrage-free pricing implies $q \cdot a' = e$, since the equity value must equal the value of the replicating asset transaction. In this case, shares of the firm provide the same return pattern as the financial asset and markets are incomplete.

By contrast, if the firm chooses production plan B, the cash-flow stream cannot be replicated by transactions in the financial asset. Consequently, there are two securities with linearly independent pay-offs and markets are complete. ∎

Since the number of securities in a stock-market economy with different state-dependent pay-offs depends on the production-finance decision of the firm, it is no longer possible to say whether markets are complete or incomplete without reference to the production allocation of the economy. However, if there are fewer firms and financial assets than states, then markets must be incomplete. For simplicity of exposition in this section, we consider the case of an economy without financial assets, $K = 0$, and with fewer firms than states of the world $J < S$. Under these conditions, markets cannot be complete.

Lemma 4.1 from Chapter 4 continues to hold even with incomplete markets. For a given set of stocks, there is a vector of Arrow securities $\hat{q} = (\hat{q}_1, \ldots, \hat{q}_s, \ldots, \hat{q}_S)$. This vector of Arrow securities is, however, no longer unique. In economic terms, with fewer assets than states, the market can no longer determine a unique rate of transformation between wealth in any state of the world and wealth in the current period. In a stock-market equilibrium where markets are incomplete, consumers will not face common rates of wealth transformation between states and dates, and their marginal rates of substitution will no longer be the same:

$$MRS_{s,0}^i \equiv \frac{\partial v^i(\cdot)}{\partial W_s^i} \bigg/ \frac{\partial v^i(\cdot)}{\partial W_0^i} \neq \frac{\partial v^j(\cdot)}{\partial W_s^j} \bigg/ \frac{\partial v^j(\cdot)}{\partial W_0^j} \equiv MRS_{s,0}^j$$

for some $s \in S$ and some $i, j \in I$.

Since consumers face no common rate of transformation for wealth in different states, one cannot conclude from arbitrage-free pricing that a change in some firm's production will be evaluated by all consumers in the same way.

The change in equity value which occurs in response to a change in production need not be equal to the evaluation of the changes in the dividend stream. Hence, with incomplete markets, we can no longer conclude from a stock-market equilibrium that

$$\Delta e^j(\Delta y^j, \Delta \beta^j) = \sum_{s \in S} MRS^i_{s,0} \cdot \Delta \delta^j_s(\Delta y^j, \Delta \beta^j). \qquad (5.6)$$

In a competitive economy, however, one would expect a stockholder to assume that equity prices reflect a firm's changes in cash flows. Equation (5.6) can therefore be reinterpreted as an assumption about the expectations of a stockholder in regard to the induced adjustments of the equity price following a change in production that changes a firm's cash flow.

ASSUMPTION 5.1 (*competitive price perceptions*). Each stockholder assumes that any change in a firm's dividend stream, evaluated with her own marginal rate of substitution, is reflected in a commensurate change of the stock price; formally, that (5.6) holds.

Notice that different stockholders hold different beliefs about the change in the stock price that follows from the same change in dividends because consumers' marginal rates of substitution between wealth in different states generally differ.[3] The assumption of competitive price perception implies, however, that no consumer believes changes in dividend streams produce gains or losses that are not captured in the equity value.

As a consequence of Assumption 5.1, the impact of a change in a firm's production plan is given once again by the term in the first square bracket of (5.5). Substituting (5.6) into equation (5.5) yields the following, now familiar, expression:

$$\Delta v^i \approx \frac{\partial v^i(\cdot)}{\partial W^i_0} \cdot \bar{\sigma}^i_j \cdot \left[\sum_{s \in S} MRS^i_{s,0} \cdot \Delta \delta^j_s(\Delta y^j, \Delta \beta^j) + \Delta \delta^j_0(\Delta y^j, \Delta \beta^j) \right]. \qquad (5.7)$$

Notice, however, that dividend changes are evaluated with a stockholder's personal marginal rate of substitution between wealth in different states. With competitive price perceptions, a stockholder would welcome any production policy of the firm which maximizes the 'present value of the firm's dividend stream evaluated at her own marginal rate of substitution'. Without complete asset markets, however, consumers are not able to adjust wealth across different states, and consequently are unable to choose a financial investment plan that equalizes their marginal rates of substitution. Thus, in contrast to the case of a complete set of asset markets, different stockholders will in general evaluate a

---

[3] Such an assumption cannot, of course, be 'rationalized', since there can be only one equity value in final equilibrium. See Grossman and Hart (1979, 300) on this problem.

firm's production decision differently, and not agree on a common objective for the firm. The following example illustrates this point.

Example 5.3. Consider again the economy of Example 5.2 without the financial asset. With one firm, markets are necessarily incomplete. Assume that there are two consumers, $I = 2$, who gain no utility from consumption in period 0 and who have an endowment in period 0 only. This economy is represented in Figure 5.3.

Without the financial asset, consumers may want the firm to produce in different points of its production set, say consumer 1 at A and consumer 2 at B. Since markets are incomplete, there is no way that consumer 1 could transfer wealth in one state to consumer 2 in exchange for wealth in the other state. Since these trades are impossible, there is no way in which the two consumers can equalize their marginal rates of substitution.

Assume now that a financial asset with returns at C becomes available. Then, together with the trade in equity, financial markets are complete. Consumers can achieve all trades between wealth in different states and an equilibrium will determine the prices of the financial asset and the stock such that both consumers' marginal rates of substitution are equalized. Hence, they will agree on the firm maximizing its present value in terms of these prices. This equilibrium is indicated by the production point D and the two consumption points E and F in the figure. Notice the common marginal rate of substitution. ∎

It remains to discuss a special case where the assumption of competitive price perceptions suffices to achieve agreement among stockholders about

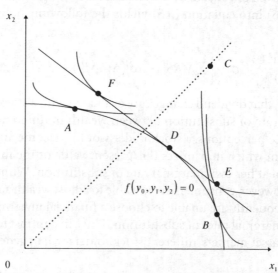

Fig. 5.3

value maximization of the firm. This special case which was introduced by Diamond (1967) is important because it has been used extensively in the applied economics literature.

Diamond (1967) considers an economy with incomplete financial markets where shareholders agree on value maximization. This shows that, under special assumptions which are outlined below, stockholders need not have equal marginal rates of substitution between wealth in different states for the evaluation of a firm's dividend stream. If consumers' marginal rates of substitution are equalized between only those states where the firms pay dividends, a common evaluation is guaranteed, and stockholders will agree on value maximization.

To study this case, we specialize our model even further by assuming that there is only one commodity in each state and date. The price of this commodity is normalized to unity. With this specialization, the vector of dividends is equal to the production vector:

$$\delta^j \equiv (\delta^j_0, \delta^j_1, \ldots, \delta^j_S) = (y^j_0, y^j_1, \ldots, y^j_S) \equiv y^j.$$

Recalling our earlier assumption that there are no financial assets, any change in a firm's production decision will induce an equal dividend change:

$$\Delta\delta^j_s(\Delta y^j) = \Delta y^j_s, \qquad \text{for all } s \in S.$$

Notice that the following definition of *equilibrium spanning* is therefore couched in terms of production vectors directly.

ASSUMPTION 5.2 (*equilibrium spanning*). A stock-market equilibrium satisfies *equilibrium spanning* if any change in a production plan of any firm can be obtained as a linear combination of the equilibrium production plans of all firms; formally, for all feasible Δy^j, $j \in J$, there exists a vector of weights $\alpha = (\alpha_1, \ldots, \alpha_J)$ such that

$$\Delta y^j_s = \sum_{k \in J} \alpha_k \cdot \hat{y}^k_s \qquad \text{for all } s \in S.$$

If the assumption of equilibrium spanning is satisfied, no feasible change in a production plan can create new trading opportunities between states that were not available in the original equilibrium. Thus, a change in production will not alter the set of assets available in equilibrium. The following example shows two economies for which equilibrium spanning is satisfied.

Example 5.4. Assume that there are two states of the world and one commodity in each state, i.e. $S = 2$, $L = 1$. Commodity prices are normalized to unity, and firms' dividend streams therefore coincide with their production plans. Consider the following two economies:

155

(i) an economy with two firms that have the following technologies:

$$Y^A = \{(y_0, y_1, y_2) \in \mathbb{R}_- \times \mathbb{R}^2_+ \mid (y_1)^2 + y_2 + y_0 \le 0\}, \text{ and}$$

$$Y^B = \{(y_0, y_1, y_2) \in \mathbb{R}_- \times \mathbb{R}^2_+ \mid y_1 + (y_2)^2 + y_0 \le 0\};$$

(ii) an economy where the firm has technology

$$Y^C = \{(y_0, y_1, y_2) \in \mathbb{R}_- \times \mathbb{R}^2_+ \mid y_1 = \varepsilon_1 \cdot \sqrt{(-y_0)}, y_2 = \varepsilon_2 \cdot \sqrt{(-y_0)}\}.$$

The diagrams below show these two technologies and indicate equilibrium allocations

$$\hat{y}^A = (\hat{y}^A_0, \hat{y}^A_1, \hat{y}^A_2), \quad \hat{y}^B = (\hat{y}^B_0, \hat{y}^B_1, \hat{y}^B_2), \quad \hat{y}^C = (\hat{y}^C_0, \hat{y}^C_1, \hat{y}^C_2),$$

respectively.

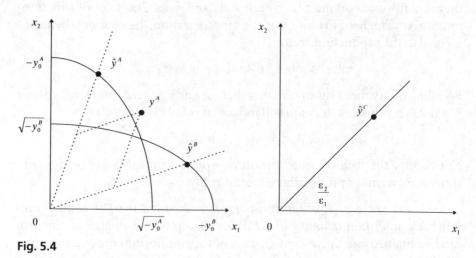

Fig. 5.4

It is easy to see in the left-hand diagram that any production vector of either firm can be achieved as a linear combination of the equilibrium production vectors $(\hat{y}^A, \hat{y}^B)$. The production plan y^A provides an example. Indeed, the equilibrium production plans $(\hat{y}^A, \hat{y}^B)$ span the whole (x_1, x_2)-space so that financial markets are complete.

Equilibrium spanning does not imply completeness of the financial market system, however, as the right-hand diagram shows. The technology of firm C has multiplicative uncertainty. All production plans open to the firm lie along a ray through the origin and provide its shareholders with the same ratio of state-contingent returns $\varepsilon_1 / \varepsilon_2$. Though the technology exhibits decreasing returns to scale, it is similar to a financial asset.[4] Clearly, in this case, all changes

---

[4] Indeed, one can view a financial asset as a special case of a technology with constant returns to scale and multiplicative uncertainty.

in production plans create state-contingent outputs that are multiples of the equilibrium production vector. ∎

It remains to show that equilibrium spanning does indeed imply unanimous acceptance of value maximization in equilibrium. To see this, recall that in any equilibrium (with or without complete markets)

$$\sum_{s \in S} MRS^i_{s,0} \cdot \hat{y}^j_s = \hat{e}^j$$

must hold for any consumer $i \in I$ maximizing utility. Furthermore, from the competitive price perceptions assumption, it follows immediately, that

$$\Delta e^j(\Delta y^j) = \sum_{s \in S} MRS^i_{s,0} \cdot \Delta y^j_s = \sum_{s \in S} MRS^i_{s,0} \cdot \left[\sum_{k \in J} \alpha_k \cdot \hat{y}^k_s \right]$$

$$= \sum_{k \in J} \alpha_k \cdot \sum_{s \in S} MRS^i_{s,0} \cdot \hat{y}^k_s = \sum_{k \in J} \alpha_k \cdot \hat{e}^k,$$

where the equilibrium-spanning assumption has been used in the second equation. Now one computes easily,

$$\sum_{s \in S} MRS^i_{s,0} \cdot \Delta \delta^j_s(\Delta y^j) + \Delta \delta^j_0(\Delta y^j) = \sum_{s \in S} MRS^i_{s,0} \cdot \Delta y^j_s + \Delta y^j_0 = \sum_{k \in J} \alpha_k \cdot \hat{e}^k + \Delta y^j_0,$$

where the second equality follows from the previous considerations. Notice that the right-hand side of this equation is the same for all consumers. Hence, with equilibrium spanning, all consumers agree that this expression should be maximized by firms.[5]

To see that $\sum_{k \in J} \alpha_k \cdot \hat{e}^k + \Delta y^j_0$ is the value of the production change in terms of the equilibrium price system, recall that arbitrage-free pricing implies that there is a set of Arrow security prices $\hat{q} \equiv (\hat{q}_1, \ldots, \hat{q}_s, \ldots, \hat{q}_S)$ such that $\sum_{s \in S} \hat{q}_s \cdot \hat{y}^j_s = \hat{e}^j$ whether or not financial markets are complete (Lemma 4.1). With incomplete markets, however, this vector of Arrow security prices is not unique and, in particular, it is not true that $MRS^i_{s,0} = \hat{q}_s$ for all consumers $i \in I$. Still, in equilibrium, $\sum_{s \in S} \hat{q}_s \cdot \hat{y}^j_s$ is the present value of the future dividends of firm j which are equal to state-contingent production in this case. Using the Arrow security prices implied by the equilibrium price system, one easily calculates:

$$\sum_{k \in J} \alpha_k \cdot \hat{e}^k + \Delta y^j_0 = \sum_{k \in J} \alpha_k \cdot \sum_{s \in S} \hat{q}_s \cdot \hat{y}^k_s + \Delta y^j_0$$

$$= \sum_{s \in S} \hat{q}_s \cdot \sum_{k \in J} \alpha_k \cdot \hat{y}^k_s + \Delta y^j_0 = \sum_{s \in S} \hat{q}_s \cdot \Delta y^j_s + \Delta y^j_0.$$

Hence, shareholders will agree on value maximization even if financial markets are incomplete provided that spanning and equilibrium price perceptions obtain.[6]

[5] This observation was made by Ekern and Wilson (1974) who did not go on to conclude unanimity, however. This last step was left to Grossman and Stiglitz (1980).

[6] Grossman and Stiglitz (1980) show that this result does not hold if there are more than two trading periods.

We conclude this section with the observation that, with incomplete financial markets, consumers in general disagree about the objective that firms should pursue. Only very special assumptions guarantee shareholder unanimity in this case. This is a major problem for the modelling of economies with firms and incomplete financial markets, and accounts for the fact that most general equilibrium treatments of financial markets neglect firms as independent agents.

It is not just a problem for economic modelling. The lack of an agreed objective for a firm operating with incomplete financial markets helps to explain the great variety of corporate governance systems one finds in real-world firms. The advantages of separating ownership and control may not be obtainable in the absence of a simple objective of the firm on which all stockholders agree. Other institutional arrangements evolve to accommodate the conflicting interests of different shareholders.[7]

5.3 The Financial Structure of the Firm

Until the early 1960s, conventional wisdom held that the cost of raising equity capital for a firm with a given return stream would be lower at low levels of debt than at higher levels of debt because the risk premium applied by the market to the firm's equity would be smaller. As the firm increased its debt, the growing risk of bankruptcy would, it was argued, require a higher risk premium, and hence raise the cost of equity. This argument implies that there is a level of debt for which the cost of equity capital is minimized, i.e. an optimal debt–equity ratio.

The prevailing view was challenged in 1958 by Modigliani and Miller who claimed that a firm's financial structure had no effect on its value, determined, as it was, solely by the firm's profit stream. Their argument is quite straightforward: the financial structure of the firm represents claims on the profit stream; if consumers can trade such claims freely, and also on the same terms as the firm itself, there can be no effect on the real transactions of the firm or consumers. If a firm increases its debt by a certain amount, shareholders lose claims to the future profit stream equal to precisely this value. They can completely offset this loss by buying exactly as many bonds as the fall in the value of their equity.

The full significance of this result and its generality remained unclear for a time since Modigliani and Miller made a number of unnecessary assumptions

---

[7] See, e.g., Hart (1995) for a new approach to corporate governance and the role of financial markets.

in their exposition. Stiglitz (1969, 1972b) clarified many of these issues and has become the main reference for the result. The model introduced in the previous section enables us to state the result clearly and to see exactly which assumptions are essential.

Denote by ω^j the value of future profits of a typical firm $j \in J$. This value accrues to the shareholders as equity value e^j or to the debt-holders, $q \cdot \beta^j$,

$$\omega^j := e^j + q \cdot \beta^j.$$

As before, the share of firm j that is held by consumer i is denoted by σ_j^i. Recall that σ_j^i indicates a percentage share in the firm's equity value and not a number of nominal titles. Furthermore, notice that the firm can raise the desired amount of debt by using any of the assets available in the economy. Thus, $\beta^j \in \mathbb{R}^K$ is the portfolio of asset holdings of firm j. If β_k^j is positive for some asset k, this indicates that firm j has sold this asset to finance input purchases; otherwise, for β_k^j negative, the firm purchases the asset. With a given production plan y^j and a given portfolio choice β^j to finance it, the firm generates the following cash flows for its equity holders:

- in period 0, equity holders have to pay for the expenditures on inputs not covered by the firm's debt: $\delta_0^j := p_0 \cdot y_0^j + q \cdot \beta^j$, and
- in each state s, equity holders receive dividends: $\delta_s^j := p_s \cdot y_s^j - r_s \cdot \beta^j$.

Recall that $q \cdot \beta^j \equiv \sum_{k \in K} q_k \cdot \beta_k^j$ and $r_s \cdot \beta^j \equiv \sum_{k \in K} r_{sk} \cdot \beta_k^j$ denote the value and the return in state s of a portfolio $\beta^j \equiv (\beta_1^j, \ldots \beta_K^j)$, respectively.

The Modigliani–Miller argument runs as follows:

Suppose some firm with a given production plan y^j decides to raise more funds issuing debt by choosing a portfolio $\beta^j + \Delta\beta^j$ with $q \cdot \Delta\beta^j > 0$. This reduces the amount an equity holder i has to contribute to the input purchase

$$\hat{\delta}_0^j = p_0 \cdot y_0^j + q \cdot (\beta^j + \Delta\beta^j) > p_0 \cdot y_0^j + q \cdot \beta^j = \delta_0^j.$$

On the other hand, the profit that the equity holder receives in any state s decreases:

$$\hat{\delta}_s^j = p_s \cdot y_s^j - r_s \cdot (\beta^j + \Delta\beta^j) < p_s \cdot y_s^j - r_s \cdot \beta^j = \delta_s^j.$$

Suppose a shareholder owns σ_j^i of the claims to this firm and uses the reduced contribution to input purchases in period 0, $\sigma_j^i \cdot q \cdot \Delta\beta^j$, to buy the portfolio of assets $\Delta a^i = \sigma_j^i \cdot \Delta\beta^j$. This consumer then receives in each state s

$$[\sigma_j^i \cdot \hat{\delta}_s^j + r_s \cdot \Delta a^i] = \sigma_j^i \cdot [p_s \cdot y_s^j - r_s \cdot (\beta^j + \Delta\beta^j)] + r_s \cdot \sigma_j^i \cdot \Delta\beta^j = \sigma_j^i \cdot \delta_s^j.$$

Thus, the consumer achieves the same cash flow in each state that she could obtain before the firm changed its financial structure. Notice, however, that in the model of this chapter the contribution of the old shareholder has decreased, since her cash flow in period 0 has risen, $\hat{\delta}_0^j > \delta_0^j$. The equity value e^j must therefore be adjusted appropriately or old shareholders would not be indifferent to such a change in the firm's financial policy.

To make this argument precise and to understand its generality and its limitations, one needs to consider carefully the extent to which a firm's shareholders are capable of maintaining their wealth in every state and date by making compensatory rearrangements in their portfolios. In this context, it is important to note that most of the literature assumes all of a firm's cash flows, including those in period 0, accrue to the new shareholders.[8] Here, however, we retain the model as presented in the previous section where the initial shareholders receive the cash flow in period 0. The following theorem puts the argument into the context of a general stock-market equilibrium.

THEOREM 5.1 (*Modigliani–Miller theorem*). Let ((p,q,e), $(x^i,a^i,\sigma^i)_{i \in I}$), be a stock-market equilibrium for production-finance plans $(y^j,\beta^j)_{j \in J}$. Then, for any production-finance plans $(y^j,\hat{\beta}^j)_{j \in J}$, ($(p,q,\hat{e})$, $(x^i,\hat{a}^i,\sigma^i)_{i \in I}$), with

$$\hat{e}^j = e^j + q \cdot (\beta^j - \hat{\beta}^j) \qquad \text{for all firms } j \in J$$
$$\hat{a}^i = a^i + \sum_{j \in J}\sigma_j^i \cdot (\hat{\beta}^j - \beta^j) \qquad \text{for all consumers } i \in I$$

is a stock-market equilibrium as well.

PROOF. It will be shown that, for any consumer $i \in I$, the budget set in period 0 and in any state $s \in S$ remains unchanged with respect to the real variables (x^i,σ^i) if the firm's financial policy is changed to $\hat{\beta}^j$ and if (i) consumers change their asset holdings to $\hat{a}^i$, and (ii) the equity value changes to $\hat{e}^j$ for all firms.

Consider a consumer's budget constraint in period 0 for a portfolio of financial assets $\hat{a}^i$ if she faces an equity price $\hat{e}^j$:

$$p_0 \cdot x_0^i + q \cdot \hat{a}^i + \sum_{j \in J}\sigma_j^i \cdot \hat{e}^j \leq p_0 \cdot \omega_0^i + \sum_{j \in J}\bar{\sigma}_j^i \cdot (\hat{e}^j + \hat{\delta}_0^j),$$

where $\hat{\delta}_0^j = p_0 \cdot y_0^j + q \cdot \hat{\beta}^j$ denotes the cash flow for the initial shareholders after the financial plan of the firm has been changed to $\hat{\beta}^j$. Substituting for $\hat{a}^i$, $\hat{e}^j$, and $\hat{\delta}_0^j$, one obtains

[8] See e.g. Duffie's (1991) exposition of the Modigliani–Miller theorem (pp. 1620, 1621).

$$p_0 \cdot x_0^i + q \cdot [a^i + \sum_{j \in J} \sigma_j^i \cdot (\hat{\beta}^j - \beta^j)] + \sum_{j \in J} \sigma_j^i \cdot [e^j + q \cdot (\beta^j - \hat{\beta}^j)]$$

$$\leq p_0 \cdot \omega_0^i + \sum_{j \in J} \bar{\sigma}_j^i \cdot ([e^j + q \cdot (\beta^j - \hat{\beta}^j)] + [p_0 \cdot y_0^j + q \cdot \hat{\beta}^j]),$$

which can be simplified to

$$p_0 \cdot x_0^i + q \cdot a^i + \sum_{j \in J} \sigma_j^i \cdot e^j \leq p_0 \cdot \omega_0^i + \sum_{j \in J} \bar{\sigma}_j^i \cdot (e^j + \delta_0^j).$$

Similarly, for an arbitrary state $s \in S$, the budget constraint

$$p_s \cdot x_s^i \leq p_s \cdot \omega_s^i + \sum_{j \in J} \sigma_j^i \cdot \hat{\delta}_s^j + r_s \cdot \hat{a}^i$$

with the adjusted dividend payment $\hat{\delta}_s^j = p_s \cdot y_s^j - r_s \cdot \hat{\beta}^j$, can be transformed by substitution for $\hat{a}^i$ to yield

$$p_s \cdot x_s^i \leq p_s \cdot \omega_s^i + \sum_{j \in J} \sigma_j^i \cdot [p_s \cdot y_s^j - r_s \cdot \hat{\beta}^j] + r_s \cdot [a^i + \sum_{j \in J} \sigma_j^i \cdot (\hat{\beta}^j - \beta^j)].$$

This is of course equivalent to

$$p_s \cdot x_s^i \leq p_s \cdot \omega_s^i + \sum_{j \in J} \sigma_j^i \cdot \delta_s^j + r_s \cdot a^i.$$

Thus a consumer can make a portfolio transaction $\hat{a}^i$ which offsets any change firm j makes to its financial structure $\hat{\beta}^j$, provided the equity value of each firm j changes to $\hat{e}^j$. Such a portfolio transaction leaves the budget set for the other choice variables (x^i, σ^i) unchanged. Hence, consumer i must find the same choices of (x^i, σ^i) optimal both before and after the portfolio and stock price change. This shows that the choice $(x^i, \hat{a}^i, \sigma^i)$ is optimal for consumers (part (1) of the equilibrium definition).

The second equilibrium condition (market clearing) needs to be checked for financial asset markets only. Since the original situation was an equilibrium, one knows $\sum_{i \in I} \sigma_j^i = 1$ for all stock markets $j \in J$ and $\sum_{j \in J} \beta_k^j = \sum_{i \in I} a_k^i$ for all financial asset markets, $k \in K$. Thus, considering an arbitrary market for a financial asset $k \in K$, one obtains

$$\sum_{i \in I} \hat{a}_k^i - \sum_{i \in I} \hat{\beta}_k^j = \sum_{i \in I} [a_k^i + \sum_{i \in I} \sigma_j^i \cdot (\hat{\beta}_k^j - \beta_k^j)] - \sum_{i \in I} \hat{\beta}_k^j = \sum_{i \in I} a_k^i - \sum_{i \in I} \beta_k^j = 0,$$

where the last equation equals zero because the financial asset markets were in equilibrium before. This establishes our theorem. ∎

The intuition behind the Modigliani–Miller result is simple. If a firm changes its debt level, the new equity owners in period 1 will experience a change in their dividend stream because of the change in debt. If consumers can borrow and lend on the same terms as firms, they can simply buy or sell financial assets to offset such a change. If the new shareholders receive the period 0 cash flow, as most derivations of the Modigliani–Miller theorem assume, no other changes are necessary.

This is easily seen by considering the budget constraint of a consumer in period 0 assuming that new shareholders do get the period 0 cash flow δ_0^j:

$$p_0 \cdot x_0^i + q \cdot a^i + \sum_{j \in J} \sigma_j^i \cdot e^j \leq p_0 \cdot \omega_0^i + \sum_{j \in J} \bar{\sigma}_j^i \cdot e^j + \sum_{j \in J} \sigma_j^i \cdot \delta_0^j.$$

Any change in firm j's portfolio $\hat{\beta}^j$ will change its cash flow in period 0 to $\hat{\delta}_0^j = p_0 \cdot y_0^j + q \cdot \hat{\beta}^j$. Suppose that consumer i chooses a new portfolio $\hat{a}^i = a^i + \sum_{j \in J} \sigma_j^i \cdot (\hat{\beta}^j - \beta^j)$ to offset the firm's portfolio changes. Notice that a shareholder adjusts her asset trade exactly by its share in the firm's portfolio change $\sigma_j^i \cdot (\hat{\beta}^j - \beta^j)$. Substituting for $\hat{a}^i$ and $\hat{\delta}_0^j$, one obtains:

$$p_0 \cdot x_0^i + q \cdot \hat{a}^i + \sum_{j \in J} \sigma_j^i \cdot e^j - \sum_{j \in J} \sigma_j^i \cdot \hat{\delta}_0^j$$

$$= p_0 \cdot x_0^i + q \cdot [a^i + \sum_{j \in J} \sigma_j^i \cdot (\hat{\beta}^j - \beta^j)] + \sum_{j \in J} \sigma_j^i \cdot [e^j - (p_0 \cdot y_0^j + q \cdot \hat{\beta}^j)]$$

$$= p_0 \cdot x_0^i + q \cdot a^i + \sum_{j \in J} \sigma_j^i \cdot [e^j - (p_0 \cdot y_0^j + q \cdot \beta^j)]$$

$$= p_0 \cdot x_0^i + q \cdot a^i + \sum_{j \in J} \sigma_j^i \cdot [e^j - \delta_0^j] \leq p_0 \cdot \omega_0^i + \sum_{j \in J} \bar{\sigma}_j^i \cdot e^j.$$

In this case, the initial shareholders are not affected at all by the change in the firm's cash flow. Therefore, no adjustment of the equity price is necessary. This is the scenario in which the Modigliani–Miller theorem is usually cast. Theorem 5.1 shows, however, that the result does not require all cash flows to go to the new shareowners provided that the equity price is adjusted accordingly.

Note carefully the exact claims of Theorem 5.1:

> Stock-market equilibria exist for any financial structure that firms may choose, but equilibria are differentiated only by the asset holdings of consumers and the equity value (if old shareholders obtain the cash flow of period 0).

Thus, as long as there is no change in firms' production plans, there need not be any change in consumption or firm ownership as a consequence of an altered financial structure.

The financial structure of firms is irrelevant, however, only if all consumers adjust their portfolios appropriately. Notice that it is important for all consumers to do so. Should some consumers fail to make the necessary portfolio adjustment, the bond market no longer clears and prices must change. Simultaneous actions by all shareholders are required to obtain the result that the *financial structure of the firm is irrelevant*.

On the other hand, the theorem is much more general than Modigliani and Miller originally thought. In particular, there is no requirement that firms use only riskless debt, nor does one need a complete set of financial markets. The essential assumption is that consumers and firms are able to buy and sell assets on the same terms. If one looks for reasons why the Modigliani–Miller theorem may fail to hold, one has to consider instances where borrowing and lending facilities are no longer equal for firms and consumers. The last part of this section indicates two possible situations.

One of the reasons why the Modigliani–Miller theorem may fail to hold is that firms may go bankrupt. A *bankruptcy* occurs when a firm cannot meet its debt obligations without further contributions by shareholders. Suppose that a firm is bankrupt in state s because it cannot repay its debt out of its own cash flows from production and sales, i.e. if $\delta_s^j < 0$. This raises the question of how the resulting deficit will be covered.

The original statement of the Modigliani–Miller theorem requires shareholders to provide the necessary additional funds in such a case. Bankruptcy laws, however, usually imply that, after all assets of the firm have been liquidated and debt has been redeemed as far as possible, the remaining debt is forgiven. Hence, if there is a *limited liability* law for firms, cash flows cannot become negative,

$$\delta_s^j = \max\{p_s \cdot y_s^j - r_s \cdot \beta^j, 0\}, \qquad \text{for } s \in S.$$

Notice that, with just two periods of activity, firms can be viewed as liquidating all assets in every state of period 1. Hence, cash flows coincide with liquidation surpluses or deficits.

Consider a stock-market equilibrium for production-finance plans such that no firm is bankrupt in any state s. Suppose that one firm, say firm j', changes its finance policy to $\hat{\beta}^{j'}$ such that bankruptcy now occurs in some state s. There is now no longer another stock-market equilibrium with only an adjustment of shareholders' financial assets:

$$p_s \cdot x_s^i \leq p_s \cdot \omega_s^i + \sum_{j \in J} \sigma_j^i \cdot \hat{\delta}_s^j + r_s \cdot \hat{a}^i.$$

If a bankruptcy of firm j' occurs in state s,

$$p_s \cdot y_s^{j'} - r_s \cdot \hat{\beta}^{j'} < 0,$$

then $\hat{\delta}_s^j = 0$ and, by substitution for $\hat{a}^i$, one obtains:

$$p_s \cdot x_s^i$$
$$\leq p_s \cdot \omega_s^i + \sum_{j \neq j'} \sigma_j^i \cdot [p_s \cdot y_s^j - r_s \cdot \beta^j] + \sigma_{j'}^i \cdot 0 + r_s \cdot [a^i + \sigma_{j'}^i \cdot (\hat{\beta}^j - \beta^j)]$$
$$= p_s \cdot \omega_s^i + \sum_{j \neq j'} \sigma_j^i \cdot \delta_s^j + r_s \cdot a^i + \sigma_{j'}^i \cdot r_s \cdot (\hat{\beta}^{j'} - \beta^{j'}).$$

The right-hand side of this inequality is larger than before the change in this firm's financing plan. Firms' returns from financial assets differ from the returns that consumers receive because the bankruptcy law allows firms to default on their debt. Shareholders would like to increase financial asset holdings and, in exchange with firms, to increase their debts. When firms have limited liability, shareholders prefer the firm to be more highly geared since they do not have to bear the negative cash flows in those states where the firm goes bankrupt. Consequently, the Modigliani–Miller argument breaks down.

A second reason why shareholders might not be indifferent to a firm's financial policy occurs when debt and equity claims are taxed differently. Suppose, for example, that interest on debt is not deductible before taxes for consumers. Clearly, shareholders would not want to take a compensatory portfolio position if a firm were to decrease its debt, since shareholders would have to pay higher taxes on income from these additional asset holdings.[9]

Notes on the Literature

Radner (1972) was among the first to note the problem of unanimity concerning a firm's objective function in an economy with incomplete markets. A symposium on 'The Optimality of Competitive Capital Markets', published in the *Bell Journal of Economics and Management Sciences* in 1974, contains articles by Leland (1974), Ekern and Wilson (1974), and Radner (1974) focusing on the question of unanimous agreement of shareholders on a firm's objective function if markets are incomplete. Grossman and Hart (1979) and Grossman and Stiglitz (1980) provide comprehensive reviews of the problem.

The literature dealing with the Modigliani–Miller theorem begins with the seminal article by these two authors (Modigliani and Miller (1958)). The vast ensuing literature covers management and economic aspects of the irrelevance theorem. Stiglitz (1969) formalizes the theorem and this is the most commonly used argument in presentations of the theorem. It is common in this literature to consider models where the financing decision of the firm affects new shareholders only, and where no adjustment of the stock price is necessary.

Most of the management literature, arguing that a firm's finance policy does matter for its value, appeals to taxation or bankruptcy laws as causes of the unequal terms for borrowing and lending by firms and shareholders. There is also a substantial literature on the importance of taxes in determining the optimal financial structure of the firms (e.g., Copeland and Weston 1988). Hart (1995) investigates the implications of the financial structure of a firm for the control of management.

[9] Exercise 7 provides an example of how taxes affect the Modigliani–Miller theorem.

Exercises

1. *Consider a farmer who plants wheat at the beginning of a year. The amount harvested at the end of the year will depend on the average rainfall during the growing seasons according to the following table:*

Acres of wheat planted: x	Average rainfall		
	≤ 10mm	$10 - 30$mm	≥ 30mm
0–10	$2 \cdot x$	$5 \cdot x$	$4 \cdot x$
10–20	$1.5 \cdot x$	$4 \cdot x$	$3.5 \cdot x$
20–40	$1 \cdot x$	$2 \cdot x$	$1.5 \cdot x$

(a) Determine the state-contingent production function of this farmer. How many states are there?

(b) Are there constant returns to scale?

2. *Consider a firm with a technology described by the production function $f(\ell) :=$ $\sqrt{\ell}$ where ℓ denotes labour input of the firm. Suppose that this firm faces a fixed wage rate w but an uncertain price for its output. Assume that the output price can be either high, p_h, or low, p_ℓ, with $p_h > p_\ell$.*

(a) Draw a diagram showing the state-contingent profit of this firm for alternative levels of labour input ℓ.

(b) Show in another diagram input–profit combinations for the two states.

(c) Explain whether asset markets can be complete if there are two firms of this type whose stocks are traded as the only assets in the economy.

3. *Consider an economy without financial assets. There is just one state, and a single commodity is available in period 0 and state 1. Each of 100 consumers is endowed with 5 units of the commodity in period 0 and 2 units in state 1. Preferences of a consumer are given by the following utility function:*

$$u(x_0, x_1) = x_0^2 \cdot x_1.$$

(a) Suppose there is a firm in this economy, owned by all consumers in equal shares, which can use quantities of the commodity in period 0 to produce output in state 1. Determine the stock-market equilibrium for a production plan

165

(−400,300). What is the cash flow of this firm and what is the equity value of the firm in equilibrium? Would all consumers want the firm to maximize profit?

(b) For the case of one consumer, draw a diagram of this stock-market equilibrium.

(c) Assume that the firm has a technology determined by a concave production function $y_1 = f(y_0)$. Draw a diagram showing the equilibrium for this case.

4. *Reconsider the model of Question 3. Assume however that consumers' preferences are given by the function*

$$u(x_0, x_1) = \min\{x_0, x_1\}.$$

5. *Consider an economy with consumers who receive endowments that differ across two states in period 1. There are two financial assets with linearly independent return vectors that pay off in these two states. In this economy, the shares of a single firm are traded which produces cash flows in period 1.*

(a) Suppose that the firm's cash flows depend on the same uncertainties as the consumers' endowments. Show that markets are complete and that the firm's equity can be priced by arbitrage.

(b) If there were just one financial asset, would markets still be complete and could the firm's equity still be priced by arbitrage?

(c) Show that the Modigliani–Miller theorem holds whether there are one or two assets in the economy.

6. *Consider an economy with a single firm and several consumers. The firm is a mining company that owns a goldmine with unknown gold deposits. In a stock-market equilibrium, equity of this firm is traded in period 0, though extraction of the mine takes place in period 1. The original owners of the firm instruct the manager of the firm to sell a bond promising a fixed return in each state of period 1.*

(a) Write down the cash flows of the firm in period 0 and for an arbitrary state in period 1 before and after the bond issue.

(b) Can stockowners make a transaction in the financial asset, i.e. buy or sell the same bond, such that their state- and date-contingent income remains unchanged?

(c) Will your answer in (a) and (b) change if bonds are issued after equity has been traded?

7. *Consider a stock-market economy with one firm and suppose that consumers have to pay income tax in each state. The firm pays no taxes.*

(a) Assume that a tax is levied on net income after deduction of interest payments on debt. Show whether the Modigliani–Miller theorem holds in this case.

(b) How does your result under (a) change if tax is levied on income without an allowance for interest payments on debt?

PART II

ASYMMETRIC INFORMATION: CONTRACTS

6
...

DEBT CONTRACTS AND CREDIT RATIONING

In previous chapters, we maintained the assumptions that all decision-makers in an economy can specify, agree on, and eventually verify states of the world, and that decision-makers know each other's preferences and beliefs. Given these assumptions, anonymous trade of state-contingent contracts in competitive markets is conceptually feasible, as we have seen in Chapters 2 to 5. In this chapter, we abandon these simplifying assumptions.

First, we will drop the assumption that all decision-makers have complete and identical information about each other's characteristics. In the context of an insurance market, asymmetric information about some players' risk characteristics may lead to a breakdown of the market on account of adverse selection. We show how other institutional arrangements, e.g. specific forms of financial contracts, may help to overcome this problem.

Next, we investigate the implications of dropping the assumption that states can be verified without costs. In this case, a standard debt contract turns out to be an optimal arrangement between borrowers and lenders. In particular, because of costly state verification, lenders charge a fixed interest rate as long as the borrowers stay solvent and assume control of the business if they default.

Finally, we analyse the consequences of using standard debt contracts in an economy where the characteristics of loan applicants are unobservable. The default possibility inherent in a standard debt contract together with the adverse selection problem for loan applicants with differing riskiness may well make a lender ration credit for seemingly identical loan applicants.

6.1 Adverse Selection in Insurance Markets

As discussed in Chapter 3, trade in assets opens insurance possibilities for individuals. With asset markets, differences in state-contingent endowments, in attitudes towards risk and in beliefs, represented by subjective probability distributions over states, can be traded off to find a Pareto-optimal allocation. In particular, we found that, if there is no aggregate uncertainty and if traders have identical von Neumann–Morgenstern utility functions and identical beliefs, agents will completely insure each other and bear no risk at all. Similarly, with identical beliefs, a risk-neutral player will always insure a risk-averse individual completely.

Reconsider this latter case with the following modifications. A risk-neutral insurer faces applicants demanding insurance against a particular loss, say fire insurance for their homes. Assume that, after consideration of relevant observable characteristics, e.g. size and construction of the insured object, the insurer faces a class of applicants who are indistinguishable from one another. All potential customers face the same loss of wealth L if their homes burn down, but a group of them has a higher probability π_H of suffering a loss than the other, π_L. The loss probability of a customer represents private knowledge held by this agent and cannot be used to condition the insurance premium. The insurer's prior assessment of the likelihood of facing an applicant with high loss probability π_H is θ. For simplicity, assume that the proportion of customers with a high loss probability in this economy is also equal to θ.

Denote the situation where a customer suffers a loss as state 1 and assume that insurance can be bought at a price ρ. Notice that this is equivalent to trading state-contingent consumption contracts at the relative price $\rho/(1 - \rho)$. To see this, note that by buying insurance coverage d at a premium rate ρ, a customer secures the state-contingent consumption vector

$$x_1 = W - L + d - \rho \cdot d, \qquad x_2 = W - \rho \cdot d.$$

Similarly, the insurer obtains a state-contingent profit from an insurance policy (d,ρ) equal to

$$y_1 = - d + \rho \cdot d = W - L - x_1, \qquad y_2 = \rho \cdot d = W - x_2.$$

An insurance policy (d,ρ) corresponds therefore to state-contingent consumption vectors (x_1,x_2) for the customer and (y_1,y_2) for the insurance firm. When there is no insurance $d = 0$, $(x_1,x_2) = (W - L, W)$ and $(y_1,y_2) = 0$ follow.

Our diagrammatic exposition of the insurance problem employs a represent-ation in terms of state-contingent consumption.

6.1.1 Competitive market failure

We show now that, due to asymmetric information, either no market equilib-rium exists at all, or an equilibrium will have all high-risk customers insuring completely[1] and the low-risk customers buying insufficient insurance or no insurance at all.

Since the insurer cannot distinguish between the two types of customers, she must supply the same amount of insurance to each customer asking for insurance at the market premium ρ. Let π be the loss probability on which the insurer's supply decision is based. The quantity offered D can be derived from the insurer's optimization problem:

$\textit{Choose D to maximize}$ $\pi \cdot (\rho - 1) \cdot D + (1 - \pi) \cdot \rho \cdot D = (\rho - \pi) \cdot D.$

A risk-neutral insurer will supply any amount of coverage D if $\rho = \pi$ holds and $D = 0$ for $\rho < \pi$. For $\rho > \pi$, the problem has no solution. It follows that in any equilibrium where trade takes place, the price of insurance must equal the probability of a loss as assessed by the insurer, $\rho = \pi$. This decision problem can be represented in a simple diagram of state-contingent consumption.

Since $y_1 = (\rho - 1) \cdot D$ and $y_2 = \rho \cdot D$, it is clear that a free choice of insur-ance coverage D for given premium ρ corresponds to a restriction of contracts to those that satisfy

$$y_2 = \frac{(\rho - 1)}{\rho} \cdot y_1,$$

or equivalently, after substitution of $y_1 = W - L - x_1$ and $y_2 = W - x_2$,

$$x_2 = \frac{W - \rho \cdot L}{(1 - \rho)} - \frac{\rho}{(1 - \rho)} \cdot x_1.$$

Note that this represents a downward-sloping line with slope $-\rho / (1 - \rho)$ pass-ing through the endowment point $(W - L, W)$. Points on this line represent the different bundles of state-contingent consumption that the insurance com-pany is willing to offer at the given premium rate ρ. This line is represented in Figure 6.1 below.

The expected profit of the insurer, G, can also be expressed in terms of x_1 and x_2 as

$$G = \pi \cdot y_1 + (1 - \pi) \cdot y_2 = \pi \cdot (W - L - x_1) + (1 - \pi) \cdot (W - x_2).$$

[1] This is of course a particular instance of Akerloff's lemon market (Akerloff 1970).

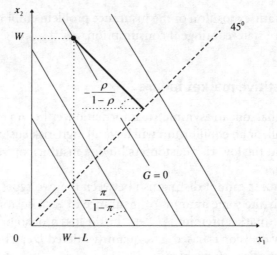

Fig. 6.1

For any given level of profit $\bar{G}$, the iso-expected-profit lines of the insurance company are then easily computed as

$$x_2 = \frac{W - \pi \cdot L - G}{(1 - \pi)} - \frac{\pi}{(1 - \pi)} \cdot x_1.$$

Note that all iso-expected-profit lines have the same slope $-\pi/(1-\pi)$ and that the zero-profit line passes through the endowment point $(W - L, W)$. Figure 6.1 contains a number of iso-expected-profit lines with a slope $\pi > \rho$. Higher-profit levels lie closer to the origin of the diagram, so obviously the firm would not want to provide insurance in this case.

This confirms our previous algebraic analysis of the profit-maximization problem for the insurer. It is left to the reader as an easy exercise to illustrate the firm's decision problem in the case where $\rho \geq \pi$.

Consider now the demand for insurance by a customer whose loss probability is π_t, where t is either H or L. This customer will

choose d_t to maximize $\quad \pi_t \cdot u(W - L + (1 - \rho) \cdot d_t) + (1 - \pi_t) \cdot u(W - \rho \cdot d_t).$

Equivalently, using $x_1 = W - L + d_t - \rho \cdot d_t$ and $x_2 = W - \rho \cdot d_t$ and, substituting for d, one can analyse this problem as follows:

Choose (x_1, x_2) to maximize $\quad \pi_t \cdot u(x_1) + (1 - \pi_t) \cdot u(x_2)$

subject to $\quad \rho \cdot x_1 + (1 - \rho) \cdot x_2 = W - \rho \cdot L.$

At full insurance, $d_t = L$, $(x_1 = x_2)$ the marginal rate of substitution equals $\pi_t/(1 - \pi_t)$. If customers are risk-averse, and $u(\cdot)$ is therefore concave, the marginal rate of substitution is falling along any indifference curve. Customers therefore want to insure completely, $d_t = L$, for any premium not exceeding their loss likelihood, $\rho \leq \pi_t$.

Figure 6.2 illustrates the optimal insurance decisions of the two types of customers for different insurance premiums. Indifference curves of customers with high loss probability π_H are indicated by broken lines, while those of low-risk customers are drawn as solid lines. As the figure illustrates, indifference curves of high-risk consumers will always be steeper than those of low-risk consumers.

In equilibrium, the beliefs of all market participants must be consistent. If both groups of customers demand the same amount of insurance, the insurer will face an average loss probability of $\pi = \theta \cdot \pi_H + (1 - \theta) \cdot \pi_L$ per unit of insurance sold. In this case, the equilibrium premium ρ^* for a unit of insurance must equal the probability of a loss as expected by the insurer, $\rho^* = \pi$. Hence,

$$\pi_H > \rho^* = \theta \cdot \pi_H + (1 - \theta) \cdot \pi_L > \pi_L.$$

At such a premium, however, all consumers with a loss probability π_H will completely insure while consumers with π_L will want to insure only partially or not at all (see Figure 6.2). The insurer would suffer a loss from the high-risk consumers that may or may not be compensated by the expected gain from the low-risk consumers.

The only equilibrium that is possible in this economy with asymmetric information has customers with a low loss probability π_L demanding incomplete

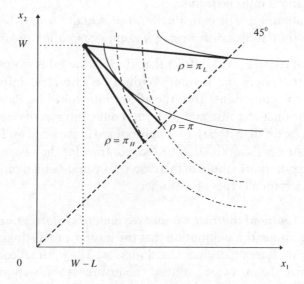

Fig. 6.2

or no insurance at an equilibrium price ρ^* between π and π_H. In contrast, customers with a high loss probability will insure completely. Hence, due to adverse selection, there are too few good risks in the insurance market. In particular, there is no equilibrium where both types of consumer demand the same amount of insurance. Anonymity breaks down and consumers reveal their types by demanding differing levels of insurance.

With asymmetric information about agents' characteristics, market equilibria exhibit the undesirable property that too many assets of the lowest quality will be traded. To overcome this problem, financial contracts can no longer offer free choice of quantity at a given price. To induce self-selection of customers with different characteristics, an insurer can offer price–quantity pairs that induce customers to reveal their true characteristics. With contracts that induce customers to reveal their true risk, however, it will no longer be possible to achieve a Pareto optimum, and to co-ordinate decisions of traders by simply adjusting the market price.

6.1.2 An optimal insurance contract

In order to derive an optimal contract under asymmetric information, the following approach is adopted:

 (i) *the insurer maximizes her objective function* subject to the following constraints:
 (ii) allocations must be *feasible,*
 (iii) allocations must be *individually rational,* and
 (iv) allocations must satisfy a set of *incentive-compatibility conditions.*

An optimal contract is a contract that gives all the gains from trade to one trading partner, here the insurer. Without asymmetric information, as reflected in the constraints (iv), the allocation would be Pareto optimal. Individual rationality, constraint (iii), rules out contracts that would make a customer worse off than if she had simply refused to participate. The following example illustrates the optimal insurance contract for the case where there is no asymmetry of information. In this case, the insurance firm can design individual contracts for all types of customers.

Example 6.1 (*optimal contract without asymmetric information*). Consider this economy under the assumption that the insurer can distinguish amongst customers with differing degrees of riskiness π_t. The optimal contract would then maximize the expected profit of the insurer from each group of customers separately. Since there is no asymmetry of information, only feasibility and individual rationality constraints need be observed (i.e. constraints (ii) and (iii)). Figure 6.3 shows such an optimal contract. Recall that iso-expected profit lines correspond to increasingly higher levels of profit as they lie closer to the origin. Furthermore, expected profits are positive for iso-expected-profit lines to the left of the one passing through the endowment point $(W–L,W)$.

Individual rationality (constraint (iii)) rules out allocations below the indifference curve passing through the endowment point. Feasibility (constraint (ii)) cannot be seen directly in the figure. It is satisfied if either (i) the proportion of customers in this risk class who suffer a loss is sufficiently small compared to the lucky ones or (ii) if the insurer can provide sufficient funds to support this insurance contract. It is, however, optimal for the insurer to provide full insurance at a premium that extracts all consumers' surplus from the customers (at A in Figure 6.3). ∎

To take into account restrictions deriving from asymmetries of information, one has to impose further constraints. To be incentive-compatible *the allocations under an optimal contract must not provide incentives for any agent to misrepresent her private information.* These *incentive,* or *truth-telling, constraints* exclude contracts that would allow individuals to secure a better allocation by falsely claiming to have the unobservable characteristics of other individuals. Contracts have to be such that individuals self-select, preferring the contract that was designed for them.

One may wonder whether the incentive constraints (iv) impose unreasonably strong restrictions on the form of the optimal contract. A famous result,

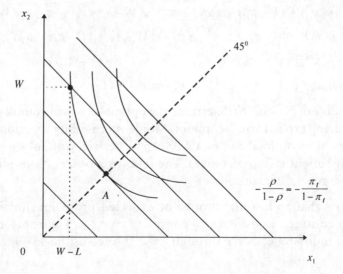

Fig. 6.3

the *revelation principle*, ensures that any incentive-compatible allocation which can be achieved under any type of contract, no matter how complicated, can also be obtained through a truth-telling contract.[2] Thus restricting choice to truth-telling contracts does not restrict the set of incentive-compatible allocations.

Returning to our insurance example, suppose that the insurer offers two contracts consisting of a premium ρ and an insurance level d. As argued above, this is equivalent to proposing a particular allocation (x_1, x_2) of state-contingent consumption. The idea is to choose these contracts (ρ, d) such that only the group of customers for whom the contract is written have an incentive to ask for it. Denote by (ρ_H, d_H) and (ρ_L, d_L), or alternatively (x_1^H, x_2^H) and (x_1^L, x_2^L), the contracts designed for the customers with high- and low-loss probabilities, respectively.

We assume that the insurer maximizes expected profit by offering such contract pairs subject to the constraint that no customer has an incentive to claim any other contract apart from the one designed for her. Furthermore, the contracts must be individually rational. The optimal contract pair must therefore solve the following optimization problem:

Choose (x_1^H, x_2^H) and (x_1^L, x_2^L) to maximize

$$\theta \cdot [\pi_H \cdot (W - L - x_1^H) + (1 - \pi_H) \cdot (W - x_2^H)] + (1 - \theta) \cdot [\pi_L \cdot (W - L - x_1^L)$$
$$+ (1 - \pi_L) \cdot (W - x_2^L)]$$

subject to

$$\pi_H \cdot u(x_1^H) + (1 - \pi_H) \cdot u(x_2^H) \geq \pi_H \cdot u(W - L) + (1 - \pi_H) \cdot u(W), \quad (IR_H)$$

$$\pi_L \cdot u(x_1^L) + (1 - \pi_L) \cdot u(x_2^L) \geq \pi_L \cdot u(W - L) + (1 - \pi_L) \cdot u(W), \quad (IR_L)$$

$$\pi_H \cdot u(x_1^H) + (1 - \pi_H) \cdot u(x_2^H) \geq \pi_H \cdot u(x_1^L) + (1 - \pi_H) \cdot u(x_2^L), \quad (IC_H)$$

$$\pi_L \cdot u(x_1^L) + (1 - \pi_L) \cdot u(x_2^L) \geq \pi_L \cdot u(x_1^H) + (1 - \pi_L) \cdot u(x_2^H). \quad (IC_L)$$

Though it is not possible to determine the optimal contract completely without specifying explicit von Neumann–Morgenstern utility functions, several properties of an optimal contract pair can be derived without such detailed knowledge about risk-preferences. The following observations allow us to draw these general conclusions.

1. Notice that each contract must be expected-profit-maximizing given the other contract. Considering a contract (x_1^A, x_2^A) in Figure 6.4, contracts along the indifference curve through (x_1^A, x_2^A) towards the 45°-line increase

2 For a brief exposition of the *revelation principle* and for further references see e.g. Laffont (1987).

the expected profit of the insurer, because the consumer's marginal rate of substitution is higher than that of the insurer, reaching equality on the 45°-line.[3] Furthermore, full-insurance contracts are more profitable the closer they lie to the origin. This is illustrated in Figure 6.4.

2. For a given insurance contract (x_1^H, x_2^H), incentive compatibility IC_L requires the contract for the low-risk customers, (x_1^L, x_2^L), to lie on or above the indifference curve of the low-risk customer through (x_1^H, x_2^H). This is illustrated in Figure 6.5. Analogously, for a given insurance contract (x_1^L, x_2^L), the incentive constraint IC_H requires contracts for the high-risk customers to lie on or above the indifference curve of high-risk customer through (x_1^L, x_2^L). The insurance contract pair in Figure 6.5 satisfies both incentive constraints.

3. Suppose that neither of the incentive constraints, IC_H and IC_L, is binding for an incentive-compatible insurance contract pair as in Figure 6.5. Keeping the insurance contract (x_1^L, x_2^L) of the low-risk customer fixed, the insurer can raise expected profit from the high-risk contract by choosing a contract where the 45°-line intersects the indifference curve of the high-risk consumer through (x_1^L, x_2^L). Figure 6.6 shows the range of contracts for the high-risk customer that are incentive-compatible given (x_1^L, x_2^L) and that improve the expected profit from the high-risk customer contract as compared with (x_1^H, x_2^H).

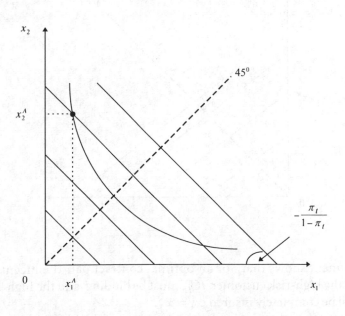

Fig. 6.4

---

[3] This argument also shows that overinsurance $(x_2 < x_1)$ cannot be in the interests of the insurer.

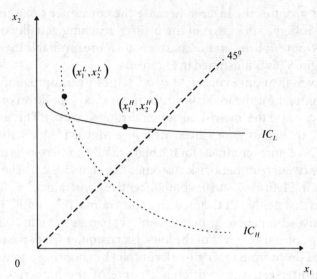

Fig. 6.5

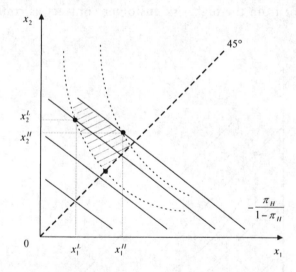

Fig. 6.6

This argument shows that, for an optimal contract pair the incentive constraint of the high-risk customer, IC_H, must be binding, and the high-risk customer will be completely insured, $x_1^H = x_2^H$.

4. Suppose now that the incentive constraint of the high-risk customer is binding and that this customer is fully insured. The shaded area in Figure 6.7 indicates all contracts for the low-risk consumer that yield a higher expected

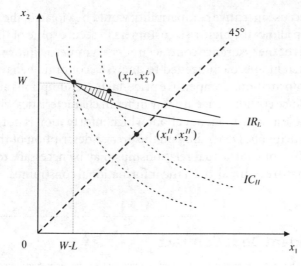

Fig. 6.7

profit for the insurer and that are individually rational for the low-risk customer.

By choosing a contract on the individual rationality constraint IR_L, the insurer can increase expected profit from the low-risk customer. Though this may violate the incentive-compatibility constraint of the high-risk customer for the given contract (x_1^H, x_2^H), lowering this contract while maintaining full insurance to maintain incentive-compatibility will increase the expected profit from this contract as well. One can therefore conclude that, for an optimal contract pair, the individual rationality constraint of the low-risk customer, IR_L, must be binding.

As indicated before, without explicit specification of the von Neumann–Morgenstern utility functions it is impossible to characterize the optimal contract pair completely. However, knowing that both customers are risk-averse and that their preferences satisfy the expected utility hypothesis is sufficient to deduce that an expected-profit-maximizing insurer will offer a contract pair such that

- the low-risk consumer obtains no surplus out of this contract and is incompletely insured, while
- the high-risk consumer will be fully insured and, in general, extract some surplus from the insurer.

At this stage, it is worth recalling that without asymmetry of information each customer would be fully insured and no surplus would go to any customer. Apart from preventing the insurer from offering full-insurance contracts to all customers, because incentive compatibility would be violated, the asymmetry in information allows the high-risk customers to secure some of the surplus.

The analysis of the insurance contract under asymmetric information illustrates the different approach needed to analyse economic behaviour under asymmetric information. Competitive price-taking assumptions are no longer appropriate, since economic agents may differ in characteristics which are important for trade among them but about which information is not available to all market participants. Depending on the precise description of the information flows, different contractual relationships may be necessary to guarantee institutions that are optimal given the informational constraints.

6.2 A Standard Debt Contract

The previous section illustrates how asymmetric information may lead to a breakdown of competitive markets on account of adverse selection. The impossibility of knowing *ex ante* the riskiness of customers forced the insurer to offer only contracts which forced customers to reveal their private information. These incentive constraints proved to be costly for the insurer. One may be tempted to presume that this problem arises because of the impossibility of knowing the personal characteristics of trading partners. This section shows that asymmetries of information determine contractual arrangements even if the required information can be gathered. In addition, as we shall see, this is the case whether or not the decision-makers involved are risk-neutral or risk-averse.

Consider the following environment for a credit relationship. There are risk-neutral entrepreneurs who have investment projects with uncertain returns but who need capital to finance the necessary input purchases. On the other hand, there are risk-neutral potential lenders with funds available who are willing to make loans to the entrepreneurs provided their opportunity costs are met.

The asymmetry of information concerns the output that the investment projects actually reap. Entrepreneurs and lenders share beliefs about the likelihood of the possible outcomes from investment. However, because the entrepreneurs run the business, they know the realized outcome while lenders do not. They can of course gather the necessary information about the actual result, perhaps by ordering an audit of the entrepreneur's business, but this is costly. The question therefore arises as to how knowledge of the impending asymmetry of information influences the contract at the time the loan is made.

Suppose that entrepreneurs have investment projects which require one unit of capital and produce a state-dependent return $f(s)$, $s \in S$. Without loss of generality, assume that states are ordered such that higher states imply higher output, i.e. $f(s)$ is a monotonically increasing function.

Ex ante, all parties share the same information about the project, i.e. the probability distribution of states is common knowledge. The set of states is finite and $p(s)$ denotes the probability of state s occurring. It will be useful to denote the probability of an event E as $P(E) \equiv \sum_{s \in E} p(s)$.

Lenders have funds which they can invest in entrepreneurs' projects. They face an opportunity cost of $I \equiv (1 + i)$ per unit of capital. Individual rationality requires that the expected return from a loan contract be at least equal to I. Lenders cannot monitor states (or equivalently output) without costs. Monitoring costs are expenses, like legal fees, fees for auditing etc., which are paid to third parties, i.e. which go neither to the borrower nor to the lender. For simplicity, assume that monitoring a state requires a fixed cost of γ.

A contract (β, ρ) is a pair of functions such that

- $\rho(s)$ determines the state-dependent pay-off which the lender receives, and
- $\beta(s) \in \{0,1\}$ specifies the states where monitoring takes place, with $\beta(s) = 1$ indicating states that are monitored according to the contract and $\beta(s) = 0$ indicating those not monitored.

It will be useful to denote the set of states where no monitoring takes place by $S_0(\beta) := \{s \in S \mid \beta(s) = 0\}$. Similarly, the set of states which are monitored will be written as $S_1(\beta) := \{s \in S \mid \beta(s) = 1\}$. Clearly, $S = S_1(\beta) + S_0(\beta)$ for any function β.

We assume that entrepreneurs have no capital of their own, so that their entire capital requirement must be raised from lenders and that, besides what they earn from the project, they have no funds available to repay loans; hence

$$0 \leq \rho(s) \leq f(s) - \gamma \cdot \beta(s).$$

Since lenders cannot observe the state of the entrepreneur's affairs directly, they have either to rely on the entrepreneur's report or they have to incur the costs necessary for auditing the entrepreneur. Hence, once the state is revealed to the entrepreneur but not to the lender, the entrepreneur has to declare that state $\hat{s}$ has occurred. Whether the entrepreneur's declaration is credible or not depends on the specified repayment $\rho(s)$, and can be determined at the time the contract is written. Hence, the contract requires monitoring in those states where an incentive exists to misrepresent the true state.

If a declared state $\hat{s}$ is designated to be monitored, then monitoring takes place and any false declaration will be detected. One can assume, therefore, that reports of states that are monitored will be correct. If the announced state is not designated as observed, no monitoring occurs and misrepresentation of the true state may be in the interests of the debtor. *Incentive-compatibility* obtains if repayments $\rho(s)$ in unmonitored states, i.e. $s \in S_0(\beta)$, do not provide incentives for the entrepreneur to make false reports. Hence, we require the contract (β, ρ) to be such that, in each state $s \in S$, the net profit of the entrepreneur from a correct report is at least as good as that from a false report:

$$f(s) - \rho(s) \geq f(s) - \rho(\hat{s}) \quad \text{for all } \hat{s} \in S_0(\beta) \quad \text{and all } s \in S \qquad \text{(IC)}.$$

The following lemma is an immediate consequence of the requirement that contracts be incentive compatible.

LEMMA 6.1. A contract (β, ρ) *is incentive-compatible* if and only if the repayment schedule $\rho(\cdot)$ is constant on $S_0(\beta)$:

$$\rho(s) = R \qquad \text{for all } s \in S_0(\beta),$$

$$R \geq \rho(s) \qquad \text{for all } s \in S_1(\beta).$$

PROOF. Suppose there are $s, s' \in S_0(\beta)$ such that $\rho(s) > \rho(s')$ and suppose that the entrepreneur observes state s. Then the entrepreneur will have an incentive to announce the state s', since $f(s) - \rho(s') > f(s) - \rho(s)$. If there is $s \in S$ such that $\rho(s) > R$, then the entrepreneur will have an incentive to announce an unobserved state in $S_0(\beta)$. ∎

Lemma 6.1 demonstrates an important feature of an incentive-compatible contract: repayments of a loan have to be state-independent, i.e. constant across states, or monitoring costs must be borne. Because auditing is costly, loan contracts do not usually specify state-contingent payments. So why then does monitoring occur at all?

If the opportunity cost of funds I were smaller than the worst outcome of the investment project, $I \leq \min\{f(s) \mid s \in S\}$, then no auditing would occur in an optimal contract, $\beta^*(s) = 0$ for all $s \in S$. The repayment would be equal to the opportunity cost in any state, $\rho^*(s) = I$, and a first-best allocation between entrepreneurs and lenders could be obtained. No monitoring is necessary and no surplus is left to an outside party. On the other hand, if there are states where the return on the investment project falls short of the opportunity costs of funds, $I > \min\{f(s) \mid s \in S\}$, a first-best contract is no longer feasible. To achieve an expected return from a loan contract that would cover the opportunity cost of funds, repayment in at least some states has to be higher than I. Hence, a constant repayment, which is a necessary condition for no monitoring in an incentive-compatible loan contract, is not feasible in every state and monitoring has to take place in some states.

To further characterize the optimal loan contract in this environment, we need to consider the expected returns of entrepreneurs and lenders from an incentive-compatible contract. Recalling the notation $P(E) \equiv \sum_{s \in E} p(s)$, an entrepreneur's return from a contract (β, ρ) can be written as

$$\pi(\beta, \rho) := \sum_{s \in S} p(s) \cdot [f(s) - \rho(s)]$$
$$= E_p f - \sum_{s \in S_1(\beta)} p(s) \cdot \rho(s) - R \cdot P(S_0(\beta)),$$

where $E_p f$ denotes the expected value of the return f. Similarly, a lender's return can be computed as

$$\sigma(\beta, \rho) := \sum_{s \in S} p(s) \cdot [\beta(s) \cdot (\rho(s) - \gamma) + (1 - \beta(s)) \cdot \rho(s)]$$
$$= \sum_{s \in S_0(\beta)} p(s) \cdot \rho(s) + R \cdot P(S_0(\beta)) - \gamma \cdot P(S_1(\beta)).$$

Notice that every contract (β, ρ) shares the expected value of the investment project minus the payment for monitoring between the entrepreneur and the lender:

$$\pi(\beta, \rho) + \sigma(\beta, \rho) = E_p f - \gamma \cdot P(S_1(\beta)).$$

Saving on monitoring costs is therefore in the best interests of both parties.

An optimal incentive-compatible loan contract (β, ρ) maximizes $\pi(\beta, \rho)$ subject to the following constraints:

$$\sigma(\beta, \rho) \geq I, \tag{IR}$$

$$f(s) - \gamma \geq \rho(s) \geq 0 \quad \text{for all } s \in S_1(\beta),$$

$$f(s) \geq R \geq 0 \quad \text{for all } s \in S_0(\beta). \tag{F}$$

Besides the individual rationality constraint (IR), feasibility constraints (F) have to be observed. Notice that the incentive-compatibility constraint,

$$f(s) - \rho(s) \geq f(s) - \rho(\hat{s}) \quad \text{for all } \hat{s} \in S_0(\beta) \text{ and all } s \in S, \tag{IC}$$

is already included through the characteristics of an incentive-compatible contract derived in Lemma 6.1.

It is easy to see that the incentive-compatibility constraint (IR) must be binding. Otherwise, one could lower R, the return on the loan in states that are not monitored, without affecting the remainder of the contract. This would increase the profit of the entrepreneur. Given $\sigma(\beta, \rho) = I$, one easily obtains

$$\pi(\beta, \rho) = E_p f - I - \gamma \cdot P(S_1(\beta))$$

for the objective function of the entrepreneur. The optimization problem for the optimal loan contract can now be rewritten as follows:

Choose (β,ρ) to maximize $E_p f - I - \gamma \cdot P(S_1(\beta))$ subject to

$$\sum_{s \in S_1(\beta)} p(s) \cdot \rho(s) + R \cdot P(S_0(\beta)) - \gamma \cdot P(S_1(\beta)) - I = 0,$$

$$\beta(s) \cdot [f(s) - \gamma - \rho(s)] + [1 - \beta(s)] \cdot [f(s) - R] \geq 0 \quad \text{for all } s \in S.$$

In this formulation, it is obvious that the optimal contract must minimize monitoring costs. The fact that an optimal contract must minimize monitoring costs and then distribute the remaining returns from the investment project such that the individual rationality constraint of the lender is satisfied, provides a further characterization of the optimal loan contract.

LEMMA 6.2. An optimal loan contract has the following form:

$$\rho(s) = \begin{cases} R & \text{for } s \in S_0(\beta) \\ f(s) - \gamma & \text{for } s \in S_1(\beta) \end{cases}, \beta(s) = \begin{cases} 0 & \text{for } f(s) \geq R. \\ 1 & \text{for } f(s) < R \end{cases}$$

PROOF. The following two claims need to be checked in order to establish the lemma: (i) monitoring where the non-monitored payment is still feasible, $\beta(s) = 1$ if $f(s) \geq R$, is not optimal, and (ii) to ask for less than the maximum when monitoring occurs, $\rho(s) < f(s) - \gamma$ for $s \in S_1(\beta)$, is not optimal.

Claim (i): Suppose (β,ρ) is an optimal contract and there is a state $\bar{s} \in S_1(\beta)$ such that $f(\bar{s}) \geq R$. Then it is feasible to give up monitoring state $\bar{s}$ and to ask for a repayment of R in this state. The individual rationality constraint is now satisfied with a strict inequality,

$$I = \sigma(\beta,\rho) = \sum_{s \in S_1(\beta)} p(s) \cdot \rho(s) + R \cdot P(S_0(\beta)) - \gamma \cdot P(S_1(\beta))$$

$$< \sum_{s \in S_1(\beta)} p(s) \cdot \rho(s) + R \cdot P(S_0(\beta)) - \gamma \cdot P(S_1(\beta)) + [R - \rho(\bar{s}) + \gamma] \cdot p(\bar{s}),$$

since $R \geq \rho(\bar{s})$ from incentive-compatibility (Lemma 6.1). By not monitoring state $\bar{s}$, one can lower the cost of monitoring without violating any other constraint. It is now possible to reduce the repayment of the entrepreneur R until the individual rationality constraint binds again. This increases the expected profit of the entrepreneur, contradicting the assumed optimality of the contract (β,ρ). Hence, for an optimal contract, $f(s) < R$ for all $s \in S_1(\beta)$.

Claim (ii): Now suppose there is $\hat{s} \in S_1(\beta)$ such that $\rho(\hat{s}) < f(\hat{s}) - \gamma$ for an optimal contract (β,ρ). Consider another repayment schedule $\tilde{\rho}(s)$ which is equal to $\rho(s)$ for all $s \neq \hat{s}$ and satisfies $\tilde{\rho}(\hat{s}) = f(\hat{s}) - \gamma$. The contract $(\beta,\tilde{\rho})$ satisfies the individual rationality constraint with strict inequality:

$$I = \sigma(\beta,\rho) < \sum_{s \in S_1(\beta)} p(s) \cdot \rho(s) + [\tilde{\rho}(\hat{s}) - \rho(\hat{s})] \cdot p(\hat{s}) + R \cdot P(S_0(\beta)) - \gamma \cdot P(S_1(\beta)).$$

Hence, one can lower R, the payment in the states that are not monitored, to some R' such that the individual rationality constraint binds again. If $R' \leq f(s)$ for some $s \in S_1(\beta)$, then this state no longer needs to be monitored, saving γ and increasing the expected profit of the entrepreneur. Otherwise, the entrepreneur and the lender will be indifferent to such a change. An optimal contract therefore requires $\rho(s) = f(s) - \gamma$ for all $s \in S_1(\beta)$. ∎

Lemma 6.2 states two further properties of an optimal contract: it does not pay an entrepreneur to specify monitoring in states where this is not necessary, and to monitor more states than is necessary given the IR constraint. The following example illustrates the optimal contract structure.

Example 6.2. Figure 6.8 shows the typical structure of an optimal loan contract. Notice that a continuous state space is used to provide a clear figure.

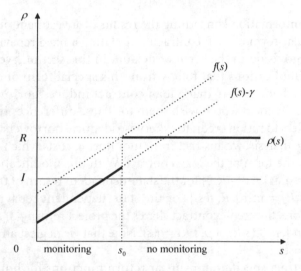

Fig. 6.8 ∎

The properties of incentive-compatible loan contracts which we derived in Lemmas 6.1 and 6.2 typically apply to debt contracts in the real world. In spite of the fact that both borrowers and lenders often know that a borrower's capacity to repay a loan depends on circumstances beyond the control of the borrower, loan contracts are very rarely contingent on outcomes. Most contracts feature a fixed repayment, even though both parties may know that there are situations in which the borrower will be unable to meet her obligations. If the latter occurs, the borrower is declared bankrupt and lenders take over to audit the failed business and recover as much as possible. These are exactly the features one finds in an optimal incentive-compatible contract:

- a fixed repayment R and no monitoring as long as this payment is made,
- if the borrower does not fulfil her repayment obligations, auditors come to the fore and lenders take control of the remaining assets.

Because of monitoring costs, it is optimal to specify a constant repayment, even if it is known in advance that there are states where the project will fail to produce enough returns to keep this promise. In this view, bankruptcy is not a 'misjudgement' of the borrower or lender or an inadequacy of contracting but a natural consequence of an asymmetry of information about a project's actual return.

6.3 Credit Rationing

Asymmetric information concerning the results of investment projects leads to the particular form of loan contracts stipulating a fixed repayment with a bankruptcy provision in the event of default. In this section, we investigate some of the implications that follow from this special form of contract. In particular, we demonstrate that a loan contract induces borrowers to take more risk than lenders would wish them to. These differences in incentives may lead lenders to ration credit to otherwise identical borrowers.

To simplify analysis, we abstract from monitoring costs which were necessary to justify the form of the loan contract. With this modification, one can write $\pi(s,R) = \max\{ f(s) - R, 0\}$ for the state-dependent return of the entrepreneur and $\rho(s,R) = \min\{ R, f(s)\}$ for the state-dependent repayment of the lender. As before, the credit contract shares the project return $f(s)$ among borrowers and lenders: $\pi(s,R) + \rho(s,R) = f(s)$. Note that we neglect any loss due to monitoring costs.

A loan contract specifies non-linear return functions for borrowers and lenders. Figure 6.9 shows graphs of the return functions for the borrower and the lender. Notice that a continuous set of states has been used to achieve a clearer diagrammatic exposition. A lender's return schedule is a concave function, for a lender participates with a constant amount R if no bankruptcy occurs. A lender is therefore particularly concerned about the lower end of the distribution. On the other hand, a borrower has a convex return schedule. In particular, once bankruptcy occurs, a borrower is no longer interested in the degree of bankruptcy. This creates a conflict of interest between borrowers and lenders in regard to the choice of contract. This conflict is demonstrated in Figure 6.10 where the entrepreneur can choose one of two projects, f_A and f_B.

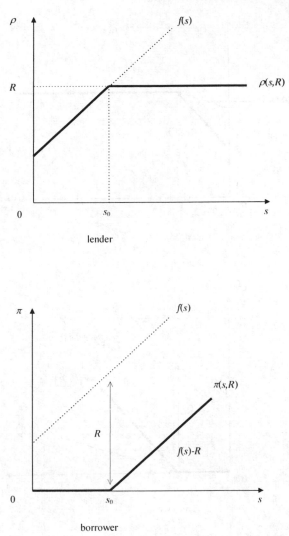

Fig. 6.9

Clearly, the entrepreneur as borrower prefers project f_A because it yields a higher return in every state. The lender however, prefers project f_B, since it yields a higher return in the case of bankruptcy. Though the two projects used to illustrate the problem in Figure 6.10 are extreme cases where a change from project A to B will lead to return schedules that can be ordered by first-order stochastic dominance, it is not difficult to see that, for any projects that are mean-preserving spreads, the borrower will always prefer the more risky and the lender the more secure project.

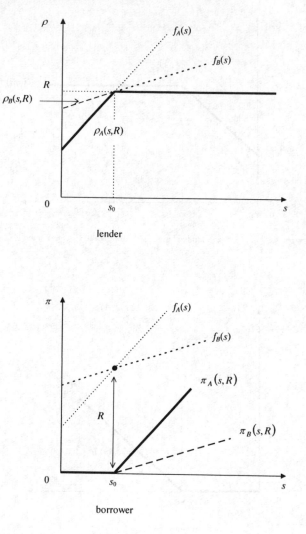

Fig. 6.10

This conflict of interest, arising from the nature of the loan contract, makes credit markets different from other markets for goods and services. In combination with other informational problems, it can explain phenomena such as *credit rationing*. Credit rationing has been advanced as a cause of the limited adjustment consumers make to shocks affecting their lifetime incomes but it was difficult to explain why lenders would react to the excess demand for loans by rationing demand rather than by raising interest rates.

Stiglitz and Weiss (1981) suggested a reason why lenders might not find it in their interests to raise interest rates in order to reduce excess loan demand. If lenders cannot observe the riskiness of a loan applicant's project, they may refrain from using the price mechanism (i.e. raising the interest rate) since this may lead to an adverse selection in respect to the project's degree of riskiness. The following model illustrates this problem.

Consider a bank, the lender, facing a group of N loan applicants. Each loan applicant needs one unit of capital to finance a project but has no funds of her own available. For simplicity, assume that there are just two types of applicants who are distinguished by their projects' degrees of riskiness. There are only two states, a high-return state and a low-return state, denoted by H and L, respectively. For simplicity, assume that the probability of each state equals 0.5. Let (x_H^t, x_L^t) be the state-contingent returns of an applicant of type t, $t = 1,2$. Assume further that the distribution of the project returns of type-2 applicants forms a mean-preserving spread of the return distribution of type-1 applicants, i.e.

$$x_L^2 < x_L^1 < x_H^1 < x_H^2$$

and

$$\mu^1 \equiv 0.5 \cdot (x_L^1 + x_H^1) = 0.5 \cdot (x_L^2 + x_H^2) \equiv \mu^2.$$

Finally, assume that it is common knowledge that half of the applicants are of type 2, but that the bank cannot distinguish applicants according to their type. The bank can raise funds from deposits at a deposit interest rate $I \equiv (1 + i)$ according to a linear supply schedule:

$$L(I) = \alpha \cdot I, \quad \alpha > 0.$$

Competition among banks forces a bank's expected profit to equal zero, i.e. $E\rho(\cdot, R) = I$. We assume further that, in the case of bankruptcy, the bank can seize some value C from the bankrupt customer which is independent of the project's success or failure. The value C may derive from some asset which the customer posts as collateral or from bankruptcy laws allowing a creditor recourse to the bankrupt debtor's private assets.

With these assumptions, one obtains the following expected return schedule for a loan applicant of type t, $t = 1,2$, as a function of the contracted interest rate R:

$$
\begin{aligned}
E\pi^t(s,R,C) &= E\max\{x_s^t - R, -C\} \\
&= \begin{cases}
0.5 \cdot [x_H^t + x_L^t] - R & \text{for} \quad x_L^t + C \geq R \\
0.5 \cdot [x_H^t - R - C] & \text{for} \quad x_H^t + C \geq R > x_L^t + C \\
-C & \text{for} \quad R > x_H^t + C.
\end{cases}
\end{aligned}
$$

A loan applicant will apply for a loan if the contracted interest rate R is such that the expected profit is non-negative. Let $\hat{R}^t$ be the interest rate for which the expected profit equals zero: $E\pi^t(s, \hat{R}^t, C) = 0$. As Figure 6.11 shows, the expected

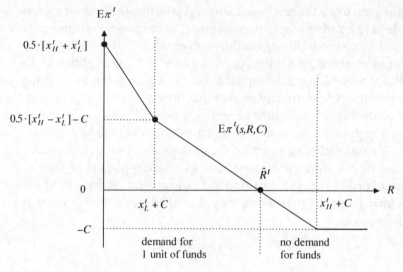

Fig. 6.11

return for this customer is positive for all $R \le \hat{R}^t$ and negative otherwise. Hence, a customer of type t will apply for one unit of funds if $R \le \hat{R}^t$. Otherwise her demand will be zero.

A straightforward calculation yields $\hat{R}^t = x_H^t - C$ as the critical value for market exit of a customer of type t. Clearly, applicants with the riskier project will have a higher critical interest rate: $\hat{R}^2 > \hat{R}^1$. High-risk customers therefore stay in the market much longer than low-risk customers.

Similarly, one can derive the expected return to the bank of a loan to an applicant of type t, $t = 1, 2$:

$$
E\rho^t(s, R, C) = E\min\{R, x_s^t + C\}
$$

$$
= \begin{cases} R & \text{for} \quad x_L^t + C \ge R \\ 0.5 \cdot [x_L^t + C + R] & \text{for} \quad x_H^t + C \ge R > x_L^t + C \\ 0.5 \cdot [x_H^t + x_L^t] + C & \text{for} \qquad R > x_H^t + C. \end{cases}
$$

Figure 6.12 displays the expected return to the bank from a loan applicant of type t.

Given our assumption that the bank cannot distinguish its customers, one obtains the expected return from a loan as the weighted average of the expected return from the two types of customers so long as both types of customers stay in the market. Figure 6.13 shows the expected return from a loan taking into account the bank's ignorance about the type of customer it faces.

The bank's expected return function is obviously not monotonic in the loan interest rate R. While it is clearly increasing as long as both types of customer

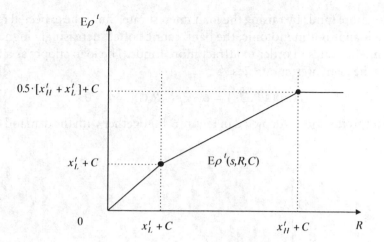

Fig. 6.12

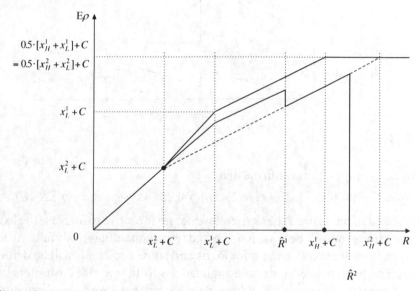

Fig. 6.13

remain in the market, it drops as soon as the low-risk applicants leave the market. It then rises again until the high-risk customers exit too. In such a situation it is clear that banks will not simply raise interest rates when they face an excess demand for loans. The reason is that higher interest rates may not decrease demand but, in addition, may change the mix of applicants in a manner detrimental to the bank.

Given our assumption that competition forces the expected return from a loan to equal its opportunity cost, $E\rho(s,R,C) = I$, the bank may not even be able to raise more funds by raising the loan interest rate. Since the expected return from a loan is not monotonic, the bank cannot offer increasingly higher deposit interest rates in order to attract more funds. The loan supply as a function of the loan interest rate R is

$$L(E\rho(s,R,C)) = \alpha \cdot E\rho(s,R,C), \quad \alpha > 0.$$

This supply function is depicted in Figure 6.14 together with the demand function.

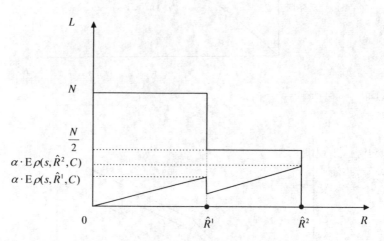

Fig. 6.14

An easy computation confirms that

$$E\rho(s,\hat{R}^1,C) = 0.25 \cdot [x_L^1 + x_L^2 + 2 \cdot x_H^1] > 0.25 \cdot [x_L^2 + x_H^2] = E\rho(s,\hat{R}^2,C),$$

as indicated in the figure. A bank therefore has no incentive to increase the loan interest rate beyond $\hat{R}^1$ because its expected return unambiguously falls. At $\hat{R}^1$, however, there is excess demand for loans and some applicants will be denied a loan. The bank may even decline applications from low-risk customers because it cannot influence demand by changing price without simultaneously changing the mix of applicants to its disadvantage.

Notes on the Literature

The failure of competitive markets on account of asymmetries of information was first analysed by Akerloff (1970). Rothschild and Stiglitz (1976) studied optimal insurance contracts with asymmetric information. The importance of monitoring costs for the contract structure was discovered by Townsend (1979) and applied to credit markets in Gale and Hellwig (1985).

There is an extensive literature on credit rationing. Clemenz (1986) contains a good introduction to this literature. The model discussed in Section 6.3 is drawn from Stiglitz and Weiss (1981).

The contracts discussed in this chapter were selected for their importance in financial economics. It should be clear, however, that there is a large literature on contracts under asymmetric information which we have not covered here. Of particular interest for financial economics is the theory on *incomplete contracts*. Hart (1995) explained the financial structure of the firm by the impossibility of writing complete contracts that specify all possible contractual contingencies. By allocating the control rights of ownership in default states to the debt holders and in all other states to the equity holders, it is still possible to provide incentives for the firm's managers.

....

Exercises

....

1. *Suppose that all consumers of a community own cars valued at $10,000. Each of them may lose the car in an accident. Risk-preferences of these consumers can be described by a von Neumann–Morgenstern utility index $u(W) := \sqrt{W}$, where W denotes the consumers' wealth.*

Suppose that consumers differ in their likelihood of suffering an accident: 80 per cent of consumers have a 10 per cent loss probability, while the remaining consumers are twice as likely to suffer a loss.

(a) A risk-neutral insurance company which cannot distinguish the consumers offers full loss insurance for $1,000. Determine whether both types of consumers will buy such a contract and determine the expected profit of the insurance company.

(b) Suppose that competitive pressure forces the insurance company to raise the premium if it makes an expected loss and to lower it if it makes an expected profit. Show that there is no premium at which the insurance company can offer full insurance and make an expected profit of zero.

(c) What could the insurer do to overcome the adverse selection problem in this economy?

2. *Reconsider the scenario of Exercise 1.*
(a) Draw a diagram showing the indifference curves of the two types of consumers over state-contingent wealth.

195

(b) Show in a diagram the state-contingent wealth combinations that can be achieved by contracts offering full insurance and varying only the insurance premium.

(c) Show in a diagram the state-contingent wealth combinations that are individually rational for both players.

(d) Show in a diagram two state-contingent wealth combinations that are *incentive-compatible* and two that are not *incentive-compatible*.

3. *Consider the problem of a monopolistic insurer discussed in Section 6.1.2 which is repeated here for convenience:*

Choose (x_1^H, x_2^H) and (x_1^L, x_2^L) to maximize

$$\theta \cdot [\pi_H \cdot (W - L - x_1^H) + (1 - \pi_H) \cdot (W - x_2^H)] + (1 - \theta) \cdot [\pi_L \cdot (W - L - x_1^L)$$
$$+ (1 - \pi_L) \cdot (W - x_2^L)]$$

subject to

$$\pi_H \cdot u(x_1^H) + (1 - \pi_H) \cdot u(x_2^H) \geq \pi_H \cdot u(W - L) + (1 - \pi_H) \cdot u(W), \quad (IR_H)$$
$$\pi_L \cdot u(x_1^L) + (1 - \pi_L) \cdot u(x_2^L) \geq \pi_L \cdot u(W - L) + (1 - \pi_L) \cdot u(W), \quad (IR_L)$$
$$\pi_H \cdot u(x_1^H) + (1 - \pi_H) \cdot u(x_2^H) \geq \pi_H \cdot u(x_1^L) + (1 - \pi_H) \cdot u(x_2^L), \quad (IC_H)$$
$$\pi_L \cdot u(x_1^L) + (1 - \pi_L) \cdot u(x_2^L) \geq \pi_L \cdot u(x_1^H) + (1 - \pi_L) \cdot u(x_2^H). \quad (IC_L)$$

(a) Write down the Lagrange function of this problem and derive the first-order conditions for an optimal contract. Are these conditions sufficient?

(b) Using the first-order conditions, show that the IR_L constraint must be binding in any solution of this problem.

4. *Consider firms with different investment projects. Each project requires \$50 of funds. Projects are distinguished by the following return distributions:*

probabilities	0.5	0.5
project 1	\$50	\$90
project 2	\$30	\$110

Assume that there are ten firms with project 1 and ten firms with project 2. Potential lenders cannot distinguish the two types of firm when deciding on whether to grant a loan or not, but are equally likely to face a firm with project 1 or one with project 2.

(a) Determine the expected returns and the variances of these two projects.

(b) A bank is willing to provide funds for a return of R if firms provide a collateral of \$20. Draw a diagram showing the expected return of the bank from each of the two projects as a function of R.

(c) Show in another diagram the expected profit of each type of firm from its project as a function of R. A firm demands a loan only if the expected profit is positive.

(d) Suppose the bank can raise $400 at an interest rate of 20 per cent and another $800 at an interest rate of 50 per cent. Draw a diagram with the supply function of the bank. Suppose the bank would behave as a price-taker and offer funds at marginal cost. Determine the loan market equilibrium.

(e) Check whether the equilibrium return derived in (d) allows the bank to make a positive expected profit. Show that credit rationing will occur and explain why the bank will not provide more credit even if firms are willing to pay a higher return R.

5. *Reconsider the situation of the Exercise 4 with the following modifications: Each project requires $100 of funds and projects are distinguished by the following return distributions.*

probabilities	0.5	0.5
project 1	$100	$180
project 2	$60	$220

(a) A lender offers funds at a return of R if firms provide a collateral of $40. Draw a diagram showing the expected return of the bank from each of the two projects as a function of R. Show in another diagram the expected profit of each type of firm from its project as a function of R. Determine the aggregate demand function for loans if a firm demands a loan only for positive expected profits.

(b) Suppose the bank can raise $400 at an interest rate of 20 per cent and another $800 at an interest rate of 50 per cent. Draw a diagram with the supply function of the bank. Suppose the bank would behave as a price-taker and offer funds at marginal cost. Determine the loan market equilibrium.

6. *A risk-neutral entrepreneur has a project that requires an investment of $100 and yields the following distribution of returns:*

returns	$70	$90	$100	$120	$140	$160
probabilities	0.05	0.10	0.10	0.25	0.30	0.20

A risk-neutral potential lender with an opportunity cost of 10 per cent interest would be willing to lend the required money but has to employ an auditor at a cost of $10 to monitor the return of the entrepreneur. If the lender were to enter a loan contract with the entrepreneur she would have to rely on the entrepreneur's *statement about the return achieved or have to spend the money to audit the entrepreneur.*

(a) What must a contract between the entrepreneur and a lender specify? What conditions have to hold for a contract to be feasible in each state?

(b) For a given contract, write down the return of the entrepreneur and the lender in a particular state of the world.

(c) Give a definition of 'incentive-compatibility' in regard to the return reported by the entrepreneur. Show that incentive-compatibility requires a constant repayment for a loan whenever no monitoring takes place.

(d) Consider a 'standard debt contract' that requires the entrepreneur to pay the lender $120 or to declare bankruptcy with the consequence that the lender audits the entrepreneur and takes the remaining value of the project. Check whether the standard debt contract is incentive-compatible. Determine the expected return of this contract for the entrepreneur and the lender.

(e) Show that the contract under (d) maximizes the expected return of the entrepreneur subject to the individual rationality constraint of the lender. *Hint*: Check whether it is possible to raise the expected return of the entrepreneur by changing the contracted amount of $120.

7. *A bank faces a large number of customers with different investment projects* $k \in [0, 2 \cdot a]$. *Each project requires one unit of funds to produce the following state-contingent return:*

$$f(s,k) = a + k \cdot (s - 0.5).$$

The distribution of states is uniform on the interval $[0,1]$.

(a) Determine mean and variance of a project of type k.

(b) Assume that the bank offers a standard debt contract at a return R with a collateral C. Determine the expected profit of a firm and the expected return of the bank for a project of type k. Show that the expected profit is increasing in k and decreasing in R.

(c) Assume that the firms carry through all projects with positive expected profit. Determine the critical level of k, $k(R)$, such that all projects $k \geq k(R)$ will be adopted. Assume further that the different types of projects k are distributed uniformly on the interval $[0, K]$. Show that the expected return of the bank is non-monotonic in R if the adverse selection of projects is taken into account. May this lead to credit rationing?

7
···

DEPOSIT CONTRACTS
AND BANKING

In this chapter, a model of a bank is presented which focuses on the liquidity aspect of the banking business. We will show that there are efficiency gains from investing liquid funds into long-term illiquid assets. However, deposit banking which achieves these efficiency gains is vulnerable to bank runs. Furthermore, uncertainty about a bank's investment projects and adverse information may trigger a bank run. Before turning to these issues, however, we need briefly to discuss the role of 'money' in an economy.

··

7.1 Money as a Means of Payment

··

The theory of financial markets developed in the previous chapters leaves no room for financial institutions like banks that one observes in all modern economies. If trade in goods and assets is carried out only *after* all prices have been determined such that the value of purchases equals the value of sales, then there is no need for settlement of net trading positions. The market equilibria studied in the first part of this book were *frictionless* in this sense. In real economies, trade takes place sequentially and buyers and sellers cannot expect to exchange goods and assets such that the value of sales equals the value of purchases for any two traders. Hence, usually, a credit relationship will arise between buyers and sellers in the course of any exchange. If trade took place only after equilibrium prices in all markets had been established, this would not matter since traders could be certain that the values of purchases and sales among all market participants would balance.

In actual economies, trade of goods and assets is not pre-co-ordinated by a general equilibrium price system. Hence, buyers and sellers must accept net credit positions based on trust that the trading partner will and can honour the obligation or they will have to settle the credit position by accepting some *means of payment*, that is *money*. In reality, exchanges of goods and assets are therefore usually accompanied by transfers of *money*. In the past, money was usually a good like gold which was easily storable and widely accepted in exchange. In modern economies, assets or portfolios of assets may serve the same purpose.

Money has value in exchange because it has a fairly stable price relative to the most commonly traded goods. It allows people to trade with each other who do not have goods or assets that they mutually desire. If money has a stable price relative to goods and assets, a seller will not hesitate to accept it in compensation for a sale, and a buyer need not find something that this particular seller is willing to accept in exchange. The value of money lies in its capacity to facilitate trade and not in its value for an individual in production or consumption.

Using a commodity or an asset as *money*, however, has a high opportunity cost since using it for exchange prevents its use in production and consumption. Furthermore, there is a risk of losing the asset while using it in exchange. Thus, there is an advantage in using *claims to the commodity or asset that serves as money* instead of the actual asset or commodity itself. By depositing their money for a fee with a trader who agrees to keep it and to pay it out on the depositor's instruction, the depositing person has the liquidity of holding the medium of exchange without actually having to carry it. In addition, if not all deposits are required for transactions, the agent can invest some of these funds to achieve a return which can be paid back as interest to the depositors. Investment of these excess deposits reduces the opportunity cost of holding money, but it requires a precise prediction of withdrawals. Hence, such a payment system depends crucially on the trustworthiness of the deposit-taking agent.

A *bank* is a firm specializing in deposit-taking. This business has obvious increasing returns to scale since a small number of employees can monitor and administer the deposits of a large number of customers. To be able to pay out all its deposits on demand, however, the bank would have to hold all the deposited money ready for withdrawal. Under normal business conditions, only a fraction of the deposited money will be called upon in a given period and a substantial part of aggregate deposits would remain unproductive as a backup for potential withdrawals which usually do not occur.

For that reason, banks usually hold reserves of money equal to the average amount required in a particular period and invest the rest of the deposited money to achieve investment returns from it. Such behaviour creates two types of risk:

(i) *Liquidity risk*: even with a perfectly riskless investment, the bank may face a liquidity crisis if for some unforeseen reason more deposits are withdrawn than the bank holds reserves.

(ii) *Investment risk*: If the investment is risky, the bank may make losses which will make it impossible to repay its liabilities to the depositors even in the long run.

In regard to investment risk, banks are no different from other firms. A bad investment decision may cause a firm to go bankrupt because it cannot pay back a loan at the specified date. Liquidity risk, however, is a problem specific to the nature of deposit contracts. Deposits are due on call because of the liquidity needs of the depositors and not at a predetermined date.

Though it is conceptually easy to distinguish between these two types of risk, it is extremely difficult to separate the two causes of a bank crisis in practice. This is because depositors' withdrawal behaviour is related to the investment performance of the bank and the return on a bank's investment depends on the accuracy of its predictions of withdrawals.

7.2 Liquid and Illiquid Assets

Imagine an economy which extends over three periods and where agents have only two types of assets to store value. The first asset, called *money*, allows the holder to store value without gains or losses. A unit of money can be used in each period for purchases of goods and other assets. In contrast, investment in the second asset, called *long-term project* or *illiquid asset*, requires a two-period commitment of funds: one unit of money invested in the illiquid asset in period t earns a return α_2 in period $t + 2$ which exceeds the return from holding money ($\alpha_2 > 1$). If the project has to be liquidated in period $t + 1$, however, only a *liquidation value* α_1 less than the return from holding money ($\alpha_1 < 1$) can be realized. All agents in this economy have access to these two assets and can buy them without restriction according to their preferences.

Assuming a liquidation value of the long-term project, α_1, which is less than the discounted present value of the future certain return, α_2, makes some implicit assumptions about market conditions. Though the return on this project is certain, it must not be possible to sell claims to it in the intermediate period at a price above α_1. The reason for this could be the absence of established markets for such claims. Organizing markets can be an expensive activity, in particular for heterogeneous goods like real estate and buildings. In addition, thin markets may give market power to some traders which may make it

impossible to realize the full present value of an investment. Such market imperfections are not explicitly modelled here. They are, however, necessary to
justify the assumption that the realizable value of the long-term investment is
less than its present value. On the other hand, such market imperfections are
the essence of a distinction between *liquid* and *illiquid* assets.

Traders in this economy are identical consumers who plan for three periods,
$t = 0,1,2$. Initially they hold m_0 units of money. They are risk-neutral and maximize wealth in period 2, the final period of their life. To model sudden liquidity needs, assume that, in period 1, consumers learn privately about an
individually available investment opportunity, called *individual project*, with
return rate θ. A fixed proportion μ of agents will obtain an individual project
with a high return rate $\theta = \beta_{\hbar}$, while the rest of the population receives a project with a low return rate $\theta = \beta_{\ell}$. Consumers with a high-return private
project want to have money available in period 1 for their private investment
opportunity. Consumers with the low-return private project prefer the long-
term investment project with return α_2. This yields the following return rate
ordering:

$$\beta_{\hbar} > \alpha_2 > \beta_{\ell} \geq 1 > \alpha_1.$$

The following diagram summarizes the return patterns of the different types
of investment in this economy.

Money	-1	1	
		-1	1
Long-term project	-1	α_1	0
		0	α_2
Individual project		-1	$\beta_{\hbar}, \beta_{\ell}$

$$0 \qquad 1 \qquad 2 \qquad \longrightarrow t$$

Negative numbers indicate the price that a consumer has to pay for a unit of
the respective investment and a positive number indicates the per-unit return
that a consumer receives.

In period 0, each consumer knows the distribution of return rates for the
private projects, $(\mu, 1 - \mu; \beta_{\hbar}, \beta_{\ell})$. The realization of θ, however, is privately observed only. *Ex ante*, in period 0, each agent has the same chance of obtaining
a high-return individual project. Hence, there is an expected return of

$$\mu \cdot \beta_{\hbar} + (1 - \mu) \cdot \beta_{\ell}$$

from holding money in period 0 and then investing it in the private project in
period 1.

To model a conflict between investment opportunities and liquidity needs

$$\mu \cdot \beta_h + (1 - \mu) \cdot \beta_\ell > \alpha_2 > \alpha_1 \cdot \beta_h$$

will be assumed. This implies immediately that consumers will hold only money, in spite of the high return earned from the illiquid asset. This assumption models a situation where the chance of a high-return rate from the individual project is so attractive and the loss from early liquidation of the long-term project is so high that consumers will decide against investing in the illiquid asset.

In period 0, each consumer owns the same initial endowment m_0 of money. We will assume further that, relative to the total amount of funds in the economy, each consumer has a negligible amount to invest.[1] Hence, an individual consumer's investment behaviour has no effect on the aggregate amounts of investment whereas a group of consumers may influence aggregate quantities. Denote by I the total number of consumers. Then $M_0 \equiv m_0 \cdot I$ is the total amount of money available for investment in the economy.

To see what role the assumption of consumers holding private information about the return rate θ plays, consider the case where this information is publicly observable. If it were known in period 1 who actually obtains the high-return individual investment project, an obvious Pareto improvement on the allocation where the whole population holds money would be achieved by pooling all agents' initial wealth M_0, investing the fraction $(1 - \mu) \cdot M_0$ in the long-term project, and holding $\mu \cdot M_0$ as reserves in the form of money.

Once the type of the agents' individual projects are known in period 1, consumers with a return rate β_h will receive a pay-out m_0 which they can invest in their private projects. Consumers with a low β_ℓ will obtain no pay-out in period 1 and earn the return α_2 in period 2. This scheme would yield an economy-wide expected return rate of $\mu \cdot \beta_h + (1 - \mu) \cdot \alpha_2$ exceeding the expected return from holding money $\mu \cdot \beta_h + (1 - \mu) \cdot \beta_\ell$. Each agent would have a higher expected return *ex ante* and, *ex post*, a return which would be at least as high as that in the absence of this scheme.

Though such a scheme dominates an allocation where agents hold only money, from an *ex ante* perspective it is not the best arrangement for consumers. Since consumers are assumed to be risk-neutral and prefer to hold money rather than to invest it in the illiquid asset in period 0, the optimal redistribution scheme would collect all initial money holdings in period 0, hold the total amount as reserves and redistribute it in period 1 to those agents with a high-return investment project. If the aggregate endowment of money M_0 is proportionally distributed to the consumers with return β_h, then each

---

[1] Formally this is modelled by the assumption of a continuum of consumers.

consumer in this group will have $M_0/(\mu \cdot I) = m_0/\mu$ to invest in the individual project in period 1. This scheme generates an expected wealth of $\beta_{\hbar} \cdot m_0 = \mu \cdot [\beta_{\hbar} \cdot m_0/\mu]) + (1 - \mu) \cdot 0$ in period 0 which exceeds both the expected value of holding money $[\mu \cdot \beta_{\hbar} + (1 - \mu) \cdot \beta_{\ell}] \cdot m_0$ and the expected value from the previous scheme $[\mu \cdot \beta_{\hbar} + (1 - \mu) \cdot \alpha_2] \cdot m_0$ because $\beta_{\hbar} > \alpha_2$. Hence a complete redistribution of money to the high-return consumers would be optimal *ex ante* if it were possible to observe the type of a consumer's investment project. The reason is that the private investment project with return $\beta_{\hbar}$ offers the best return in this economy. Being risk-neutral, it is optimal for consumers to put all money in this project even if there is a risk of losing everything with probability $(1 - \mu)$.

On the other hand, this scenario makes it completely obvious why this scheme does not work if the type of a consumer's project is private information. Even if consumers agree in period 0 to redistribute all funds in period 1 to the consumers with the high-return project, any consumer who afterwards obtains the low-return project and, hence, would miss out on all pay-off in period 2, would have good reason to report a high return in order to receive a share of the aggregate funds. If all low-return consumers behaved in this way, the scheme would break down and everyone would end up with the allocation that would arise had they decided to keep their money in the first place.

7.3 The Optimal Contract

These considerations raise the question of what kind of scheme or contract will be optimal given the informational constraints. Private information of consumers about their returns implies that a redistribution of funds contingent on the type of the individual project is possible only if there is no incentive for a consumer to misrepresent this information. Thus, an optimal contract has to maximize the expected pay-off of the consumers in period 0 subject to feasibility constraints and to *incentive constraints.*

Denote by R the part of the total funds M_0 held as money, and by K the amount invested in the illiquid project. Let $\xi_t(\theta)$ be the amount of money paid back in period t to a consumer of type θ, where θ is either $\beta_{\hbar}$ or β_{ℓ}. A contract must specify an aggregate investment strategy (R,K) and the payments to consumers with high- and low-return projects respectively, $(\xi_1(\beta_{\hbar}), \xi_2(\beta_{\hbar}), \xi_1(\beta_{\ell}), \xi_2(\beta_{\ell}))$.

The optimal contract $(R,K,\xi_1(\beta_{\hbar}),\xi_2(\beta_{\hbar}),\xi_1(\beta_{\ell}),\xi_2(\beta_{\ell}))$ must maximize the *ex ante* expected utility of consumers

$$\mu \cdot [\beta_h \cdot \xi_1(\beta_h) + \xi_2(\beta_h)] + (1 - \mu) \cdot [\beta_\ell \cdot \xi_1(\beta_\ell) + \xi_2(\beta_\ell)]$$

subject to constraints which guarantee that (i) pay-outs are feasible for the investment strategy, and that (ii) in period 1 when consumers know their types, no consumer has an incentive to pretend to have any other than her true type.

Feasibility of the contract requires

$$R + K = M_0,$$

$$Z \leq R + \alpha_1 \cdot K \qquad \text{and}$$

$$[\mu \cdot \xi_2(\beta_h) + (1 - \mu) \cdot \xi_2(\beta_\ell)] \cdot I = \alpha_2 \cdot [K - \frac{1}{\alpha_1} \cdot \max\{0, Z - R\}]$$
$$+ \max\{0, R - Z\},$$

where $Z \equiv [\mu \cdot \xi_1(\beta_h) + (1 - \mu) \cdot \xi_1(\beta_\ell)] \cdot I$ denotes the aggregate amount of money paid out in period 1.

The return of the individual project is private information to the consumer. To guarantee truthful revelation[2] of this information, the contract must be *incentive-compatible*, i.e. provide no incentive for a consumer to lie about the type of the project. Therefore, pay-outs in period 1, when the consumer knows her type, must satisfy:

$$\beta_h \cdot \xi_1(\beta_h) + \xi_2(\beta_h) \geq \beta_h \cdot \xi_1(\beta_\ell) + \xi_2(\beta_\ell)$$

and

$$\beta_\ell \cdot \xi_1(\beta_\ell) + \xi_2(\beta_\ell) \geq \beta_\ell \cdot \xi_1(\beta_h) + \xi_2(\beta_h).$$

The first inequality guarantees that a consumer of type β_h will prefer the payment schedule $(\xi_1(\beta_h), \xi_2(\beta_h))$ that the optimal contract specifies for her over the payment schedule $(\xi_1(\beta_\ell), \xi_2(\beta_\ell))$ which is designed for the other type. Similarly, the second constraint makes it optimal for a consumer with a low-return project to claim the payment schedule $(\xi_1(\beta_\ell), \xi_2(\beta_\ell))$ rather than $(\xi_1(\beta_h), \xi_2(\beta_h))$.

It is not difficult to derive the following properties of an optimal contract $(R^*, K^*, \xi_1^*(\beta_h), \xi_2^*(\beta_h), \xi_1^*(\beta_\ell), \xi_2^*(\beta_\ell))$:

  (i) The optimal level of reserves is exactly the quantity of money to be paid out in period 1, $R^* = Z^* \equiv [\mu \cdot \xi_1^*(\beta_h) + (1 - \mu) \cdot \xi_1^*(\beta_\ell)] \cdot I$.
  (ii) It is never optimal to make a pay-out in period 1 to a consumer with a low-return project or to make any payment in period 2 to a consumer with a high-return project, $\xi_1^*(\beta_\ell) = \xi_2^*(\beta_h) = 0$.

---

[2] It is a well-known result that there is no loss of generality in restricting attention to *direct mechanisms* which require an agent to report her type; compare e.g. Laffont (1987).

To see that (i) is true, suppose reserves exceed pay-outs in period 1, $R' > Z^*$. Reducing reserves to $R^* = Z^*$ will leave $(\xi_1^*(\beta_\ell), \xi_1^*(\beta_\ell))$ unchanged but will earn an additional return $(\alpha_2 - 1) \cdot (R' - Z^*)$ which can be distributed to consumers in period 2. Hence $R' > Z^*$ cannot be optimal. For $R' < Z^*$, the amount $Z^* - R'$ must be obtained from early liquidation of the illiquid asset. This is costly, since liquidation of one unit of investment returns only α_1 units of money. Increasing reserves to $R^* = Z^*$ will yield an extra return of $\alpha_2 \cdot ((1/\alpha_1) - 1) \cdot (Z^* - R')$ which can be shared out in period 2. Thus, $R' < Z^*$ cannot be optimal either.

To check claim (ii), suppose that $\xi_1^*(\beta_\ell) > 0$ holds. Reducing the pay-out in period 1 to consumers with a low-return project by ε, $0 < \varepsilon < \xi_1^*(\beta_\ell)$, the contract $(\xi_1^*(\beta_h), \xi_2^*(\beta_h), \xi_1^*(\beta_\ell) - \varepsilon, \xi_2^*(\beta_\ell) + \alpha_2 \cdot \varepsilon)$ with reserves $R' = R^* - \varepsilon \cdot (1 - \mu) \cdot I$ and an investment $K' = K^* + \varepsilon \cdot (1 - \mu) \cdot I$ is feasible. This contract, however, is strictly preferred by consumers with a low-return project because $\beta_\ell < \alpha_2$ holds. Similarly, if $\xi_2^*(\beta_h)$ were strictly positive, reducing this pay-out by ε, $0 < \varepsilon < \xi_2^*(\beta_h)$, yields the following feasible contract: $(\xi_1^*(\beta_h) + \varepsilon, \xi_2^*(\beta_h) - \alpha_2 \cdot \varepsilon, \xi_1^*(\beta_\ell), \xi_2^*(\beta_\ell))$ with reserves $R' = R^* + \varepsilon \cdot \mu \cdot I$ and investment in the long-term project $K' = K^* - \varepsilon \cdot \mu \cdot I$. Since $\beta_h > \alpha_2$ holds, a consumer with a high-return project will prefer this contract.

This result allows us to simplify the optimal contract problem. Substituting for $R^* = \mu \cdot \xi_1^*(\beta_h) \cdot I$ and $K^* = [(1 - \mu) \cdot \xi_2^*(\beta_\ell) \cdot I]/\alpha_2$ in $K^* + R^* = M_0$ simplifies the feasibility constraints to

$$\alpha_2 \cdot \mu \cdot \xi_1^*(\beta_h) + (1 - \mu) \cdot \xi_2^*(\beta_\ell) = \alpha_2 \cdot (M_0/I), \qquad (7.1)$$

and the incentive-compatibility constraints to

$$\beta_h \cdot \xi_1^*(\beta_h) \geq \xi_2^*(\beta_\ell) \geq \beta_\ell \cdot \xi_1^*(\beta_h). \qquad (7.2)$$

An optimal contract can therefore be determined as a solution to the following, much simpler, optimization problem:

Choose $(\xi_1(\beta_h), \xi_2(\beta_\ell))$ *to maximize*

$$\mu \cdot \beta_h \cdot \xi_1(\beta_h) + (1 - \mu) \cdot \xi_2(\beta_\ell)$$

subject to (7.1) *and* (7.2).

Figure 7.1 illustrates this problem and its solution.

The indifference curves of the objective function are linear and steeper than the feasibility constraint because $\beta_h > \alpha_2$ holds. The optimum occurs where the lower incentive constraint is binding, $\xi_2^*(\beta_\ell) = \beta_\ell \cdot \xi_1^*(\beta_h)$. Substituting this into the feasibility constraint (7.1), one obtains the following optimal contract

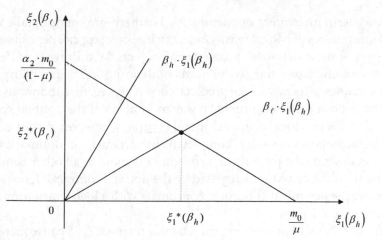

Fig. 7.1

$$\xi_1^*(\beta_k) = \frac{\alpha_2}{\mu \cdot \alpha_2 + (1-\mu) \cdot \beta_1} \cdot m_0, \quad \xi_2^*(\beta_k) = 0,$$

$$\xi_1^*(\beta_\ell) = 0, \qquad\qquad \xi_2^*(\beta_\ell) = \frac{\beta_1 \cdot \alpha_2}{\mu \cdot \alpha_2 + (1-\mu) \cdot \beta_1} \cdot m_0,$$

$$R^* = \frac{\alpha_2}{\mu \cdot \alpha_2 + (1-\mu) \cdot \beta_1} \cdot \mu \cdot M_0, \quad K^* = \frac{\beta_1}{\mu \cdot \alpha_2 + (1-\mu) \cdot \beta_1} \cdot (1-\mu) \cdot M_0.$$

One can easily check that the following inequalities hold:

$$m_0 < \xi_1^*(\beta_k) \le \xi_2^*(\beta_\ell) < \alpha_2 \cdot m_0.$$

The optimal contract specifies that consumers with a high-return project obtain a repayment in period 1 which exceeds their initial money holdings. A low-return consumer gets a larger pay-out in period 2 than a high-return consumer in period 1 but generally less than α_2, the return on investments in the illiquid asset. This is optimal because consumers favour the highest pay-out possible in period 1 given the incentive-compatibility constraints. Thus, an optimal contract requires the payment of less interest on deposits than on long-term savings, $(\xi_2^*(\beta_\ell) - m_0) > (\xi_1^*(\beta_k) - m_0)$, in order to prevent early withdrawals of consumers with low-return projects.

7.4 Banks as Deposit-Taking Institutions

The scenario presented in the previous sections models the situation in which banks do business: consumers with random short-term liquidity needs do not use long-term investment opportunities. Furthermore, an optimal contract has some features of bank deposit contracts: banks accept call deposits and invest part of these deposits in long-term projects. Withdrawals of deposits occur randomly according to the needs of depositors. The feasibility of the bank's business depends on the predictability of aggregate withdrawals.

Bank deposit contracts provide a way to implement the optimal contract derived in the previous section. Optimal contracts, however, do not describe the interactions of consumers completely. In particular, an optimal contract does not describe the pay-offs of a consumer if some or all other consumers deviate from the behaviour suggested by the optimal contract. Here, we need to specify the pay-offs that occur if consumers with a low-return project also withdraw their deposits.

Suppose that withdrawals exceed a bank's reserves. As a consequence, the bank has to call back loans, i.e. it has to liquidate part or all of its long-term investment which is costly because $\alpha_1 < 1$ holds. Such early liquidation will reduce the interest that can be paid to depositors who do not withdraw in period 1. Falling interest rates, however, may in turn induce depositors to withdraw who would not have done so at the original interest rate. This can create a spiral of withdrawals and early liquidations ending in a bank run.

A *deposit contract* specifies a repayment of $(1 + r_1)$ units of money on call per unit of money deposited in period 0, and a repayment of $(1 + r_2)$ units of money in period 2 for each unit deposited in period 0 and not withdrawn in period 1. Thus, a deposit contract is characterized by a pair of interest rates (r_1, r_2). If a proportion μ of total deposits is withdrawn in period 1 and if the bank holds $(1 + r_1) \cdot \mu$ per unit deposited as reserves and invests $[1 - \mu \cdot (1 + r_1)]$ per unit of deposit in the illiquid long-term project, then the following set of interest-rate pairs will be feasible:

$$Q(\alpha_2, \mu) \equiv \{(r_1, r_2) \in \mathbb{R}^2 \mid r_2 \le (\alpha_2 - 1) - \alpha_2 \cdot \frac{\mu}{1 - \mu} \cdot r_1\}.$$

For interest rate pairs $(r_1, r_2) \in Q(\alpha_2, \mu)$ which satisfy

$$r_2 < (\alpha_2 - 1) - \alpha_2 \cdot \frac{\mu}{1 - \mu} \cdot r_1,$$

the bank will make a positive profit. If an equality holds, the bank's profit is zero. Interest-rate pairs satisfy the incentive-compatibility condition if $\beta_h \cdot (1 + r_1) \ge (1 + r_2) \ge \beta_\ell \cdot (1 + r_1)$ holds. The interest rate combinations (r_1, r_2) in the shaded area of Figure 7.2 are feasible and incentive-compatible.

The optimal contract of the previous section corresponds to the interest-rate pair (r_1^*, r_2^*). It requires payment of as much interest in period 1 as is incentive-compatible. Since the optimal contract maximizes consumers' welfare, the bank will make no profit. The analysis of the next sections, however, is supposed to apply for general bank deposit contracts and will therefore also cover

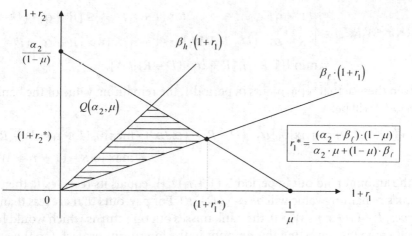

Fig. 7.2

the case of banks which are profitable. Hence, general feasible and incentive-compatible deposit contracts $(r_1, r_2) \in Q(\alpha_2, \mu)$ will be the object of our study.

Whether a contract $(r_1, r_2) \in Q(\alpha_2, \mu)$ can be carried out as planned depends crucially on the correctness of a bank's prediction of aggregate withdrawals in period 1. If the withdrawals in period 1 deviate from the predicted amount, which is held as reserve, the interest rate actually paid in period 2 must be lowered. To study the implications of incorrect predictions, one has to specify the *actual repayment schedule* of a deposit contract (r_1, r_2).

Denote by D the total amount of funds deposited with the intermediary in period 0 and let W be the amount withdrawn in period 1. The returns which a deposit contract (r_1, r_2) actually pays in period 1, $\rho_1(r_1, r_2; W, R, D)$, and in period 2, $\rho_2(r_1, r_2; W, R, D)$, depend on the amount of deposits D and reserves R as well as on the amount of funds withdrawn in period 1. If the amount of deposits withdrawn in period 1 is not equal to the reserves held by the bank, then the actual return in period 2 will be affected.

It may happen that the amount that the bank can liquidate, $\alpha_1 \cdot (D - R)$, together with its reserves R is insufficient to meet the contracted payments in period 1, $(1 + r_1) \cdot W$. An explicit description of the *actual repayment scheme* $(\rho_1(\cdot), \rho_2(\cdot))$ therefore requires assumptions about how funds are to be distributed among depositors if funds that can be liquidated in period 1, $R + \alpha_1 \cdot (D - R)$, are insufficient to pay the contracted amount $(1 + r_1) \cdot W$. For simplicity, it is assumed here that remaining funds are shared out proportionally to the claiming depositors.[3] This assumption implies the following actual repayment schedule for period 1:

[3] Since consumers are assumed to be risk-neutral, a proportional rationing scheme is equivalent to an anonymous stochastic rationing scheme, as the *sequential service constraint* in Diamond and Dybvig (1983).

$$\rho_1(r_1,r_2;W,R,D) = \begin{cases} (1 + r_1) & \text{for } (1 + r_1) \cdot W \le [R + \alpha_1 \cdot (D - R)] \\ [R + \alpha_1 \cdot (D - R)]/W & \text{for } (1 + r_1) \cdot W > [R + \alpha_1 \cdot (D - R)] \end{cases}$$

$$= \min \{(1 + r_1), [R + \alpha_1 \cdot (D - R)]/W\}.$$

Given these actual repayments in period 1, the remaining value of the bank in period 2 will be:

$$V(r_1;W,R,D) = \max\{0, [\alpha_2 \cdot (D - R) - (\alpha_2/\alpha_1) \cdot \max\{0, (1 + r_1) \cdot W - R\}$$
$$+ \max\{0, R - (1 + r_1) \cdot W\}]\}.$$

If the amount paid out in period 1, $(1 + r_1) \cdot W$, equals its reserves R, then the bank's remaining value will be $\alpha_2 \cdot (D - R)$. For pay-outs that are less than reserves, $R - (1 + r_1) \cdot W > 0$, the bank misses out on returns which would have been earned by investing this amount in the long-term project. On the other hand, if reserves are less than pay-outs $R - (1 + r_1) \cdot W < 0$, then some investment in the illiquid asset has to be liquidated prematurely at a cost. Therefore, $V(r_1;W,R,D)$ reaches a maximum for $(1 + r_1) \cdot W = R$ and becomes zero for all $W \ge \bar{W} \equiv [\alpha_1 \cdot D + (1 - \alpha_1) \cdot R]/(1 + r_1)$.

The actual return that the bank can pay in period 2 is therefore

$$\rho_2(r_1,r_2;W,R,D) = \min \{(1 + r_2), V(r_1;W,R,D)/(D - W)\}.$$

It will be equal to the contracted return $(1 + r_2)$ if the bank correctly predicts withdrawals $W = \mu \cdot D$ and holds reserves $R = \mu \cdot (1 + r_1) \cdot D$. Figure 7.3 shows the actual return structure of the deposit contract as a function of withdrawals W.

The main question arising in the context of these deposit contracts concerns the implications of a possible divergence of *actual* from *contracted* returns for consumers' decisions to deposit or not to deposit in period 0, and to withdraw or not to withdraw in period 1. If the contracted return rates (r_1,r_2) are incentive-compatible, then only consumers of type $\beta_{\hbar}$ will withdraw, while consumers of type β_{ℓ} will leave their deposits with the bank, *provided the bank can pay the contracted return rates*. With actual returns deviating from contracted ones, however, consumers with a low-return project may also find it optimal to withdraw their deposits in period 1. Given the actual return schedules for arbitrary aggregate withdrawals, one can analyse how consumers' behaviour will change as the aggregate level of withdrawals and, therefore, the actual return rates vary.

Given that no consumer wants to invest directly in the long-term project, a consumer's strategy is described by the amount d_i deposited with the bank in period 0 and type-contingent withdrawals in period 1 $(w_i(\beta_{\hbar}), w_i(\beta_{\ell}))$. The set of strategies is given by the following inequalities, $\theta = \beta_{\hbar}, \beta_{\ell}$,

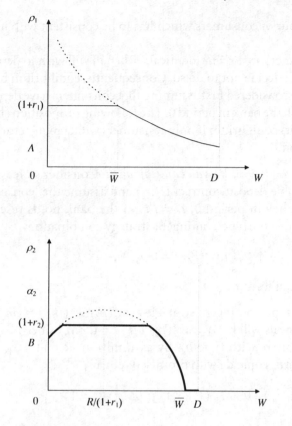

$$A \equiv \alpha_1 + (1-\alpha_1) \cdot R/D \qquad B \equiv \alpha_2 + (1-\alpha_2) \cdot R/D \qquad \overline{W} \equiv \frac{\alpha_1 \cdot D + (1-\alpha_1) \cdot R}{(1+r_1)}$$

Fig. 7.3

$$0 \le d_i \le m_0, \qquad 0 \le w_i(\theta) \le d_i.$$

The amount $m_0 - d_i$ is held as money. The pay-off function of consumer i for a deposit and withdrawal strategy $(d_i, w_i(\beta_{\ell}), w_i(\beta_{\ell}))$ can be written as

$$\mathcal{P}_i(d_i, w_i(\beta_{\ell}), w_i(\beta_{\ell})) \equiv [\mu \cdot \beta_{\ell} + (1-\mu) \cdot \beta_{\ell}] \cdot (m_0 - d_i)$$

$$+ \mu \cdot [\beta_{\ell} \cdot \rho_1(\cdot) \cdot w_i(\beta_{\ell}) + \rho_2(\cdot) \cdot (d_i - w_i(\beta_{\ell}))]$$

$$+ (1-\mu) \cdot [\beta_{\ell} \cdot \rho_1(\cdot) \cdot w_i(\beta_{\ell}) + \rho_2(\cdot) \cdot (d_i - w_i(\beta_{\ell}))].$$

Note that the actual returns $(\rho_1(\cdot), \rho_2(\cdot))$ are independent of a consumer's choice by virtue of the assumption that a single consumer holds a negligible amount of aggregate deposits. Actual returns, however, depend on the

211

aggregate behaviour of consumers which has to be consistent with individual behaviour.

Since all consumers are *ex ante* identical, either all will wish to deposit with the bank or all will decide not to do so. Consequently, equilibrium behaviour in period 1 will be considered first assuming that consumers have deposited all their funds m_0 with the bank in period 0. The following proposition shows that it is a (Bayes–Nash) equilibrium if only consumers with a high-return project withdraw in period 1.

PROPOSITION 7.1 (*withdrawal equilibrium*). Consider a feasible and incentive-compatible deposit contract (r_1, r_2) and assume that consumers deposit all their money in period 0, $D = M_0$. If the bank holds reserves $R = (1 + r_1) \cdot \mu \cdot M_0$, then the type-contingent strategy combination

$$(w_i^*(\beta_k), w_i^*(\beta_\ell)) = (m_0, 0), \quad i \in I,$$

is a Bayes–Nash equilibrium.

PROOF. Given type-contingent strategies $(w_i^*(\beta_k), w_i^*(\beta_\ell)) = (m_0, 0)$, $i \in I$, aggregate withdrawals will be $W = w_i^*(\beta_k) \cdot \mu \cdot I = \mu \cdot M_0$, since μ is the proportion of consumers with type β_k. By assumption, $R = (1 + r_1) \cdot \mu \cdot M_0$. Hence, actual returns coincide with promised returns,

$$\rho_1(r_1, r_2; \mu \cdot M_0, (1 + r_1) \cdot \mu \cdot M_0, M_0) = 1 + r_1$$

and

$$\rho_2(r_1, r_2; \mu \cdot M_0, (1 + r_1) \cdot \mu \cdot M_0, M_0) = 1 + r_2.$$

It remains to show that $w_i^*(\cdot)$ is indeed optimal for this return structure. Since consumers are risk-neutral, it is clear that they will either withdraw their full deposit, m_0, or not withdraw it, 0, depending on the return expected from either action. This fact, together with the independence of the repayment schedule from a single consumer's behaviour, makes it possible to represent the choice situation of a consumer by the game tree in Figure 7.4. By incentive compatibility, $\beta_k \cdot (1 + r_1) \geq (1 + r_2) \geq \beta_\ell \cdot (1 + r_1)$. Hence, one concludes immediately that $w_i^*(\beta_k) = m_0$ and $w_i^*(\beta_\ell) = 0$ are optimal choices for the two types. ∎

As an immediate consequence of Proposition 7.1, we see that a bank deposit contract can implement the optimal contract $(r_1^*, r_2^*) \in Q(a_2, \mu)$. The optimal contract is therefore an equilibrium even if the return schedule is fully specified. The following section will, however, show that there are other, less attractive, equilibria as well.

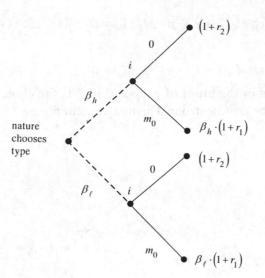

Fig. 7.4

7.5 Problems of Deposit Contracts: Bank Runs

Proposition 7.1 establishes that any feasible and individually rational deposit contract can be implemented as a Bayes–Nash equilibrium. This is, however, not the only possible equilibrium outcome in this bank model. Since actual returns may fall short of the promised returns if more deposits are withdrawn than there are reserves, the illiquidity of the bank's assets may create a situation where it is optimal for all depositors to withdraw. Such an equilibrium, a *bank run*, is not caused by the *riskiness* of the bank's assets but by the *illiquidity* of its assets. The next proposition shows that it is an equilibrium if all consumers withdraw their deposits.

PROPOSITION 7.2 (*bank-run equilibrium*). Consider a feasible and incentive-compatible deposit contract (r_1, r_2) and assume that consumers deposit all their money in period 0, $D = M_0$. If the bank holds reserves $R = (1 + r_1) \cdot \mu \cdot M_0$, then the type-contingent strategy combination

$$(w'_i(\beta_h), w'_i(\beta_\ell)) = (m_0, m_0), \quad i \in I,$$

is a Bayes–Nash equilibrium.

PROOF. Given the type-contingent strategies $(w'_i(\beta_h), w'_i(\beta_\ell)) = (m_0, m_0)$, $i \in I$, $W = M_0 = D$ follows. Hence, actual returns will be

$$\rho_1(r_1,r_2; M_0,(1+r_1)\cdot\mu\cdot M_0,M_0)= \alpha_1 + (1-\alpha_1)\cdot(1+r_1)\cdot\mu$$

and

$$\rho_2(r_1,r_2; M_0,(1+r_1)\cdot\mu\cdot M_0,M_0)= 0$$

respectively. As in the proof of proposition 7.1, the choice situation of a consumer can be represented in a game tree as in Figure 7.5. The minimum

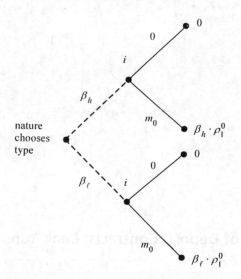

Fig. 7.5

repayment in period 1, $\rho_1^0 \equiv [\alpha_1 + (1-\alpha_1)\cdot(1+r_1)\cdot\mu]$, is always positive. Thus, the type-contingent strategy $w_1'(\cdot)$, to withdraw in any case, is obviously optimal. ∎

As proposition 7.2 shows, bank runs can occur as a consequence of perfectly rational behaviour. The logic of this result is easy to see: if every other consumer withdraws in period 1, then it is best also to withdraw because the return on deposits in period 2 will be zero while there remains a positive return from liquidation in period 1. It is not hard to check that these are the only Bayes–Nash equilibria in pure strategies for this game.

Of course, intuition suggests that no consumer would want to deposit with the bank in the first place if a bank run were expected for period 1. Hence, there are exactly two subgame-perfect equilibria in this game which reflect this intuition.

PROPOSITION 7.3. Consider a feasible and incentive-compatible deposit contract (r_1,r_2) and assume that the bank holds reserves $R = (1+r_1)\cdot\mu\cdot D$. Then there are two subgame-perfect equilibria:

(i) $d_i^* = m_0$, $w_1^*(\beta_4) = d_i^*$, $w_i^*(\beta_\ell) = 0$ for $i \in I$;

(ii) $d_i' = 0$, $w_i'(\beta_4) = d_i'$, $w_i'(\beta_\ell) = d_i'$ for $i \in I$.

PROOF. *Claim (i):* Suppose each consumer deposits d_i in period 0. It follows from proposition 7.1 that $w_i^*(\beta_4) = d_i$ and $w_i^*(\beta_\ell) = 0$, for $i \in I$, is a Nash equilibrium of the subgame following these moves. Incentive-compatibility implies $(1 + r_1) \geq 1$ and $(1 + r_2) \geq \beta_\ell \cdot (1 + r_1)$. The expected return from depositing a unit of money, $\mu \cdot \beta_4 \cdot (1 + r_1) + (1 - \mu) \cdot (1 + r_2)$, therefore exceeds the expected return from holding money, $\mu \cdot \beta_4 + (1 - \mu) \cdot \beta_\ell$. Hence, it is optimal to deposit all money, $d_i^* = m_0$, in the first stage of the game. This proves claim (i).

Claim (ii): Suppose each player has deposited d_i in period 0. Proposition 7.2 shows that $w_i'(\beta_4) = d_i$ and $w_i'(\beta_\ell) = d_i$, for $i \in I$, is a Nash equilibrium of the ensuing subgame. Hence, depositing a unit of money with the bank yields an expected return of $[\mu \cdot \beta_4 + (1 - \mu) \cdot \beta_\ell] \cdot \rho_1^0$ which is less than the expected return from holding money since $\rho_1^0 \leq 1$. Thus, $d_i' = 0$ is optimal as claimed in (ii). ∎

Figure 7.6 illustrates this argument. Suppose that nature chooses the agent's type before, not knowing this choice, the agent decides whether to deposit her money with the bank, m_0, or not to deposit it, 0. Then the consumer learns her

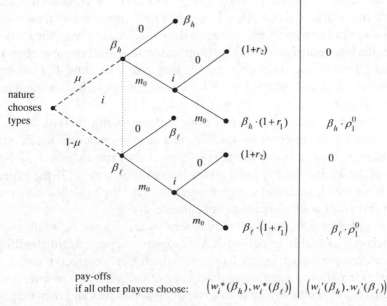

Fig. 7.6

type and decides whether to withdraw her funds, m_0, or not to withdraw them, 0. The pay-offs for the two second-stage equilibrium strategies are represented.

The analysis of a deposit contract which specifies the actual return pattern for a feasible and incentive-compatible interest rate pair (r_1, r_2) has shown that there is a bank-run equilibrium in period 1, given that consumers deposit their money holdings with the bank in period 0. This bank-run equilibrium is, however, irrational in the sense that no agent would deposit in period 0 if she assumed a bank-run equilibrium to follow.

Note, however, that a bank-run equilibrium in period 1 is not irrational in its own right. What is irrational is first to deposit and then to withdraw in all circumstances, since nothing happens between period 0 and 1 which would justify such behaviour. The following section will show that some uncertainty in regard to the outcome of the illiquid project together with privately observed adverse information may create an environment where a bank run can occur in period 1, even if the bank's investment is sound.

7.6 Adverse Information, Bank Failures, and Bank Runs

The analysis in the previous section suggests that bank runs do not pose a problem in a world with a riskless long-term investment project, even if this asset is illiquid. For a consumer who has deposited money with the bank and receives the low-return project, there is no reason to withdraw early other than fear that all other low-return consumers may also withdraw. If a consumer were concerned about such a possibility, however, it would be irrational to deposit in the first place.

Riskiness of the long-term project alone will not change this conclusion. Of course, with a risky outcome for the illiquid asset, the bank may fail in certain circumstances. Since consumers are risk-neutral, the *expected* return of the deposit will determine their deposit and withdrawal behaviour. If the expected return from the illiquid asset is high enough to make the bank business viable, then the previous analysis remains unchanged.

For a bank run to occur as an equilibrium phenomenon, new information must become available in period 1. A newspaper report about the illiquid asset, for example, may trigger a bank run, whether it is correct or not. A new piece of information, a signal, may affect depositors' behaviour in several ways. The signal may become available to some or all depositors and they may react to it simultaneously. This is the approach chosen in this section.

Alternatively, a group of depositors may obtain the new information and reveal it to others by acting on it. This latter case corresponds to a contagious bank run where depositors withdraw their deposits simply because they observe that others withdraw theirs. Modelling a bank run as induced by the observed withdrawals of other consumers requires a precise description of the sequence in which withdrawals and observations occur. Such a model would explain how a signal is transmitted among consumers[4] but would not provide further insights about the role of information in the intermediate period. To avoid unnecessary complications, the assumption that consumers, whether they obtain new information or not, decide on their withdrawals simultaneously will be maintained here.

Consider the case where there is a small chance $\varepsilon > 0$ that the illiquid investment project may fail in period 2. The following scheme indicates the modified return structure of the project:

$$\text{long-term project} \qquad -1 \qquad\qquad \alpha_1 \qquad\qquad \alpha_2 = \begin{cases} \alpha_H & w.p. \quad (1-\varepsilon) \\ 0 & w.p. \quad \varepsilon \end{cases}$$

$$\underset{0}{\bullet} \qquad\qquad \underset{1}{\bullet} \qquad\qquad \underset{2}{\bullet} \longrightarrow t$$

As argued before, riskiness of the illiquid asset alone makes a bank failure possible, but does not induce bank runs. Since consumers are risk-neutral, it would suffice to replace the certain return α_2 with the expected return $(1 - \varepsilon) \cdot \alpha_H$ for the analysis of the previous section to apply unaltered.

Uncertainty about the pay-off of the illiquid asset may, however, have an effect on the deposit and withdrawal behaviour of consumers if one assumes in addition that, at the beginning of period 1, consumers receive new information, a signal σ, about the success of the long-term investment. This signal σ may take either of the following two values: σ_H indicating that the return of the illiquid asset is α_H, and σ_L warning of an impending failure of the illiquid project. The signal σ is informative since it is correlated with the failure of the illiquid asset. We consider three states of the world characterized by different combinations of the return rate of the illiquid asset and the signal σ that consumers observe. Table 7.1 summarizes these three states and their probabilities. The probabilities in the right-hand column are *ex ante* probabilities for the three states. A state is characterized by a particular return of the illiquid asset and a particular state of information of the consumers.

---

[4] There is a small, but growing, literature on information transmission through observation of the behaviour of other agents. This literature on 'herding behaviour' appears to provide a way of modelling bank runs as induced by the observed withdrawals of other consumers. Compare, e.g., Banerjee (1992) and Bikhchandani, Hirshleifer, and Welch (1992).

State	Return of the illiquid asset	Information	Probability of state
s_1	α_H	σ_H	$1 - \varepsilon - \delta$
s_2	α_H	σ_L	δ
s_3	0	σ_L	ε

Table 7.1

The signal is informative: σ_H indicates that there is no risk for the return of the illiquid asset, while σ_L allows the consumers to reassess the likelihood of a failure. Note, however, that a signal is not necessarily 'correct': δ is the probability that consumers receive a warning signal σ_L and that the illiquid asset has a return α_H. Clearly, in this state, the signal is misleading. If the signal were completely unrelated to the outcome of the illiquid asset, then the signal would become a pure 'sunspot'. This corresponds to the special case $\varepsilon = 0$.

In period 0, when consumers make their decision about depositing with the bank, states are unknown. At the beginning of period 1, depositors learn the returns of their private investment opportunities θ and which signal σ has occurred. In the light of this information each depositor will update beliefs about the success or failure of the illiquid project. Table 7.2 lists the updated beliefs of a depositor.

Information in period 1	Updated belief that state is		
	s_1	s_2	s_3
σ_H	1	0	0
σ_L	0	$\delta/(\delta + \varepsilon)$	$\varepsilon/(\delta + \varepsilon)$

Table 7.2

Withdrawal strategies of consumers in period 1 will be conditioned on the signal σ which a consumer holds and on the type of her private project θ,

$$(w(\beta_k, \sigma_H), w(\beta_k, \sigma_L), w(\beta_\ell, \sigma_H), w(\beta_\ell, \sigma_L)).$$

A strategy of a consumer now specifies

- how much to deposit in period 0, d, and
- a type-contingent withdrawal plan

$$(w(\beta_k, \sigma_H), w(\beta_k, \sigma_L), w(\beta_\ell, \sigma_H), w(\beta_\ell, \sigma_L)) \text{ for period 1.}$$

Given such a withdrawal plan, aggregate withdrawals $W(\cdot)$ can now be written as a function of the state, because observations of the warning signal σ vary with states:

$$W(s_i) = [\mu \cdot w(\beta_h,\sigma) + (1 - \mu) \cdot w(\beta_\ell,\sigma)] \cdot I, \quad \text{for } i = 1,2,3.$$

Risk-neutrality implies that consumers will either deposit all their money, m_0, or nothing at all. Similarly, in period 1, they will withdraw all their deposits or leave them all with the bank. Consumers with a high-return private project will withdraw their deposits no matter what signal they receive. Consumers with a low-return signal, on the other hand, will make their withdrawal decision dependent on their reassessed beliefs about the success of the illiquid asset, because a failure of this investment will lead to a bank failure.

Observing the good signal, σ_H, a consumer with a low-return project knows that the bank will pay the promised interest. Incentive-compatibility of the returns on deposits, $(1 + r_2) > \beta_\ell \cdot (1 + r_1)$, then guarantees that it is optimal not to withdraw the deposit.

From a bad signal σ_L, consumers can conclude that the bank will fail with probability $\varepsilon/(\delta + \varepsilon)$. If this updated probability of a bank failure is small enough, then only high-return consumers will withdraw even if the bad signal is observed. But if the information of a bad signal induces a strong belief that a bank failure is imminent, then it is optimal for all consumers to withdraw early. In particular, for

$$(1 + r_2) \cdot [1 - (\varepsilon/(\delta + \varepsilon))] < \beta_\ell \cdot (1 + r_1),$$

there is a unique equilibrium where all consumers withdraw their deposits. The following type- and state-contingent behaviour forms an equilibrium in period 1:

$$(w(\beta_h,\sigma_H), w(\beta_h,\sigma_L),\ w(\beta_\ell,\sigma_H), w(\beta_\ell,\sigma_L)\ ) = (m_0, m_0, 0, m_0).$$

If all consumers have deposited their funds with the bank, $D = M_0$, and follow this withdrawal strategy, then aggregate withdrawals will be

$$W(s_1) = [\mu \cdot m_0 + (1 - \mu) \cdot 0] \cdot I = \mu \cdot M_0,$$

$$W(s_2) = [\mu \cdot m_0 + (1 - \mu) \cdot m_0] \cdot I = M_0, \quad \text{and}$$

$$W(s_3) = [\mu \cdot m_0 + (1 - \mu) \cdot m_0] \cdot I = M_0.$$

Suppose the bank offers a contract $(r_1,r_2) \in Q(\alpha_2,\mu)$ and holds sufficient reserves for the case of normal business, $R = (1 + r_1) \cdot \mu \cdot M_0$. Given aggregate withdrawals $W(s_i)$, one easily computes the following state-contingent actual returns:

$$\rho_1(\cdot \mid s_1) = (1 + r_1) \quad \text{and} \quad \rho_2(\cdot \mid s_1) = (1 + r_2),$$
$$\rho_1(\cdot \mid s_2) = \rho_1^0 \quad \text{and} \quad \rho_2(\cdot \mid s_2) = 0,$$
$$\rho_1(\cdot \mid s_3) = \rho_1^0 \quad \text{and} \quad \rho_2(\cdot \mid s_3) = 0,$$

with $\rho_1^0 \equiv \alpha_1 + (1 - \alpha_1) \cdot (1 + r_1) \cdot \mu < (1 + r_1)$.

An individual consumer's behaviour has no impact on aggregate variables and, therefore, on returns. Hence, one can check the optimality of a consumer's strategy in regard to the other consumers' behaviour in a decision tree. In state s_1, no bank failure is possible. This explains why there is a single node for the decision in period 1 in this case. In the other states, s_2 and s_3, consumers obtain the same signal σ_L. Thus, they do not know whether a bank failure occurs or not. In Figure 7.7, the decision to deposit (not to deposit) is denoted by m_0 (0) and the decision to withdraw (not to withdraw) in period 1 by m_0 (0) respectively.

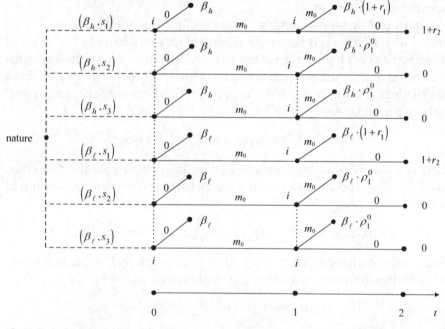

Fig. 7.7

It is easy to check that the assumed withdrawal behaviour in period 1

$$(w(\beta_h, \sigma_H), w(\beta_h, \sigma_L), w(\beta_\ell, \sigma_H), w(\beta_\ell, \sigma_L)) = (m_0, m_0, 0, m_0)$$

is indeed optimal. In state s_3 the bank fails and consumers, regardless of their private project, are justified in withdrawing their funds early. In state s_2, however, all consumers withdraw because the bad information about the illiquid asset makes even consumers with a low-return project find it too risky to stay with the bank. Though the illiquid asset has a good pay-off in this case, the bank will break down due to false information about a pending bank failure. Note that this bank run is caused by an information problem, not by any actual problem of the bank.

It remains to check whether depositing may be an optimal strategy in period 0 given such withdrawal behaviour. One computes the expected returns from depositing and following this withdrawal strategy as

$$(1 - \varepsilon - \delta) \cdot [\mu \cdot \beta_k \cdot (1 + r_1) + (1 - \mu) \cdot (1 + r_2)]$$
$$+ (\varepsilon + \delta) \cdot [\mu \cdot \beta_k + (1 - \mu) \cdot \beta_\ell] \cdot \rho_1^0$$

and the return from holding money as $[\mu \cdot \beta_k + (1 - \mu) \cdot \beta_\ell]$. Since

$$[\mu \cdot \beta_k \cdot (1 + r_1) + (1 - \mu) \cdot (1 + r_2)] > [\mu \cdot \beta_k + (1 - \mu) \cdot \beta_\ell]$$
$$> [\mu \cdot \beta_k + (1 - \mu) \cdot \beta_\ell] \cdot \rho_1^0,$$

depositing is optimal provided that $(\varepsilon + \delta)$, the probability of receiving a bad signal σ_L, is sufficiently small.

Though there are other equilibria in this game, these arguments demonstrate that informational problems can lead to bank runs. In contrast to the case of a certain return, however, it can be subgame-perfect to deposit with the bank if the risk of a bad signal is sufficiently low.

In Chapter 8, we will take up the question whether regulation of a bank may help to avoid problems arising in a bank model based on liquidity considerations.

....

Notes on the Literature

....

Since formal modelling of banks began, a substantial literature has emerged that concerns itself with the nature of the banking business. One cannot do justice to the many issues raised and the many contributions made in a single chapter of a book. Moreover, this literature has been surveyed several times over the past 20 years. The surveys by Baltensperger (1980) and Santomero (1984) organize the literature according to the different aspects of the banking business, and Hellwig (1991) provides a highly stimulating account of the most recent research from the perspective of the banking system's role in corporate finance. We content ourselves with a brief discussion of the three types of model that have emerged from this literature.

The oldest type of model views a bank as an enterprise that transforms indivisible and risky assets issued by firms into assets of small denomination with little or no risk. In this way, banks intermediate between small investors who seek low-risk investment opportunities and profitable but risky business investment. Banks manage their asset and liability structure for exogenously given risk and return characteristics of the assets and for exogenously given random withdrawals of deposits. The correct evaluation of the bank's asset risk and the correct pricing of liabilities becomes a major concern in this context. Baltensperger (1980) and Santomero (1984) offer examples for this type of model.

A second, more recent, strand of literature models investors and firms explicitly. Although direct investment in firms is feasible, banks can provide services for both parties. Diamond (1984) shows that banks may be more efficient in monitoring firms and therefore able to provide a portfolio of assets in firms at lower cost than an individual investor. By choosing a sufficiently diversified portfolio of assets the bank can provide deposits for investors with reduced or, by the law of large numbers, no risk at all. This model provides an endogenous justification for a bank. Diamond's (1984) model of investors and firms resembles the model of monitoring costs in Section 6.2, which was used to justify the standard debt contract.

The third type of banking model focuses on the special characteristic of a bank deposit contract to be due on call. Diamond and Dybvig (1983) sparked off a sequence of papers dealing with bank models based on illiquid assets and random needs for liquidity. Most of these models assume risk-averse consumers and view deposit contracts as insurance instruments. Jacklin (1987) shows that a mutual fund type of bank can implement the optimal contract in a Diamond and Dybvig environment. Jacklin and Bhattacharya (1988) show that this is no longer true if the illiquid asset has risky returns. Some of the literature investigates the role of a different rationing scheme called *sequential service constraint* (Diamond and Dybvig 1984 and Anderlini 1990). Chari and Jagannathan (1988) were the first to suggest that a bank run may be triggered by adverse information about the returns of the long-term project. The fact that 'sunspots' can induce a bank run was observed by Diamond and Dybvig (1983), and is explicitly modelled in Anderlini (1990). The model presented in this chapter is based on Eichberger and Milne (1991) and Eichberger (1992). Bhattacharya and Thakor (1993) and Dowd (1992) provide recent surveys of this literature.

Exercises

1. *Consider a consumer who has preferences over wealth in period 1 and period 2, W_1 and W_2 respectively, which are represented by the following von Neumann–Morgenstern utility function: $\beta_t \cdot W_1 + W_2$. The discount parameter β_t is uncertain but known to take the values β_e with probability μ and β_ℓ with probability $(1 - \mu)$, $\beta_e > \beta_\ell$.*

In period 0, this consumer has to invest her initial wealth W_0. She can

- *either hold 'money' which stores wealth from period to period without gain or loss,*
- *or invest it in an asset that returns per unit invested either α_1 in period 1 and 0 in period 2, or 0 in period 1 and α_2 in period 2, $\alpha_2 > \alpha_1$.*

(a) Draw a diagram with the indifference curves for the two types of consumers.

(b) Suppose that the consumer holds half of her initial wealth as money and invests the other half. Show in a diagram the feasible $W_2 - W_1$ combinations of the consumer. At what rate can she transform wealth of period 2 into wealth of period 1?

(c) Analyse in a diagram how the set of feasible wealth combinations changes as the consumer varies her investment in period 0.

(d) Solve the optimal choice problem for both types of the consumer given a decision about the initial investment level.

2. *Suppose that a bank has deposits D which it can hold as reserves R or invest in an asset that returns per unit either $0.80 in period 1 and $0 in period 2, or $0 in period 1 and $1.60 in period 2.*

(a) For a given amount of reserves R and the remainder of its deposits invested, show in a diagram how the bank's wealth in period 2 varies as withdrawals W change from zero to D.

(b) Prove that it is optimal to hold reserves exactly equal to the pay-out that is necessary for withdrawals in period 1.

(c) Suppose that the bank holds half of its deposits as reserves and promises to pay 20 per cent interest on deposits withdrawn in period 1. Show that the bank's wealth in period 2 falls to zero if withdrawals exceed 75 per cent of deposits.

3. *Reconsider the model of Section 7.6 where the investment project may fail and consumers get a signal which is correlated with success or failure of the project.*

(a) How many types of consumers have to be distinguished in period 1 in this case? Write down the type-contingent contract for the representative consumer.

(b) How many states of the world must be distinguished in this scenario? For each state of the world, write down the feasibility constraints if all consumers use the same type-contingent contract.

4. *A Bayes–Nash equilibrium is defined as a type-contingent strategy for each player such that the strategy assigned to each type of player maximizes the expected utility of this type*

- *given the behaviour described by the type-contingent strategy combination, and*
- *given the information revealed by the player's type.*

(a) Show that the bank-run equilibrium described in Section 7.5 is a Bayes–Nash equilibrium. What is the information revealed by a player's type?

(b) Show that the optimal contract described in Section 7.3 is a Bayes–Nash equilibrium.

5. *Reconsider the model of Section 7.2. Suppose that, in period 0, consumers form a mutual fund which invests $(1 - \mu) \cdot M_0$ and holds $\mu \cdot M_0$ as liquid reserves. In period 1, the fund pays each consumer $\mu \cdot m_0$ and in period 2 $\alpha_2 \cdot (1 - \mu) \cdot m_0$. After they learn their type in period 1, consumers are allowed to trade their shares in the fund.*

(a) Determine supply and demand for shares of the fund in period 1.

(b) What is the equilibrium price of a share?

(c) Show that this mutual fund with retrading of shares also implements the optimal contract derived in Section 7.3.

8
...

REGULATION OF BANKS

Chapter 7 suggested that transformation of liquidity is a bank's main role in a modern economy. Taking deposits on call and investing them, at least partially, in long-term illiquid assets entails the risk of bank runs. Because of the intrinsic risk these institutions face, regulation has been part of the institutional framework from the earliest days of banking. In this chapter, we study the effectiveness of different regulatory measures and the capacity of these instruments to achieve their objectives.

8.1 Bank Regulation: The Rationale

We have argued in Chapter 7 that rational consumers would not deposit their funds with a bank if they expected a bank run to occur in period 1. However, once the decision to deposit has been made, these funds are committed and a bank-run equilibrium is as much a possibility as an equilibrium implementing the optimal contract. Indeed, existence of these two equilibria is a prerequisite for adverse information triggering a bank run.

In most countries, banks have been considered to be firms with special risks and broader obligations than other businesses. A major concern has always been the possibility of a banking panic which may be triggered by a failure of or a run on a single bank. Such a panic, leading to the collapse of a number of banks and associated firms, may arise because some of a bank's long-term investment will often be with other banks which may be forced to liquidate funds in turn. Selling assets of many financial institutions simultaneously may severely reduce the liquidation value of the assets, thus re-enforcing the need to liquidate. Such banking panics have been observed historically and have provided a reason for extensive regulation of banking business.

Regulation of banks has taken many forms. Some of the practices found are easy to understand in the context of our model. For example, banks were often constrained by regulation to purchase only 'safe' assets, like mortgages, excluding banks from trade in equity and other security markets altogether. Such measures were aimed at making the pay-off of a bank's assets as predictable as possible, for, as the bank model in the previous chapter shows, certainty may prevent bank failures. However, certain returns of a bank's long-term assets do not shelter it from bank runs. A disadvantage of such regulation is that it makes a bank's assets more predictable but not necessarily more stable. By preventing diversification of a bank's assets, the long-run risk of a bank's portfolio may even be higher.

Bank failures cause disruptions of the payment system and may have large repercussions on all sectors of an economy, because other firms and banks may break down as a consequence. Prudential control of the banking system with the objective of preventing further bank failures has a certain appeal therefore. Our model shows that bad news may trigger a bank run, even if it is objectively false. Thus, observing the breakdown of a bank may induce depositors of another bank to withdraw their funds, even if the two banks are not even linked.

The model presented in the previous chapter is suitable for analysing and assessing different forms of regulation designed to prevent bank runs. Among the many possible ways of regulating banks, the following four types of intervention are most commonly proposed:

- reserve requirements,
- suspension of convertibility,
- deposit insurance, and
- capital adequacy requirements.

These methods will be analysed in the context of the bank model with a certain return of the illiquid asset, and also for the case of uncertainty about the illiquid asset's return with new information arriving in period 1. The analysis will focus on the suitability of these regulatory measures for the stated objective, to avoid bank crises, and the costs involved for the banks. Further issues concerning regulation of banks will be discussed at the end of this chapter.

Most of the arguments about the impact of prudential regulation on withdrawal behaviour can be conducted in Figure 8.1 which shows the repayment schedule of period 2 as a function of aggregate withdrawals, $\rho_2(W)$, and the return of consumers with a low-return investment opportunity if they withdraw their funds in period 1, $\beta_\ell \cdot \rho_1(W)$. A consumer who leaves funds with the bank will achieve a return of $\rho_2(W)$ while a consumer with a low-return project obtains a return of $\beta_\ell \cdot \rho_1(W)$ from withdrawing in period 1. It is optimal for a consumer with a low-return project

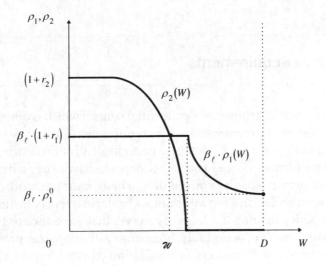

Fig. 8.1

- to withdraw the deposit if $\beta_\ell \cdot \rho_1(W) \geq \rho_2(W)$, and
- to leave the deposit in the bank if $\beta_\ell \cdot \rho_1(W) \leq \rho_2(W)$.

Thus, there is a critical level of aggregate withdrawals, $\mathcal{W}$, such that consumers with a low-return project will withdraw their funds, if and only if the aggregate withdrawals exceed $\mathcal{W}$. Notice that $\mathcal{W}$ is always larger than reserves, $\mathcal{W} > R$, which equal the aggregate withdrawals of the consumers with a high-return investment opportunity, who will withdraw their deposits in any case. Hence, there are two equilibria[1] associated with two aggregate withdrawal levels,

- an equilibrium at $W^* = R$, where only consumers with the high-return project withdraw, and
- an equilibrium at $W' = D$, where all consumers withdraw their deposits prematurely.

From Figure 8.1, it is immediately obvious that the bank-run equilibrium, $W = D$, will exist as long as the return schedules satisfy the inequality

$$\rho_2(D) < \beta_\ell \cdot \rho_1(D).$$

Regulation which is effective in preventing a bank-run equilibrium must change the pay-off schedules such that this case is impossible. This will be the leading question in the following sections where we discuss the particular forms of prudential regulation.

[1] Indeed, there is a third equilibrium at $W = \mathcal{W}$ where consumers with the low-return project are indifferent between withdrawing and leaving the deposit with the bank if the right proportion of indifferent consumers withdraws. This equilibrium will not be further analysed here.

8.2 Reserve Requirements

One of the earliest instruments of prudential control which is often applied in practice is *reserve requirements*. Reserve requirements usually specify that a minimum fraction of a bank's deposits, or equivalently of its assets, be held as reserves in the form of a liquid asset. Since deposits have to be paid back on demand rather than at a predetermined date, a bank must have sufficient liquid funds to meet the demand for withdrawals by depositors at any time. An optimal bank policy requires holdings of reserves that are sufficient to meet the expected withdrawals in period 1. Hence, banks will voluntarily provide for reserves in order to avoid unnecessary liquidation costs arising from premature liquidation of long-term assets.

The amount of reserves which banks hold voluntarily will be insufficient, however, if more consumers than expected withdraw their deposits. In particular, they are inadequate for a bank run where all depositors reclaim their money. Mandatory reserve requirements are supposed to guarantee adequate reserves for withdrawals. Considering the following three cases makes it absolutely clear that there is a fundamental problem with reserve requirements as an instrument of prudential control.

(1) If the bank is required to hold reserves which are adequate for just withdrawals in the non-bank-run equilibrium, then the bank will voluntarily comply with these requirements. No protection from bank runs is provided by this level of reserves, as the analysis in the previous chapter shows.

(2) If required reserve holdings exceed the amount of reserves voluntarily held by a bank but fall short of a 100 per cent reserve ratio, then no extra protection against bank runs is achieved. Actual returns on deposits in period 2 will still fall to zero if all consumers withdraw,

$$\rho_2(D) = 0 < \beta_\ell \cdot \rho_1(D),$$

making it optimal for all consumers to withdraw early. Such extended reserve requirements impose costs on the bank because reserves in excess of those needed for the non-run case could have been invested in the illiquid asset yielding a higher return. These costs reduce the interest payment that the bank can make to consumers and/or the bank's profit. Thus, there are costs from such a policy without offsetting benefits in terms of greater security of the bank.

(3) Finally, if the regulator imposes a 100 per cent reserve requirement, then full protection against bank runs is achieved. The bank can, however, no longer

invest any deposits in the illiquid asset, thus forgoing any returns from holding deposits. Hence, the bank cannot pay a return on deposits. This destroys the possibility of achieving a superior return by depositing with the bank. In this case, protection from bank runs is provided at the cost of all potential benefits from depositing.

Figure 8.2 shows that, with a 100 per cent reserve ratio, the bank simply stores the deposits and cannot pay any return on deposits. It is therefore optimal for all consumers, irrespective of their investment opportunity, to withdraw the funds that they have deposited with the bank. In fact, depositing is like holding money.

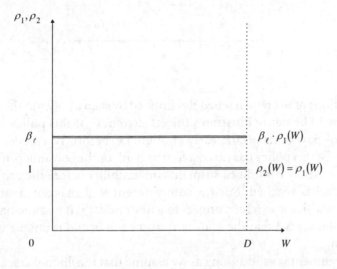

Fig. 8.2

This analysis will not change at all if the return of the illiquid asset uncertain and if information on the quality of the bank's investment becomes publicly known in period 1. In conclusion, reserve requirements are a particularly inefficient way to achieve protection against bank runs.

8.3 Suspension of Convertibility

An alternative way of securing the bank against bank runs is an early closure of the bank. If the pay-out in period 1 is stopped before the return on deposits in period 2, $\rho_2(\cdot)$, falls below $\beta_\ell \cdot \rho_1(\cdot)$, then there remains no incentive for the consumers with a low-return project to withdraw early. Figure 8.3 shows the

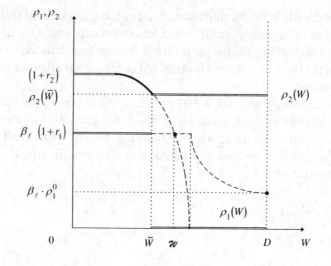

Fig. 8.3

modifications of the return schedules implied by such a policy as the schedules marked ⬄. The figure illustrates the effectiveness of this policy if the suspension of payments occurs early enough, i.e. before $\tilde{W}$ exceeds $\mathbf{w}$. More importantly, this policy has no cost for the bank or the consumers if the regulator can credibly commit to suspend convertibility before the critical withdrawal level is reached. Such a commitment will make it irrational for consumers with a low-return project to withdraw early. It is immediately obvious from Figure 8.3 that the non-bank-run equilibrium is unique under this regulation.

This argument is valid as long as we assume that the illiquid asset has a certain return in period 2. If one assumes instead that, with small probability, the illiquid asset may fail in period 2, then suspending convertibility cannot prevent returns in period 2 from falling to zero if this event occurs. If the likelihood of this event is small enough, then consumers with the low-return project may not withdraw their funds in period 1. However, in this case, consumers will actually lose their deposits if the bank's illiquid asset fails. Protection from a bank run may come at the cost of 'efficient' liquidation should the project actually fail.

Moreover, if consumers receive a signal concerning the likelihood of a bank failure, then this signal may trigger the bank-run equilibrium even if the authorities tried to stop the pay-out from the bank. Consumers who are concerned about their investment may then run to recover as much as possible before the bank is closed. A credible commitment to close banks in the case of excessive withdrawals may even increase the likelihood of a run, since consumers face the prospect of losing even the liquidation return ρ_1^0.

8.4 Deposit Insurance

Compared to reserve requirements and suspension of convertibility, deposit insurance has been a regulatory institution of more recent times. The first comprehensive system was introduced in the USA following the series of bank collapses in the early 1930s. Since then a number of other countries have adopted similar schemes to protect depositors against bank runs.

Deposit insurance usually works as follows. A regulatory agency collects mandatory contributions from financial institutions covered by the scheme to accumulate funds which will be used to pay back deposit claims in case of a bank run or failure. Different countries vary this basic arrangement by

- guaranteeing only part of a depositor's funds,
- restricting payments to a maximum amount,
- making contribution schemes dependent on some risk measure, or
- requiring contributions in proportion to some balance sheet item.

In the context of the bank model of the previous chapter, it becomes obvious that deposit insurance does not affect consumers' withdrawal behaviour if it only guarantees a fraction or all of the promised repayment in period 1, $(1 + r_1)$. Consumers with a low-return project β_ℓ will withdraw their deposits whenever

$$\beta_\ell \cdot \rho_1(\cdot) > \rho_2(\cdot).$$

If all consumers withdraw their deposits, the second-period return will be zero, $\rho_2(\cdot, D) = 0$. Hence, consumers will find it optimal to withdraw if everyone else withdraws irrespective of how much the deposit insurance agency guarantees to repay in period 1.

To prevent consumers from withdrawing early, repayments in period 2 must exceed the return which consumers achieve from their private project if they withdraw their deposits in period 1. Since a low-return consumer could recover ρ_1^0 in period 1, even if all other consumers withdraw, a guaranteed return in period 2 of $\beta_\ell \cdot \rho_1^0$ would break the incentive to withdraw in period 1. This argument shows that a guaranteed repayment in period 1, $\hat{\rho}_1$, which is not accompanied by a repayment in period 2, $\hat{\rho}_2$, of at least $\beta_\ell \cdot \hat{\rho}_1$, cannot prevent bank runs.

Figure 8.4 shows a deposit insurance scheme where depositors are guaranteed a minimum repayment of $(1 + r_1)$ in period 1 and a minimum repayment of $\beta_\ell \cdot (1 + r_1)$ in period 2. Though depositors with a low-return project would

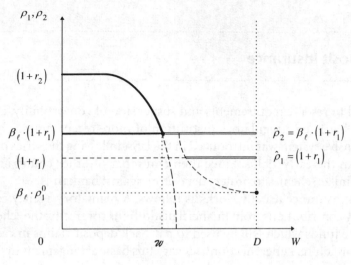

Fig. 8.4

be indifferent between withdrawing and leaving their deposits in the bank for $W > \mathcal{w}$, the non-bank-run equilibrium will dominate all other equilibria. There are many different deposit insurance schemes distinguished by the repayment schedules that they guarantee depositors. It is possible to give precise conditions for a deposit insurance scheme to render a bank run impossible.

The following proposition holds for the case of a certain return on the illiquid asset α_2 if the bank offers a deposit contract $(r_1, r_2) \in Q(\alpha_2, \mu)$ and holds reserves $R = (1 + r_1) \cdot \mu \cdot M_0$.

PROPOSITION 8.1. If a deposit insurance agency guarantees a repayment $\hat{\rho}_2 > \beta_\ell \cdot \hat{\rho}_1$, then a bank run is not a Bayes–Nash equilibrium in period 1.

PROOF. A bank run is a situation where all consumers irrespective of their project withdraw their deposit, $(w(\beta_h), w(\beta_\ell)) = (m_0, m_0)$. Consider a consumer with a low-return project. If this consumer withdraws in period 1, she will earn a return rate of $\beta_\ell \cdot \hat{\rho}_1$. By not withdrawing in period 1, a consumer obtains $\hat{\rho}_2 > \beta_\ell \cdot \hat{\rho}_1$ from the deposit insurance. Hence, withdrawing in period 1 cannot be optimal for a consumer with a low-return project. ∎

With a deposit insurance system satisfying this condition, bank-run equilibria are no longer compatible with optimizing behaviour of consumers because the repayment schedule in period 2 has been changed by guaranteeing repayment $\hat{\rho}_2$. Notice that the guarantee of the deposit insurer will never have to be exercised, since no bank run will occur in equilibrium. Thus, deposit insurance appears to be an attractive way to prevent bank runs arising from a coordination problem among consumers.

This conclusion depends, however, on the assumed risklessness of the illiquid asset. To see this, reconsider the model with an illiquid asset that has a risky return α_H. Repeating the argument in the proof of Proposition 8.1 shows that a deposit insurance scheme that pays $\hat{\rho}_2 > \beta_L \cdot \rho_1^0$ in period 2 will make early withdrawals by low-return consumers suboptimal. Hence, no bank run equilibrium exists in this case either. In state s_3, however, a bank failure occurs because the illiquid asset has a return of zero. In this case, the deposit insurer actually has to cover the loss, and deposit insurance is no longer a free good.

If bank failures are a possibility, then the deposit insurance agency will have to pay for losses by the bank. This may be very costly and lead the deposit insurance agency itself into bankruptcy if government agencies do not inject further funds. The problem arises because it is impossible for a regulator to predict whether unexpected early withdrawals by depositors are a pure coordination problem causing short-term liquidity problems for the bank, or a rational reaction to a pending failure of the bank's investment. The difficulty faced by a regulator in distinguishing bank runs caused by sudden liquidity problems from bank failures caused by bad investment decisions has been a major problem afflicting the deposit insurance scheme in the USA over the last decade.

8.5 Capital-Adequacy Requirements

Up to this point, a bank has been treated as a business institution without owners. Indeed, if the deposit contract were optimal, i.e. the contracted returns on deposits were (r_1^*, r_2^*), then the bank would not make any profit.

There are, however, incentive-compatible deposit contracts $(r_1, r_2) \in Q(\alpha_2, \mu)$ which create a surplus for the bank. Profitable ownership of a bank is therefore possible in the environment modelled in the previous chapter.

If owners participate in the investment of a bank and if they offer repayments on deposits that generate some profit, then the owners' profits provide a cushion against unexpected withdrawals in period 1 and the associated decline in actual returns on deposits in period 2. Capital participation by the bank's owners reduces the risk of a bank-run equilibrium. The owners' capital and profits work like a collateral for the contracted return schedules of the deposit contract. Indeed, with sufficient capital and a certain return on the illiquid investment, owners can guarantee the contracted returns.

Capital-adequacy requirements impose a minimal capital participation by owners, usually expressed as a fraction of certain assets of the bank. Denoting the amount of capital contributed by the owners of a bank by E and the amount invested in the illiquid asset by K, one can write the balance sheet equation of the bank in this model as

$$K + R = D + E.$$

With equity participation E the amount of funds invested in the illiquid asset would be $K = D + E - R$. This raises the question of how much equity is necessary to guarantee those depositors who do not withdraw in period 1 the contracted return $(1 + r_2)$. Clearly, if the funds deposited by those consumers who stay with the bank until period 2 remain invested in the illiquid asset, then they will reap a return α_2 which is high enough to pay the contracted amount $(1 + r_2)$.

In a bank without own-capital participation by its owners, the bank has to liquidate funds invested in the illiquid asset if withdrawals in period 1 exceed reserves, $(1 + r_1) \cdot W > R$. Since liquidation of a unit of money invested in the illiquid asset raises only α_1 units of money in period 1 while the bank has to pay out $(1 + r_1)$ per unit of withdrawal, it has to cover a deficit of $(1 + r_1 - \alpha_1)$ per unit of withdrawal by additional liquidation of funds. If the bank held no reserves, $R = 0$, then a bank deficit of $(1 + r_1 - \alpha_1) \cdot W$ would have to be covered by liquidation in period 1. Since withdrawals cannot be greater than total deposits, $D \geq W$, the maximal possible deficit is $(1 + r_1 - \alpha_1) \cdot D$.

Holding reserves saves $(1 - \alpha_1) \cdot R$ and liquidating equity invested in the illiquid asset raises $\alpha_1 \cdot E$. It is therefore unnecessary to liquidate deposits invested in the illiquid asset if

$$\alpha_1 \cdot E + (1 - \alpha_1) \cdot R \geq (1 + r_1 - \alpha_1) \cdot D$$

holds. Using the balance sheet equation to substitute for R, one can express this condition equivalently as

$$E \geq (1 - \alpha_1) \cdot K + r_1 \cdot D.$$

In this form, it becomes clear that equity must suffice to cover any shortfall on investments in the illiquid asset plus the promised interest payments for period 1.

For the case of an illiquid asset with riskless return α_2, the following proposition shows that this condition is in fact sufficient to guarantee a return of $(1 + r_2)$ in period 2 independent of withdrawals in period 1.

PROPOSITION 8.2. For any amount of deposits D and reserves R, suppose that the owners of the bank invest equity in the illiquid asset such that

$$E \geq [(1 + r_1 - \alpha_1) \cdot D - (1 - \alpha_1) \cdot R]/\alpha_1.$$

Then the actual return on a unit of deposit in period 2 satisfies

$$\rho_2(W) = (1 + r_2)$$

for all levels of aggregate withdrawals $W \leq D$.

PROOF. From the definition of the actual return function $\rho_2(\cdot)$ in Chapter 7, it follows that $\rho_2(W) = (1 + r_2)$ holds if and only if

$$V(r_1;W,R,D) \geq (1 + r_2) \cdot (D - W).$$

Recalling the definition of $V(r_1;W,R,D)$ given in Chapter 7, modified such that the investment in the illiquid asset is $E + D - R$ rather than $D - R$, it is easy to see that, for $(1 + r_1) \cdot W > R$,

$$V(r_1;W,R,D) = \max\{0, \alpha_2 \cdot (E + D - R) - (\alpha_2/\alpha_1) \cdot [(1 + r_1) \cdot W - R]\}$$

holds. Hence, $V(r_1;W,R,D) \geq (1 + r_2) \cdot (D - W)$ if and only if

$$\alpha_2 \cdot (E + D - R) - (\alpha_2/\alpha_1) \cdot [(1 + r_1) \cdot W - R] \geq (1 + r_2) \cdot (D - W).$$

This inequality can be transformed into the following equivalent inequality

$$(\alpha_2/\alpha_1) \cdot [\alpha_1 \cdot E + (1 - \alpha_1) \cdot R + \alpha_1 \cdot [1 - (1 + r_2)/\alpha_2] \cdot D$$
$$- [(1 + r_1) - \alpha_1 \cdot (1 + r_2)/\alpha_2] \cdot W] \geq 0.$$

Note that $(1 + r_1) \geq 1 \geq \alpha_1 \cdot (1 + r_2)/\alpha_2$ holds since $1 \geq (1 + r_2)/\alpha_2$ by feasibility $(r_1,r_2) \in Q(\alpha_2,\mu)$. Because $W \leq D$, the last inequality is necessarily satisfied if

$$(\alpha_2/\alpha_1) \cdot [\alpha_1 \cdot E + (1 - \alpha_1) \cdot R + \alpha_1 \cdot [1 - (1 + r_2)/\alpha_2] \cdot D$$
$$- [(1 + r_1) - \alpha_1 \cdot (1 + r_2)/\alpha_2] \cdot D]$$
$$= (\alpha_2/\alpha_1) \cdot [\alpha_1 \cdot E + (1 - \alpha_1) \cdot R - (1 + r_1 - \alpha_1) \cdot D] \geq 0$$

holds. This is, however, guaranteed by the condition of the proposition. ■

Proposition 8.2 demonstrates that sufficient equity can guarantee depositors the contracted return $(1 + r_2)$ no matter how many depositors withdraw their funds in period 1. It is therefore never optimal for a depositor with a low-return project to withdraw his deposit in period 1 since $(1 + r_2) \geq \beta_\ell \cdot (1 + r_1)$ for all levels of aggregate withdrawals W. Hence, there cannot be a bank-run equilibrium if the owners of the bank provide sufficient capital. Figure 8.5 illustrates the return functions of deposits for this case.

Though it has been shown that the owners of a bank can guarantee the second-period return on deposits and, by doing so, protect the bank from bank runs, it is not clear whether the owners of the bank would want to invest the necessary capital in the bank business. It may well be that a requirement to

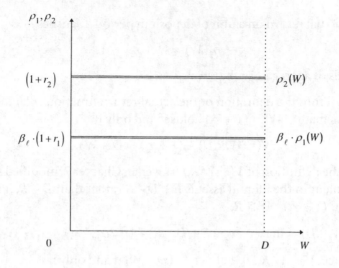

Fig. 8.5

invest sufficient funds in the banking business will make banking non-profitable. Whether the banking operation is undertaken or not depends on the return that the owners' investment in the bank will generate and on the opportunity cost of such an investment.

To gain some insight into the incentives of the bank owners and the scope for profitable banking in this model, consider the case of a monopolistic bank with an inelastic supply of deposits for $r_1 \geq 0$. If the bank is a monopolist, it can offer the lowest incentive-compatible interest rate in period 2, $r_2 = \beta_\ell \cdot (1 + r_1)$ $- 1$. The profit-maximizing pair of interest rates subject to the supply of deposits is therefore the pair $(r_1, r_2) = (0, \beta_\ell - 1)$. Given this interest rate pair all consumers will initially deposit with the bank and consumers with a high-return project will withdraw in period 1 while all other consumers stay with the bank up to period 2 if the actual return rate in period 2 is at least $\beta_\ell - 1$.

Suppose that the bank satisfies the capital-adequacy constraint for this interest pair,

$$E \geq [(1 - \alpha_1)/\alpha_1] \cdot (D - R) = [(1 - \alpha_1)/\alpha_1] \cdot (1 - \mu) \cdot M_0.$$

Note that the profit-maximizing choice of interest rate in period 1 is zero, $r_1 = 0$, and the optimal level of reserves is equal to the amount withdrawn by the consumers with a high-return project, $R = W = \mu \cdot M_0$. Given sufficient equity, there is a unique withdrawal equilibrium where only high-return consumers withdraw their deposits in period 1, as Figure 8.5 shows.

The profit from the banking business for the owners is therefore

$$\Pi(E) := \alpha_2 \cdot (E + D - R) - \beta_\ell \cdot (D - R) = \alpha_2 \cdot E + (\alpha_2 - \beta_\ell) \cdot (1 - \mu) \cdot M_0.$$

There is a constant profit rate from the business with those depositors that do not withdraw in period 1, $(\alpha_2 - \beta_\ell) \cdot (1 - \mu) \cdot M_0$. The marginal profit for any unit of own-capital invested is α_2, the return rate of the illiquid asset in which the bank invests its equity. Whether the bank is willing to invest voluntarily in the riskless illiquid asset depends on the opportunity costs of the bank's owners. If alternative investment opportunities have a return rate which is less than or equal to α_2, then a capital-adequacy requirement which guarantees the non-bank-run equilibrium will be without cost to the bank's owners.

If, however, the opportunity costs of the bank's owners per unit of funds invested in the bank business, say $\tilde{r}$, exceeds the return on the illiquid asset, $\tilde{r} > \alpha_2$, then investors may not be willing to provide sufficient equity to guarantee the return schedule for depositors. More precisely, the profitability condition $\Pi(E) \geq \tilde{r} \cdot E$ imposes an upper bound on profitable equity participation by the bank's owners,

$$\frac{(\alpha_2 - \beta_1)}{(\tilde{r} - \alpha_2)} \cdot (1 - \mu) \cdot M_0 \geq E.$$

Note that this upper bound depends on the minimum interest that has to be paid on deposits, β_ℓ, because that limits the profit margin on deposits that are not withdrawn, and on the amount of deposits that will not be withdrawn under normal business conditions. This upper bound may well be in conflict with the lower bound on equity participation required to secure the return schedule on deposits. These considerations point to the crucial importance of the bank owners' opportunity costs of funds for their willingness to comply with capital-adequacy requirements.

As in the case of deposit insurance discussed before, the potentially costless protection from bank runs through a guarantee of the repayment schedule on deposits, this time, however, by the bank owners rather than by a public agency, depends again on the assumption that the illiquid asset be riskless. If there is a chance that the illiquid asset may fail, then it is impossible to protect return rates by investing sufficiently in the illiquid asset.

This is easy to see by considering the actual return rate function $\rho_2(W)$ for the case where $\alpha_2 = 0$ holds. No level of equity will stabilize the actual return in this case. Information about a pending bank failure can therefore induce early withdrawals which indeed may be justified, as in state s_3, or may not be justified, as in state s_2. Thus, one has to conclude that capital-adequacy requirements cannot prevent bank run equilibria if there remains a risk of a bank failure.

8.6 Summary

The discussion of different regulatory measures for prudential control in this section has led to the following conclusions:

- Reserve requirements provide protection against bank runs only in the case of a 100 per cent reserve requirement which eliminates the efficiency-enhancing deposit business of a bank.
- Suspension of convertibility achieves protection from bank-run equilibria for the case of an illiquid asset with a riskless return. Otherwise it prevents efficient liquidation of a failing investment.
- Deposit insurance can provide effective protection from bank runs whether the illiquid asset is risky or riskless. This is possible because outside funds are injected in the case of a bank failure. The costs of such a protective measure depend therefore on the distortion created by raising the necessary funds for the deposit insurance scheme.
- Capital-adequacy requirements can provide protection from bank runs if the illiquid asset is riskless; otherwise there is no possibility of preventing bank runs through capital-adequacy requirements. The costs of this regulation for the bank owners depend crucially on the opportunity costs of their funds.

Up to this point, the analysis has neglected the question of how incentives for depositors to monitor the bank's assets are affected by regulatory protection. Moral hazard of this kind is often considered to be a major problem for a smoothly working deposit market. The standard argument for this view supposes that, without regulation, the market for deposits would operate just like any other market for financial assets: equilibrium interest rates for deposits reflect the risks of the respective bank's asset portfolio and deposits are claims against a bank's portfolio which can be priced as described in the first part of this book. Any kind of regulation will interfere with this process and lead to distorted asset prices and allocations.

This view rests on the presumption that there is no asymmetric information and that the pay-off stream of a bank's assets is not affected by consumers' decisions to withdraw or to deposit, i.e. to buy or sell claims to these assets. From this perspective, there is no difference between deposits and other securities. In the model proposed in the previous chapter, however, deposits are a special contract form which solves an investment problem due to asymmetric information about depositors' characteristics. The decision by depositors to withdraw their funds does not leave the returns on deposits unaffected. The actual returns on deposits with a bank are endogenously determined and depend on the equilibrium that will obtain. It is therefore inadequate to apply the equilibrium-pricing methods of the first part of this book to these deposit contracts. Therefore, the standard argument for a moral hazard problem due to regulation is not applicable.

Of course, this argument does not rule out incentive problems due to prudential control. It asks, however, for an argument in the framework of asymmetric information which was used to establish this contract form as potentially optimal.

Notes on the Literature

There is a large literature on bank regulation. In particular, during the last decade much of this literature has been concerned with the moral hazard problem implicit in all forms of outside guarantees. This part of the literature was stimulated by the experiences in the USA in the mid-1980s which are analysed in Kane (1985).

Formal analysis of different prudential control concepts is limited because there is no generally agreed model of a bank. Diamond and Dybvig (1983) discuss deposit insurance and suspension of convertibility. Anderlini (1990) argues for a lender-of-last-resort facility which we did not discuss here.

In recent years, the debate about prudential control has shifted more to capital adequacy requirements and their impact on the banking business. This shift in interest is linked to the introduction of capital standards for banks internationally agreed upon by the members of the Bank for International Settlements.

Exercises

1. *Consider the case of deposit insurance and assume that there is a fixed fee for insuring the bank which has to be paid in period 0.*

(a) Show in a diagram how this fee affects the return schedules in period 1 and in period 2.

(b) Analyse in the diagram the effects of such a fee on the degree of protection the insurance scheme provides and on the feasibility of the bank.

(c) How would this analysis be changed if the fee had to be paid in period 1?

2. *Consider a deposit insurance scheme that would guarantee only the deposit in each period.*

(a) Draw a diagram showing the repayment schedules that a depositor faces in this case. Will such an insurance scheme provide protection from a bank run?

(b) By how much must the guaranteed repayment in period 2 exceed the repayment in period 1 to prevent a bank run?

(c) Discuss the effectiveness of an insurance scheme which guarantees a repayment in period 2 that exceeds the repayment that the bank can provide in period 1 by a fixed margin.

3. *It is argued in this chapter that deposit insurance and suspension of convertibility can effectively prevent bank-run equilibria at no cost.*

(a) Explain this proposition.

(b) Will this proposition remain true if the bank's investment can fail but consumers get no signal about the state of the investment project?

9

TOWARDS APPLICATION: FINANCIAL MARKETS AND FINANCIAL INTERMEDIARIES

In this final chapter, we present an overview of the theoretical material contained in earlier chapters, and attempt to relate the current state of the theory of financial economics to events unfolding in actual financial institutions and markets. One of the exciting features of financial economics is that both theory and practice have advanced considerably in recent decades. More than that, a number of practical developments have followed almost immediately upon new theoretical insights. A prominent example of this latter point is the rapid practical implementation of the theoretical breakthrough achieved by Fischer Black and Myron Scholes in their solution of the option pricing problem.

A theme of the chapter is the continuing rivalry between financial intermediaries and financial markets as alternative means of effecting intertemporal trade. Outside the theoretical world of perfect markets, financial intermediaries have a role to play in bringing borrowers and lenders together. As information technology becomes more sophisticated and transaction costs are lowered, some, at least, of the obstacles to the operation of markets are removed, and direct finance via market exchange of financial instruments displaces indirect finance via financial intermediaries. Financial intermediaries, in turn, respond with more elaborate products and processes in order to recapture lost opportunities. The evolution of intertemporal trade in the real world is marked by this dialectic struggle between alternative institutional arrangements: financial markets and financial intermediaries.

9.1 Financial Markets and Financial Intermediaries in Theoretical Context

In a world of perfect markets, the intertemporal choice problem is solved by agents interacting directly with one another in financial markets. The objects of choice are financial claims. Such claims are enforceable contracts which specify the precise conditions, including time and states of nature, under which particular actions will be undertaken by the contracting parties. In such an imaginary world, taken to the extreme, it is possible for agents to insure fully against any conceivable contingency. Within the limits of their budget constraints, agents can rearrange their consumption of goods and services in an infinite variety of ways, both through time and across states of nature, so as to achieve maximum satisfaction or utility.

The extension of the standard choice paradigm of atemporal micro-economics to an intertemporal context is the starting-point for a discussion of financial economics. At this level of generality and abstraction, it is clear that extension to an intertemporal context adds nothing of substance to the standard problem of consumer utility maximization. Financial economics is a mere derivative of general economics, albeit with a more elaborate set of commodities which are the objects of trade. A seminal statement of this approach is Debreu (1959).

Several strands of literature evolve from the foundation of perfect financial markets. The first is what we recognize as the traditional Theory of Finance. This involves the application of restrictive assumptions either to the preferences of economic agents or to the probability distributions attaching to the return vectors of financial assets. Either way, the restrictions produce a theoretical framework within which agents choose amongst assets based on the mean and variance of the probability distributions of asset returns.

This approach leads immediately to the familiar mean-variance analysis of portfolio choice theory and subsequently to the development of the Capital Asset-Pricing Model. The focus throughout is on financial markets in which defined claims are traded amongst agents. The questions of interest concern the demands for different assets in equilibrium and the prices which clear asset markets in equilibrium.

A second approach, conceptually distinct from the first and yet also growing out of the perfect markets paradigm, is arbitrage pricing. In this case, no restrictions are placed on agents' preferences. The foundation for developing pricing rules in equilibrium is the fundamental notion in economics that perfect substitutes trade at the same price in equilibrium. This 'law of one price' becomes the basis upon which a variety of pricing relationships can be developed. Perhaps the most famous is the Black–Scholes option-pricing model. For all its complexity, the Black–Scholes formula represents nothing beyond the outworking of the forces of arbitrage in a model of contingent claims markets.

The concept of arbitrage is also useful in developing much simpler pricing relationships. The concept of net present value, viewed in this light, is an arbitrage relationship. When markets exist in which the individual elements of a sequence of cash flows can be separately traded, the net present value of the sequence is simply the sum of the separate market prices. This 'linear' property of arbitrage models conveys a powerful insight into the pricing of complex financial claims. The key to pricing complex claims in equilibrium is determining precisely how such complex claims can be decomposed into their constituent elements. The price of the complex claim in equilibrium will be the simple linear sum of the prices of the constituent elements. This assumes, of course, that the constituent elements are separately traded in discrete markets.

A third stream of literature to flow from the paradigm of perfect financial markets focuses on the financial structure of the firm. Publication of the Modigliani–Miller (MM) 'irrelevance' results turned conventional wisdom on its head. It would have been hard to imagine results more contrary to established wisdom in corporate finance than the twin propositions that the financial structure of the firm and its dividend policy had no impact on firm value. After all, 'everybody knew' that gearing was of vital importance to the success of a firm, and how sensitive the stock market was to a firm's dividend policy.

The significance of the MM findings was widely misinterpreted. Rather than implying the futility of corporate finance, the MM results pointed to the inadequacy of models based on the assumption of perfect financial markets. Rather than denying the good sense in the advice given by corporate financiers, both then and now, the results pointed to the inadequacy of the theory in explaining the rationale for such advice.

The intellectual legacy of the MM theorems is the research agenda they spawned seeking to establish precisely which aspects of the perfect markets paradigm were responsible for their unexpected results. Subsequent explorations of the roles of taxes, clientele effects, and the like, have been singularly productive of valuable insights into how financial markets work in reality.

A fourth development in the literature is the investigation of the incompleteness of financial markets. This represents an attempt to relax one of the conditions of the perfect markets paradigm, namely the existence of a complete set of markets in which elementary financial claims can be traded.

The absence of complete markets does not disturb the main results of the theory. It is still possible to derive the CAPM, for example, and the Modigliani–Miller results generally remain intact. Incompleteness compromises the efficiency properties of a general equilibrium. It is no longer true that a general equilibrium allocation in financial markets is necessarily Pareto-optimal.

Perhaps of greater practical relevance is the fact that market incompleteness destroys 'value maximization' as the unanimous choice of utility-maximizing shareholders for the objective function of the firm. In short, the Fisher Separation Theorem no longer holds. In practical terms, this undermines the use of profit maximization and its related capital budgeting rules, including net present value maximization, as legitimate decision criteria in corporate finance. In a world of incomplete markets, it is simply not true that shareholders are uniquely served by managerial attempts to maximize profit. The shareholders in fact face a collective choice problem of the Arrow type in attempting to devise instructions for management. This raises the spectre of owner– owner and owner–manager conflict.

The assumption of incompleteness represented a departure from one of the tenets of the perfect markets paradigm. A more radical departure occurred with the assumption of asymmetric information. A willingness to allow agents to possess differential information about economic outcomes and the actions of their fellows altered fundamental aspects of the paradigm of market exchange. In a world where agents are unable to observe the objects of trade with equal facility or to observe each other's actions, market exchange becomes difficult if not impossible. The literature dealing with the implications of asymmetric information investigates the existence of optimal arrangements (if any) between would-be borrowers and would-be lenders in a world where information is not common to both parties.

The introduction of information asymmetries opens the way for incentive problems. Once two parties to a contract cannot independently observe the same set of outcomes at identical cost, there is the potential for one party to dissemble, and in so doing, to induce the other party to make a decision contrary to his or her self-interest. Incentive problems of this type play havoc with contracts, and hence with free exchange based on the anticipation of mutual benefit. In short, incentive problems can close markets. At the same time, incentive problems stimulate the development of alternative institutional arrangements designed to contain or control information problems sufficiently to allow borrowers and lenders to interact profitably.

One of the earliest investigations of asymmetric information in financial markets was the study of adverse selection in insurance. When the insured party knows more about the true risk of loss than the insurer can discover, there is an obvious tendency for bad risks to be attracted to the insurer. There is no outright solution to this problem but it can be controlled at some cost by imposing certain conditions in the insurance contract designed to induce bad risks to reveal themselves.

In analogous fashion, the debt contract is a device for eliciting behaviour on the part of a borrower which is consistent with the interests of a lender, in the absence of the lender being able to (costlessly) observe all states of nature. The debt contract is a solution to the problem of asymmetric information in financial markets. Likewise, credit-rationing behaviour represents an efficient response by lenders in the face of imperfect information and the incentive for borrowers not to reveal their true circumstances. Both types of arrangement seek to align incentives facing the two parties to a transaction so that mutually beneficial intertemporal exchange can occur in circumstances where it would otherwise be impossible.

Perhaps the most elaborate institutional response to the problem of asymmetric information is the financial intermediary. When one combines asymmetric information facing borrowers and lenders with their differing demands for liquidity, it is easy to show that a bank issuing deposit contracts as liabilities and holding loan contracts as assets is an optimal institutional arrangement. The bank acts as a liquidity insurer, guaranteeing access to liquid funds on demand to lenders while simultaneously meeting the needs of borrowers for funds committed over the longer term. The key to this balancing act is the bank's ability to pool risks and release lenders from their fear of being caught short of liquid funds.

One difficulty with this arrangement, as Diamond and Dybvig (1983) point out, is that it can be subject to destabilizing bank runs. This possibility leads naturally to a discussion of deposit insurance and bank regulation more generally. Such external intervention has traditionally been used to 'patch up' this particular institutional response to asymmetric information in financial markets.

9.2 Financial Markets and Financial Intermediaries in Evolutionary Context

The focus of financial economics is intertemporal trade. In perfect markets, such exchange takes place between economic agents directly without the services of an intermediary. Financial intermediaries are superfluous in a world of perfect financial markets. To establish a role for financial intermediaries requires imperfection in some dimension of the operation of financial markets. Financial intermediaries then provide a superior means of effecting exchange between ultimate parties to intertemporal trade, superior, that is, to no trade at all or to the imperfect variety possible through direct exchange on financial markets.

The evolution of financial systems is characterized by a continuing struggle between financial intermediaries and financial markets. As imperfections in the operation of markets recede with the development of new transactions technology and/or new ways of harnessing information, intertemporal trade on markets substitutes for financial intermediation. In turn, financial intermediaries find ways of improving their services so as once again to establish their supremacy, at least in certain dimensions, over market-based alternatives.

There is a sense in which 'the writing is on the wall' for financial intermediaries. Evolution of financial systems is consistently in the direction of ameliorating obstacles to the more efficient operation of financial markets. Theory is quite unequivocal in its prediction that efficient financial markets render financial intermediaries obsolete.

While one can cast the history of financial systems in terms of attempts to reconcile the competing claims of financial intermediaries and financial markets, the process is far from complete. One can break into history and observe both the phenomenal advance in the use of financial markets and also the considerable counter-reaction of financial intermediaries seeking to retain their *raison d'être* and to specialize in those services which, for the present at least, remain beyond the reach of financial markets. In this section, we review the current state of play and suggest some directions the evolutionary struggle might take in the future. For convenience, we restrict our attention to banks. This is not to imply that non-bank financial intermediaries are unaffected by current developments but rather that banks, as quintessential financial intermediaries, are most exposed to evolutionary change in financial markets, and are, accordingly, the best exemplar of the outworking of challenge and response in financial systems.

9.2.1 Disintermediation

Two related developments have transformed the practice of banking in recent years. The first is disintermediation—the tendency of firms and, in some cases also individuals, to access financial markets directly and independently of a financial intermediary. It is increasingly the case that large firms, especially multinational corporations, can raise funds directly in capital markets. Whereas in the past, an intermediary would guarantee access to ultimate lenders on superior terms to those available to non-financial corporations, nowadays large corporations can raise funds in their own names at least as cheaply, and in many cases more cheaply, than financial intermediaries. This has led to a developing trend whereby firms large enough to access capital markets directly bypass intermediaries.

The increasing capacity of large firms to disintermediate is partly a result of improved information technology which allows ultimate lenders to inform themselves about the characteristics of borrowers more easily and at lower cost. It is also the result of the sheer size and multinational presence of the world's largest corporations. Institutions which were once known only in local markets now have an international presence and recognition. This is a growing trend.

The development was abetted by substantial deterioration in the credit ratings of some of the world's largest banks on account of defaults on loans to certain developing countries (notably, but not exclusively, in Latin America). As the credit ratings of banks fell, large corporations found themselves with superior credit ratings to those of their bankers, and were therefore induced to access capital markets themselves so as to secure cheaper funding. The eventual recovery of banks' balance sheets did not reverse the situation since, by then, banks were subject to more stringent capital requirements under guidelines laid down by the Bank for International Settlements. Tougher capital regulations on banks have helped to preserve the funding advantage some large companies have in accessing international capital markets on their own.

Having recognized the importance of disintermediation, it should be pointed out that the process has not left banks completely at a loss. The most powerful effect of disintermediation is elimination of banks' balance sheet funding of large corporate credits. Large corporations tend not to borrow from banks. This does not mean that banks have no involvement with corporate fund-raising but rather that the nature of the involvement is changing. Banks are more likely to act as advisers and/or underwriters than outright lenders. Such ancillary functions are still important in securing direct access to capital markets by corporate borrowers. James (1987) provides convincing evidence of the continuing importance of the involvement of banks in facilitating corporate access to financial markets.

Nevertheless, the fact remains that the role of banks in fund-raising for large firms has become the more limited one of accessory rather than intermediary. The funds are raised by the firms themselves, albeit with advice and support by banks, and do not come via the balance sheet intermediation of banks. This is a development which is exercising the minds of bank strategists the world over. Is it possible that banks may eventually outlive their usefulness to large corporations?

For the present at least, the involvement of a financial intermediary is still required at some stage during the fund-raising process. Corporates have discovered, however, that the financial intermediary need not be an independent bank. Another challenge to traditional financial intermediaries has come from corporate treasuries or 'in house banks'. Such involvement of financial intermediaries as is required can be provided as easily and, in some cases more cheaply, by the corporation's own financial subsidiary. And if the subsidiary can do this for its parent company, why not for others? Banks are facing competition not only from corporations themselves but also from their financial subsidiaries. The financial arms of General Electric and British Petroleum are now larger than many banks and compete directly with banks in offering ancillary financial services, both to their parents and to the corporate world more generally.

Banks have responded to this development in two ways. The first is to try to get closer to their corporate clients by forming 'relationships'. Such relationships involve special treatment of the kind a firm might expect from its own subsidiary. In some cases, explicit equity involvement of the bank with its client, as is traditional in Germany and Japan but less common in Anglo-Saxon banking systems, has developed to enhance the closeness of the relationship. Banks' ability to adopt this strategy is limited in some countries by central bank regulatory proscription of equity links between banks and their commercial clients.

The second response of banks to disintermediation by their larger clients is to concentrate their efforts in those sectors of the market less able to take advantage of direct finance. Banks have moved 'down market' towards medium-size and small firms and personal clients. At present, such clients are mostly unable to disintermediate on account of the absence of sufficient information about their creditworthiness to enable them to access markets directly. Such firms and individuals can only raise funds via an intermediary whose creditworthiness substitutes for that of the client and grants access to ultimate lenders.

Such a strategy is feasible so long as this sector of the market is unable to disintermediate. The question posed to bank strategists is how long it will be before disintermediation is a possibility for these clients as well. Is it a just a matter of time or will there always be a large enough constituency of firms and individuals unable to access markets directly who will need the services of an intermediary?

9.2.2 Securitization

The second trend in financial systems around the world is known by the somewhat awkward term: *securitization*. This refers to the process whereby financial intermediaries, banks in particular, convert claims held as assets on their balance sheets into marketable securities. The genesis of this process was once again associated with the Latin American debt crisis of the 1980s. Banks found themselves with large tranches of poor-quality credits on their books and declining credit ratings as a result. We noted above that this helped to promote disintermediation by large corporates. Banks responded by trying to find ways to rid themselves of the bad loans. In ordinary circumstances, they might have foreclosed on the borrower but this option was not available with sovereign creditors. Securitization was the answer to their dilemma.

Securitization involves sales of loans from the books of banks into a specially designed trust which then issues securities against the loans directly into the capital market. The banks gain by removing non-performing loans from their balance sheets. The capital market gains by being able to purchase sovereign credits, albeit low-quality, high-risk credits, at appropriately discounted market prices. The securities which resulted from this first instance of securitization were suitably known as 'junk' bonds.

From these inauspicious beginnings, securitization has grown to become a major force in corporate finance. It has also found its way into retail consumer markets, including mortgage finance, consumer finance, and student loans. The attraction for banks is that the funding of loans can be separated from their origination. When banks hold loans on their balance sheets, they must obtain sufficient capital to meet the capital adequacy requirements imposed by central banks. Where these are onerous, such requirements may erode the competitive advantage of banks in acting as an intermediary. One response is to restrict the involvement of banks to loan origination. The funding of the loans can take place via the capital market once they are sold by the bank to a special purpose trust which issues securities against the loans.

The arrangement suits banks because it enables them to bring forward their revenue flows from lending by crystallizing them in the form of fees. The more loans are written and securitized, the larger the volume of revenue from fees, without the need to service the loans written with capital on the balance sheet. Borrowers gain by being given access to funds on a cheaper basis than would ordinarily be available through bank 'on-balance-sheet' finance. Lenders gain by being able to earn capital market interest rates on their funds rather than bank deposit rates, while at the same time knowing exactly what types of credits secure their claims on the trust.

Securitization has been described as a technological breakthrough with the potential to displace traditional balance sheet borrowing and lending by intermediaries (Bryan 1991). It need not eliminate a role for intermediaries but certainly restricts the range of their activities. Rather than handle both origination and funding, intermediaries are restricted to origination, where they still possess some competitive advantage, while funding becomes a matter of issuing securities directly to the capital market.

Like disintermediation, securitization represents the substitution of trade on financial markets for functions traditionally performed by financial intermediaries. Intermediaries become involved in cases where ultimate borrowers cannot meet ultimate lenders face to face in the financial markets on account of excessive transaction costs, imperfect information, or both. Securitization represents a method whereby financial intermediaries can add enough information to the promises of ultimate borrowers for the market once again to take over. By originating loans and allowing recourse in the event of default, financial intermediaries screen loans and enhance their creditworthiness sufficiently for them to be traded in open financial markets. The role of the intermediary is not displaced entirely by this process but is substantially restricted in scope.

Securitization may not spell the end of intermediaries but it may mean the end of intermediation as we know it, at least in areas where credits can be securitized. Again, the question arises as to whether there are any natural limits to securitization. Are there any loans which could not, even in principle, be securitized? At present, the advance of securitization seems inexorable, with assets as diverse as car loans and credit card receivables having been securitized in recent years. The test will come with less homogenous assets like loans to small businesses and personal loans. There may still be too little information about the borrowers and too little security available in such cases to enable securitization to proceed. Small business lending and personal sector loans may yet prove to be the final stronghold of balance sheet intermediation. Or, alternatively, it may be the last frontier of securitization and the scene of the final conquest by financial markets.

9.3 Conclusion

Financial economics studies the interaction of borrowers and lenders as they seek to optimize their choices amongst an unlimited variety of intertemporal options. In recent years, both the theory and the praxis of financial economics have advanced substantially, making financial economics one of the most exciting fields of the discipline in which to work.

Many aspects of the operation of financial markets and financial institutions remain a mystery. While the basic motivation for, and form of, intertemporal exchange is understood, detailed explanations of a variety of phenomena, including such fundamental processes as price determination, still elude even the most advanced researchers. This book is written in the hope that today's students will be sufficiently fascinated by the unravelling story of financial economics to make their own contribution to a deeper understanding of these unique markets, their institutions, and their practices.

REFERENCES

Akerloff, G. (1970). 'The Market for Lemons: Qualitative Uncertainty and the Market Mechanism', *Quarterly Journal of Economics*, 84: 488–500.

Allais, M. (1952). 'Le comportement de l'homme rationnel devant le risque: critiques des postulats et axiomes de l'école Américaine', *Econometrica*, 21: 503–46.

Anderlini, L. (1990). 'Theoretical Modelling of Banks and Bank Runs', in F. Hahn (ed.), *The Economics of Missing Markets, Information, and Games*. Oxford: Clarendon Press.

Arrow, K. J. (1964). 'The Role of Securities in the Optimal Allocation of Risk Bearing', *Review of Economic Studies*, 31: 91–6.

Baltensperger, E. (1980). 'Alternative Approaches to the Theory of the Banking Firm', *Journal of Monetary Economics*, 6: 1–37.

Banerjee, A. V. (1992). 'A Simple Model of Herd Behavior', *Quarterly Journal of Economics*, 107 (August): 797–817.

Bernoulli, D. (1738). 'Specimen theoriae novae de mensura sortis', trans. into English by L. Sommer (1954), 'Exposition of a New Theory on the Measurement of Risk', *Econometrica*, 22: 23–36.

Bhattacharya, S., and Thakor, A. V. (1993). 'Contemporary Banking Theory', *Journal of Financial Intermediation*, 3: 2–50.

Bikhchandani, S., Wirshleifer, D., Welch, I. (1992). 'A Theory of Fads, Fashion, Custom, and Cultural Change as Informational Cascades', *Journal of Political Economy*, 100: 992–1026.

Black, I., and Scholes, M. (1973). 'The Pricing of Options and Corporate Liabilities', *Journal of Political Economy*, 81: 637–59.

Brennan, M. J. (1989). 'Capital Asset Pricing Model', in J. Eatwell, M. Milgate, and P. Neumann (eds.), *The New Palgrave Dictionary of Finance*. London: Macmillan Press.

Bryan, L. L. (1991). 'Structured Securitized Credit: A Superior Technology for Lending', in D. Chew (ed.), *New Developments in Commercial Banking*. Oxford: Basil Blackwell, 55–68.

Chari, V. V., and Jagannathan, R. (1988). 'Banking Panics, Information, and Rational Expectations Equilibrium', *Journal of Finance*, 43: 749–63.

Clemenz, G. (1986). *Credit Markets with Asymmetric Information*. Berlin, Heidelberg: Springer-Verlag.

Copeland, T., and Weston, J. (1988). *Financial Theory and Corporate Policy*. Reading, Mass.: Addison-Wesley.

References

Cox, J., Ross, S., and Rubinstein, M. (1979). 'Option Pricing: A Simplified Approach', *Journal of Financial Economics*, 7: 229–63.

Debreu, G. (1959). *Theory of Value*. New York: Wiley.

Diamond, D. (1984). 'Financial Intermediation and Delegated Monitoring', *Review of Economic Studies*, 51: 393–414.

—— and Dybvig, P. H. (1983). 'Bank Runs, Deposit Insurance and Liquidity', *Journal of Political Economy*, 91: 401–19.

—— —— (1986). 'Banking Theory, Deposit Insurance and Bank Regulation', *Journal of Business*, 59: 55–68.

Diamond, P. (1967). 'The Role of a Stock Market in a General Equilibrium Model with Technological Uncertainty', *American Economic Review*, 57: 759–76.

Dowd, K. (1992). 'Models of Banking Instability: A Partial Review of the Literature', *Journal of Economic Surveys*, 6: 107–32.

Duffie, D. (1989). *Futures Market*. London: Prentice Hall.

—— (1991). 'The Theory of Value in Security Markets', in W. Hildenbrand and H. Sonnenschein (eds.), *Handbook of Mathematical Economics*, iv. Amsterdam: North-Holland.

Dybvig, P. H., and Ross, S. A. (1989). 'Arbitrage' in P. Neumann, M. Milgate, and J. Eatwell (eds.), *The New Palgrave Dictionary of Money and Finance*. New York: Macmillan, Stockton Press.

Eichberger, J. (1992). 'A Simple Model of a Bank', Research Paper No. 351, University of Melbourne.

—— and Milne, F. (1991). 'Bank Runs and Capital Adequacy', Melbourne: Dept. of Economics, University of Melbourne.

Ekern, S., and Wilson, R. (1974). 'On the Theory of the Firm in an Economy with Incomplete Markets', *Bell Journal of Economics and Management*, 5: 171–80.

Fama, E. F., and Miller, M. H. (1972). *The Theory of Finance*. Hinsdale, Ill.: Dryden Press.

Feller, W. (1966). *An Introduction to Probability Theory and its Applications, ii.* New York: John Wiley & Sons.

Fisher, I. (1930). *The Theory of Interest,* repr. 1965. New York: A. M. Kelley.

Gale, D., and Hellwig, M. (1985). 'Incentive-Compatible Debt Contracts: The One-Period Problem', *Review of Economic Studies*, 52: 647–63.

Grossman, S. J., and Hart, O. D. (1979). 'A Theory of Competitive Equilibrium in Stock Market Economies', *Econometrica*, 47: 293–328.

—— and Stiglitz, J. (1980). 'Stockholder Unanimity in Making Production and Financial Decisions', *Quarterly Journal of Economics*, 94: 543–66.

Hart, O. (1979). 'On Shareholder Unanimity in Large Stock Market Economies', *Econometrica*, 47: 1057–1083.

—— (1995). *Firms, Contracts, and Financial Structure*. Oxford: Clarendon Press.

Hellwig, M. (1991). 'Banking, Financial Intermediation and Corporate Finance', in A. Giovannini and C. Mayer (eds.), *European Financial Integration*. Cambridge: Cambridge University Press, 35–72.

Hirshleifer, J. (1970). *Investment, Interest and Capital*. London: Prentice-Hall.

Hirshleifer, J., Riley, J. G. (1992). *The Analytics of Uncertainty and Information.* Cambridge: Cambridge University Press.

Huang, C., and Litzenberger, R. (1988). *Foundations for Financial Economics.* New York: North-Holland.

Ingersoll, J. (1987). *Theory of Financial Decision Making.* Totowa, NJ: Rowman & Littlefield.

Jacklin, Ch. J. (1987). 'Demand Deposits, Trading Restrictions and Risk Sharing', in E. Prescott and N. Wallace (eds.), *Contractual Arrangements for Intertemporal Trade.* Minneapolis: University of Minnesota Press.

—— and Bhattacharya, S. (1988). 'Distinguishing Panics and Information-Based Bank Runs: Welfare and Policy Implications', *Journal of Political Economy,* 96: 568–92.

James, C. (1987). 'Some Evidence on the Uniqueness of Bank Loans', *Journal of Financial Economics,* 19: 217–35.

Jarrow, R. A. (1988). *Finance Theory.* London: Prentice Hall.

Johnson, N. L., and Kotz, S. (1972). *Distributions in Statistics: Continuous Multivariate Distributions.* New York: Wiley.

Kane, E. J. (1985). *The Gathering Crisis in Federal Deposit Insurance.* Cambridge: MIT Press

Laffont, J.-J. (1987). 'Revelation of Preferences', in J. Eatwell, P. Milgate, and P. Newman (eds.), *The New Palgrave: A Dictionary of Economics.* London: Macmillan.

—— (1989). *The Economics of Uncertainty and Information.* London: MIT Press.

Leland, H. E. (1974). 'Production Theory and the Stock Market', *Bell Journal of Economics and Management,* 5: 125–44.

—— and Pyle, D. H. (1977). 'Information Asymmetries, Financial Structure and Financial Intermediation', *Journal of Finance,* 32: 371–87.

Lintner, J. (1965a). 'The Valuation of Risk Assets and the Selection of Risky Investments in Stock Portfolios and Capital Budgets', *Review of Economics and Statistics,* 47: 13–37.

—— (1965b). 'Security Prices, Risk, and Maximal Gains from Diversification', *Journal of Finance,* 20: 587–616.

Machina, M. J. (1987a). 'Choice Under Uncertainty: Problems Solved and Unsolved', *Journal of Economic Perspectives,* 1: 121–54.

—— (1987b). 'Expected Utility Hypothesis', in J. Eatwell, P. Milgate, and P. Newman (eds.), *The New Palgrave: A Dictionary of Economics.* London: Macmillan.

Magill, M., and Shafer, W. (1991). 'Incomplete Markets', in W. Hildenbrand and H. Sonnenschein (eds.), *Handbook of Mathematical Economics,* iv. Amsterdam: North-Holland.

Markowitz, H. (1952). 'Portfolio Selection', *Journal of Finance,* 7: 77–91.

Mas-Collel, A., Whinston, M., and Green, J. R. (1995). *Microeconomic Theory.* New York, Oxford: Oxford University Press.

Merton, R. C. (1977). 'An Analytic Derivation of the Cost of Deposit Insurance and Loan Guarantees', *Journal of Banking and Finance,* 1: 3–11.

Milne, F. (1995). *Finance Theory.* Oxford: Oxford University Press.

References

Modigliani, F., and Miller, M. H. (1958). 'The Cost of Capital, Corporate Finance and the Theory of Investment', *American Economic Review*, 48: 262–97.

Mossin, J. (1966). 'Equilibrium in a Capital Asset Market', *Econometrica*, 34: 768–83.

Radner, R. (1972). 'Existence of Equilibrium of Plans, Prices and Price Expectations in a Sequence of Markets', *Econometrica*, 40: 289–303.

—— (1974). 'A Note on Unanimity of Stockholders' Preferences among Alternative Production Plans: A Reformulation of the Ekern-Wilson Model', *Bell Journal of Economics and Management*, 5: 181–4.

Roll, R. (1977). 'A Critique of the Asset Pricing Theory's Tests: Part 1: On Past and Potential Testability of the Theory', *Journal of Financial Economics*, 4: 129–76.

Ross, S. A. (1976). 'Arbitrage Theory of Capital Asset Pricing', *Journal of Economic Theory*, 13: 341–60.

Rothschild, M., and Stiglitz, J. (1976). 'Equilibrium in Competitive Insurance Markets: An Essay on the Economics of Imperfect Information', *Quarterly Journal of Economics*, 90: 629–49.

Santomero, A. M. (1984). 'Modeling the Banking Firm. A Survey', *Journal of Money, Credit, and Banking*, 16 (November): 576–602.

Sharpe, W. F. (1964). 'Capital Asset Prices: A Theory of Market Equilibrium Under Conditions of Risk', *Journal of Finance*, 19: 425–42.

Stiglitz, J. E. (1969). 'A Re-examination of the Modigliani-Miller Theorem', *American Economic Review*, 59: 784–93.

—— (1972*a*). 'On the Optimality of the Stock Market Allocation of Investment', *Quarterly Journal of Economics*, 86: 25–60.

—— (1972*b*). 'Some Aspects of the Pure Theory of Corporate Finance: Bankruptcies and Take-Overs', *Bell Journal of Economics and Management Science*, 3: 458–82.

—— and Weiss, A. (1981). 'Credit Rationing in Markets with Imperfect Information', *American Economic Review*, 71: 393–410.

Tobin, J. (1958). 'Liquidity Preference as Behaviour Towards Risk', *Review of Economic Studies*, 25: 65–86.

Townsend, R. (1979). 'Optimal Contracts and Competitive Markets with Costly State Verification', *Journal of Economic Theory*, 21: 417–25.

Treynor, J. (1961). 'Toward a Theory of the Market Value of Risky Assets', Unpublished MS.

Varian, H. (1992). *Microeconomic Analysis*, 3rd edn. New York: Norton.

Von Neumann, J., and Morgenstern, O. (1944). *Theory of Games and Economic Behavior*. Princeton, NJ: Princeton University Press.

Williamson, S. D. (1987). 'Recent Developments in Modeling Financial Intermediation', *Federal Reserve Bank of Minneapolis Quarterly Review*, 11: 19–29.

Ziemba, W. T., and Vickson, R. G. (eds.) (1975). *Stochastic Optimization Models in Finance*. New York: Academic Press.

INDEX

Page ranges in roman (e.g. 57–67) indicate references *passim*; page ranges in italic type (e.g. *57–67*) indicate continuous treatment.

Index

Index

standard deviation 29
state 35–6
  indexes 93
  space 38
state of the world 2, 3, 36
state-contingent
  commodities 110
  consequences 2
  consumption: vectors 12, 172; contracts 172–4, 178
  outcomes 8–9, 11–12
  pay-off 118, 129–32 & *fig.*; vector 59, 102, 125–6
  returns 132 *fig.*, 219
  wealth combination 66, 119–21
  wealth mean 73
  wealth pair 122–3
  wealth space 61, 65
  wealth standard deviation 73
  wealth vector 69
state-dependent
  consequences 2
  wealth vector 60
state-preference approach 8
state-space approach 6
statistical moments 29–30
Stiglitz 157 n., 159, 190
stochastic dominance *14–29*
  first-order 16
  second-order *18–21*
stock
  market equilibrium *140–5*, 160, 162–3
  price 130
  return 130
strike price 128
subgame-perfect 221
  equilibria 214
support 39–41
suspension of convertibility 226, 229–30, 238

transformation curve 151 *fig.*
transitivity 9–11, 29, 43
truth-telling constraints 177
truth-telling contract 178
type-contingent
  behaviour 219
  strategy (combination) 212–14

uncertainty, decisions taken under 1–56
uniform distribution 36
utility
  expected 44
  function 11–12, 29, 33, 43, *47–51*, 118–19; continuous 42; indirect 143; quadratic 30–1; von Neumann–Morgenstern 172
  index number 42, 79; unbounded 50
utility function over probabilities 11

value maximization *149–51*, *151–8*, 244
variance 29
vector
  of dividends 155
  of security prices 124
  production vector 155
von Neumann 11, 13, 44, *47–51*, 79, 97
von Neumann–Morgenstern utility functions 172, 178, 181

wealth
  combination 119, 121
  pair, state-contingent 123
Weiss 190
Welch 217 n.
Wilson 157 n.
withdrawal
  behaviour 226
  equilibrium 236 & *fig.*
  strategies 218–19, 220–1

260